C000089825

EMPLOYM

Seventh Edition

C J Carr

MA, BCL

Sometime Dean of Faculty of Cultural, Legal and Social Studies,
University of Central Lancashire

P J Kay

BA, LLM

Principal Lecturer, Department of Legal Studies,
University of Central Lancashire

M&E
PITMAN
PUBLISHING

London · Hong Kong · Johannesburg · Melbourne · Singapore · Washington DC

PITMAN PUBLISHING
128 Long Acre, London WC2E 9AN
Tel: 0171 447 2000 Fax: 0171 240 5771

A Division of Pearson Professional Limited

Seventh edition 1998

A CIP catalogue record for this book can be obtained from the British Library

ISBN 0 7121 1079 8

Typeset by WestKey Limited, Falmouth, Cornwall
Printed and bound in Great Britain by Bell and Bain Ltd. Glasgow

The Publishers' policy is to use paper manufactured from sustainable forests.

CONTENTS

PREFACE

The period since the publication of the last edition has seen a slowing-down in the pace of new legislative material in Employment Law, but there has been considerable consolidation and tidying-up. The opportunity has been taken in this edition of incorporating the relevant provisions of the Employment Rights Act 1996, the Industrial Tribunals Act 1996 and the Disability Discrimination Act 1995. We have also covered a number of important changes introduced by statutory instrument, and in particular the Collective Redundancies and Transfer of Undertakings (Protection of Employment) (Amendment) Regulations 1995 and the Employment Protection (Part-Time Employees) Regulations 1995.

The rate at which the tribunals continue to interpret and apply the statutory provisions has, of course, continued apace. We have been able to include a large number of new cases in this edition and in particular we have dealt in some detail with the still-unconcluded litigation in *R.* v. *Secretary of State ex p. Seymour-Smith and Perez* (1997). We now await the deliberations of the European Court of Justice on the questions referred to it by the House of Lords, but we have been able to include coverage of the case as it has progressed through the domestic legal system.

We hope that this book provides a clear, straightforward and succinct account of the law as it stands in April 1997. We are, of course, responsible for any errors which we may have inadvertently made.

Peter Kay
Christopher Carr

INTRODUCTION

1. Scope of employment law

Employment law is that part of English law which deals with the legal problems arising from the employment relationship. The relationship between employer and employee is based on the contract of employment and any book must necessarily concentrate on this relationship. However, with the development of trade unions, employers' organisations and, in particular, state intervention, the subject covers many aspects other than simply the contract of employment. Indeed with the passing of the Employment Acts 1988 and 1990 the relationship between a trade union and its members has become a subject of increased importance (*see* 17: **20–21**). The legislation relating to Trade Unions is now consolidated in the Trade Union and Labour Relations (Consolidation) Act 1992 and the legislation relating to individual employment rights is consolidated in the Employment Rights Act 1996.

2. Sources of employment law

As with all legal subjects, employment law is based upon legislation and case law (judicial precedent). There is also the concept of custom and practice which still regulates a substantial number of employment relationships (*see* 4: **14–18**). At this stage it must be emphasised that legislation is playing an increasingly important role; indeed there is hardly a Parliamentary session which passes without a major piece of employment legislation being passed. Further, the nature of this legislation is often controversial as it has been introduced as a result of political parties seeing such legislation as a major plank of their political platforms. The economic and political changes brought about by this legislation therefore cannot be ignored.

3. Function of employment law

Traditionally it has been thought that employment law, perhaps more than any branch of law, exists largely to prevent the need for the parties to a dispute to resort to the tribunals or courts. Recent trends, such as the 'right of management to manage', have meant increased confrontation in the employment sphere and parties in such disputes seem more willing to resort to legal redress in order to test the legal merits of their actions. The law, therefore, is becoming increasingly important in such areas. The use of practice and procedures, which are based on the legal framework, are obviously still important but so is the use of the legal remedy.

Note: The cross-references in the text consist of the relevant chapter number followed by the section number in bold type.

TABLE OF CASES

1

ADMINISTRATION OF EMPLOYMENT LAW

INTRODUCTION

Until relatively recent times, labour law was regarded merely as an aspect of the law of contract, being administered in the ordinary civil courts. However, the industrial tribunal system was established in 1964 and, since that time, various other courts and non-judicial bodies have been created, thus recognising that the problems arising from employment and industrial relations require specialised courts, tribunals etc. The procedures in these bodies are relatively informal and the 'judges' have special knowledge of employment and industrial relations. It would, however, be misleading to deal with bodies which resolve these disputes without first referring to the voluntary procedures which exist for dealing with such problems prior to their being taken to the courts and tribunals.

THE VOLUNTARY PROCEDURES

1. Introduction

It is most unusual for a person with a grievance relating to his employment to have immediate resort to the legal institutions. The majority of such problems are settled informally at the work-place between the employer and employee and/or their representatives. The law encourages such procedures by recommending their creation in the Code of Practice (*see* **15**) and by requiring a reference in the written statement to a grievance procedure (*see* **2:7**).

2. Nature of voluntary procedures

Clearly the nature of such procedures varies considerably from one place of work to another and between different types of employment. In some cases these procedures will have been determined by national negotiations between employer(s) and trade union(s), whereas in others it may simply consist of the employee having an opportunity to put their grievance to the employer or their representative. In addition to such procedures there is an increasing number of 'policies' governing the employment relationship. Such policies are wide ranging in their nature and usually aimed at dealing with specific problems in the employment sphere; examples of such policies include equal opportunities and sexual harassment. Policies can also deal with current social and medical problems which employees may potentially face and these include policies on AIDS, smoking and alcohol.

INDUSTRIAL TRIBUNALS

3. Creation and composition

The industrial tribunals were established by the Industrial Training Act 1964 to deal with certain disputes arising under that Act but, since that time, their jurisdiction has been considerably extended, notably in respect of claims for redundancy payments, unfair dismissal and, now, certain breach of contract of employment claims. The tribunals are organised on a regional basis and each tribunal consists of a legally qualified chairman and two lay members appointed from a panel. Normally one of the lay members would have been nominated by an employers' organisation and the other by a trade union. The governing statute is now the Industrial Tribunals Act 1996 (ITA 1996).

4. Jurisdiction

Industrial tribunals are empowered to deal with a wide range of matters arising from a number of legislative provisions, the most important of which are as follows:

(a) Complaints of unfair dismissal.

(b) Applications for a redundancy payment.

(c) References regarding the written particulars of terms of employment.

(d) Complaints regarding guarantee payments.

(e) Complaints regarding suspension from work on medical grounds.

(f) Complaints regarding trade union membership and activities.

(g) Complaints regarding the time off work provisions.

(h) Complaints regarding the right to maternity pay and leave.

(i) Complaints under the Sex Discrimination Act 1975.

(j) Complaints under the Equal Pay Act 1970.

(k) Complaints regarding time off work for ante-natal care.

(l) Complaints regarding secret ballots on employer's premises.

(m) Complaints regarding unreasonable expulsion from trade union membership.

(n) Complaints by trade unions relating to failure of consultation on redundancies.

(o) Complaints by trade unions relating to failure to inform or consult them about transfers of undertakings.

(p) Complaints of unlawful refusal of employment on grounds relating to trade membership under s. 137 of the Trade Union and Labour Relations Act 1992.

Section 3 of the Industrial Tribunals Act 1996 enables the appropriate Minister to confer jurisdiction on Industrial Tribunals in respect of damages for breach of contract of employment. The Minister had in fact exercised this power in 1994 and the ability for Industrial Tribunals to hear such claims is contained in The Industrial Tribunals Extension of Jurisdiction Order 1994. Rule 4 of this Order outlines the claims which the tribunal has jurisdiction over; crucially the claim must arise on the termination of the contract of employment. Rule 5 lists claims which are outside the jurisdiction of Industrial Tribunals, including terms relating to intellectual property, those imposing an obligation of confidence and covenants in restraint of trade. Such claims remain within the jurisdiction of the ordinary courts.

Section 4 of the ITA 1996 specifies situations where the chairman of a tribunal may sit alone in certain cases. Such cases include claims relating to unauthorised wage deductions, breach of contract claims and where both parties consent. Further, the Employment Appeal Tribunal (EAT) in *Tsangacos* v. *Amalgamated Chemicals Ltd* (1997) held that Industrial Tribunals should allow the chairman to sit alone in hearings concerning preliminary jurisdictional matters, the rationale being to allow for the efficient disposal of cases.

5. Procedure

Section 7 of the ITA 1996 allows the Secretary of State to make regulations with respect to proceedings before Industrial Tribunals. The regulations in question are the Industrial Tribunals (Constitution) and Rules of Procedure Regulations 1993 (as amended). Further s. 9 of ITA 1996 allows these regulations to include provision for Pre-Hearing reviews and preliminary matters. The detail of these provisions is contained in Rules 6 and 7 of the 1993 Regulations. The essence of a Pre-Hearing is that an Industrial Tribunal is allowed to require a deposit, up to a maximum of £150, to be paid by parties as a condition of continuing a claim. In addition an Industrial Tribunal has a general power to warn a party to a case, as a preliminary matter, that if he continues with the case then costs may be awarded against him. Clearly the purpose of these regulations is to deter some claimants from pursuing their cases. The EAT in *Wellcome Foundation* v. *Darby* (1996) provided guidance on the issue of preliminary hearings. The EAT stated tribunals should think whether the issue is one properly to be taken in advance and suggested that not every issue should be seen as one which is suitable for this procedure. The EAT thought that questions relating to time limits and qualifying periods of employment could be appropriate as preliminary matters.

Appeals on questions of law lie in respect of most of the jurisdictions of the industrial tribunals to the Employment Appeal Tribunal: s. 21 of the ITA 1996.

6. Conciliation

In respect of most of the kinds of application which may be made to the industrial tribunals, before there is a hearing, an attempt is made to settle the matter by conciliation using the services of a conciliation officer. Section 203 of the Employment Rights Act (ERA) 1996 now allows a settlement to be binding without the services of ACAS, provided that the agreement made is in writing, relates to the particular matter in question and the employee has received independent legal advice from a qualified lawyer as to the nature and effect of the agreement.

Interestingly under s. 18(3) of the ITA 1996, ACAS is now able to become involved in a matter even if no Tribunal application has been lodged. Both parties must request and agree to this and information given to ACAS during this consultation remains confidential (s. 18(7) of ITA 1996).

7. Tribunal statistics: 1993–94 and 1994–95

Table 1.1 Outcome of tribunal cases by jurisdiction 1994–95 (1993–94 figures in brackets)

	Total cases disposed of	ACAS settlement*	Successful at hearing	Unsuccessful hearing	Withdrawn	Other
Unfair dismissal	40,039 (42,757)	15,485 (15,249)	4,829 (5,952)	7,464 (7,558)	11,389 (12,680)	872 (1,308)
Redundancy pay	6,926 (8,567)	N/A	2,463 (3,193)	1,182 (1,314)	3,013 (3,752)	268 (318)
Collective redundancies	553 (442)	120 (65)	135 (114)	34 (28)	247 (233)	17 (2)
Sex discrimination	4,052 (1,969)	1,005 (824)	340 (176)	350 (285)	2,276 (632)	81 (52)
Race discrimination	1,365 (1,304)	325 (272)	72 (151)	390 (369)	507 (461)	71 (51)
Breach of contract	597	262	47	49	221	18
Equal pay	418 (780)	98 (50)	8 (19)	17 (24)	286 (685)	9 (2)
Wages Act	10,119 (11,281)	2,664 (2,105)	2,096 (2,082)	1,344 (1,152)	3,950 (5,554)	65 (388)

* ACAS does not conciliate in the following jurisdictions: redundancy pay, solvency pay, written statements of terms of employment, interim relief, paid time off for safety representatives and certain health and safety matters.

(Source: *Labour Market Trends*, July 1996)

8. Proposals of reform

The Government, in July 1996, published the draft Employment Rights (Dispute Resolution) Bill which contained proposals for reform. Two of these proposals include granting ACAS the power to fund and provide an arbitration scheme for unfair dismissal and to allow employers and employees to refer any individual employment dispute to independent arbitration. At the time of writing there is no legislative timetable for this proposed legislation.

9. Preliminary hearings

An important recent trend is the increased use of preliminary hearings. The purpose of such a hearing is to prevent cases going forward which do not have a reasonable chance of success. In 1994–95 a total of 618 preliminary hearings were held out of 1,298 cases in total; of these 618 preliminary hearings 382 cases were dismissed and 236 allowed to proceed. This shows a clear shift in the way the EAT operates. Further the EAT in 1996 issued a Practice Direction outlining the procedure which applies to all appeals before the EAT.

EMPLOYMENT APPEAL TRIBUNAL (EAT)

10. Creation and composition

The EAT was established in 1975 and continued by ss. 22–28 of ITA 1996. It consists of judges of the High Court and Court of Appeal (and their Scottish equivalents), one of whom is appointed President, and lay members drawn from a panel of persons having special knowledge or experience of industrial relations. On each case heard, there will be a judge and, normally, two lay members sitting. The EAT is a superior court of record based in London but entitled to sit anywhere within the jurisdiction.

11. Jurisdiction

The essential function of the EAT is to hear appeals on questions of law from the industrial tribunals on most of the jurisdictions exercised by the tribunals (s. 21 of ITA 1996). In a limited number of situations, however, the EAT does have jurisdiction to hear appeals on points of law or fact: for example from the decisions of industrial tribunals under s. 179 of the 1992 Act (unreasonable expulsion or exclusion from a trade union). Further it has the ability to hear appeals (some on questions of law only and others on questions of law or fact) from the Certification Officer (*see* **18** below). The EAT has only limited original jurisdiction under s. 5(2) of the Employment Act 1980, allowing it to determine some applications for compensation following the refusal of a trade union to admit or re-admit a person to membership of a closed shop.

12. Procedure and powers

The EAT regulates its own procedure subject to the provisions of the Employment Appeal Tribunal Rules 1993 (SI 1993/2854). The amending regulations give effect to the changes in the industrial tribunal procedures (*see* 5 above). A party who wishes to appeal from an industrial tribunal's decision must submit a copy of the full written reasons for the decision in addition to a notice of appeal and a copy of the decision within 42 days. The EAT does, however, have a discretion to authorise the institution of the appeal before the full written reasons are sent if it considers it would lead to the 'more expeditious or economic disposal of any proceedings or would otherwise be desirable in the interests of justice'.

An appeal from the EAT on a question of law lies to the Court of Appeal and thence to the House of Lords.

ADVISORY CONCILIATION AND ARBITRATION SERVICE (ACAS)

13. Creation and composition

ACAS was established in 1974 and placed on a statutory basis in 1975: Employment Protection Act 1975. All the functions of ACAS are now contained in the Trade Union and Labour Relations (Consolidation) Act 1992. In a general sense, its forerunner was the Commission on Industrial Relations (1969–74). It is independent of Government and is managed by a Council normally consisting of a full-time chairman and nine other members including three appointed after consultation with the representatives of employers' organisations and three appointed after consultation with the representatives of workers' organisations. ACAS is based in London with offices in regional centres. To exercise its functions, ACAS has the power to appoint staff, including conciliation officers, and to request other persons to perform services, e.g. arbitration.

14. Functions

ACAS is charged with the general duty of 'promoting the improvement of industrial relations, in particular, by exercising its functions in relation to the settlement of trade disputes under sections 210 and 212 (of the 1992 Act)'. *See* s. 209 of the 1992 Act. Its specific functions include the following:

(a) *Conciliation in trade disputes.* The provision of assistance by conciliation or otherwise in actual or apprehended trade disputes (*see* Chapter 19) on request or otherwise: s. 210 of the 1992 Act.

(b) *Conciliation in individual cases.* The provision of conciliation facilities with a view to promoting the settlement of those disputes in which an individual has made application to an industrial tribunal: EPA 1975, s. 211 of the 1992 Act.

(c) *Arbitration*. The provision of arbitration services either through the Central Arbitration Committee (*see* **16**) or otherwise to the parties to a trade dispute, provided that all parties consent and, normally, provided that all voluntary procedures have been exhausted. Such arbitration awards may be published with the consent of the parties: s. 212 of the 1992 Act.

(d) *Advice*. The provision of specific and general advice upon a wide range of matters (e.g. negotiating machinery) to interested parties; this advice can be given to both sides of industry: s. 213 of the 1992 Act (as amended).

(e) *Inquiry*. The conducting of general and specific inquiries into industrial relations questions, the results of which may be published: s. 214 of the 1992 Act.

(f) *Disclosure of information*. The investigation of disputes relating to disclosure of information: ss. 181–185 of the 1992 Act.

(g) *Codes of practice*. The issuing of relevant Codes of Practice: s. 199 of the 1992 Act.

ACAS is not a judicial body, but if it exceeds its jurisdiction or powers, its action may be subject to judicial review.

Section 251A of the 1992 Act now allows ACAS to charge for some of its services. It is for the Secretary of State to decide which of its services ACAS may charge for and at what rate.

15. Codes of Practice

The publication and use of Codes of Practice is becoming of increasing importance in the regulation of employment and industrial relations. In this context Codes issued by ACAS are under discussion but other bodies such as the Health and Safety Commission and the Equal Opportunities Commission have powers to issue Codes. In addition the Secretary of State is also empowered to issue Codes of Practice, following consultation with ACAS (*see* **23**).

The status in law of such Codes is that, although a failure to observe any provision of a Code cannot of itself give rise to legal proceedings, in proceedings before industrial tribunals and other bodies the provisions of a Code are admissible in evidence and are to be taken into account in determining the question at issue. In *Polkey* v. *A.E. Dayton Services Ltd* (1987), the House of Lords re-affirmed the importance of the appropriate Codes (*see* 13:**12**) in determining the fairness of dismissal.

ACAS has issued the following Codes:

(a) Disciplinary practice and procedures in employment (*see* 13:**12**).

(b) Disclosure of information to trade unions for collective bargaining purposes (*see* 18:**5**).

(c) Time off for trade union duties and activities (*see* 8:**9**).

CENTRAL ARBITRATION COMMITTEE (CAC)

16. Creation and composition

CAC was established in 1975, replacing the Industrial Arbitration Board (which itself had replaced the Industrial Court established in 1919). Although independent of Government and ACAS, CAC is served by ACAS staff. CAC has a chairman and members appointed by the Secretary of State for Employment.

17. Functions

The main functions of CAC are as follows: see ss. 259–265 of the 1992 Act:

(a) Determining matters relating to sex discrimination in collective agreements and pay structures.

(b) Making an award following an employer's failure to disclose information for collective bargaining purposes (*see* 18:7).

The decisions of CAC are published. There is no appeal from CAC, but it is subject to judicial review if it exceeds its jurisdiction or powers: *see*, for example, *R*. v. *CAC ex parte Deltaflow Ltd* (1977).

CERTIFICATION OFFICER (CO)

18. Creation of office

The office of CO was established in 1975 (s. 254 of the 1992 Act) although some of its functions were previously exercised by the Chief Registrar of Friendly Societies. The office has become of increased importance due to the recent legislation (Trade Union and Labour Relations Act 1992). One of the purposes of this legislation is to ensure that individual trade union members' rights are maintained and in this respect the CO has enforcement powers.

19. Functions

The main functions of the CO are as follows:

(a) To determine whether a trade union is entitled to a certificate of independence: ss. 6–9 of the 1992 Act.

(b) To maintain a list of trade unions and employers' associations: ss. 2–4 of the 1992 Act.

(c) To perform certain duties under the 1992 Act in relation to the 'political fund' of trade unions (*see* 17:**10**). The 1992 Act gives two further powers in this respect. Firstly, s. 80 creates the right to complain to the CO (or the High Court) where a trade union member claims a political fund ballot has been or will be held otherwise than in accordance with the rules drawn up by the CO. Secondly, s. 256 allows the CO to regulate its own procedure, including a power 'to restrict the circumstances in which the identity of an individual who has made, or is proposing to make, any such application, or complaint is disclosed to any person.' The purpose of this is to prevent a complainant from being victimised.

(d) To receive complaints and, if necessary, make a declaration that a trade union has failed to comply with ss. 46–53 of the 1992 Act. These sections of the Act (see 17:16) deal with the duty of trade unions to hold elections for certain posts.

(e) Further important new powers are given to the Certification Officer by s. 10 of TURER Act 1993, which inserts five new sections s. (A–E) after s. 37 of TULR(C) Act 1992. The thrust of these new provisions is to enable the certification officer to investigate a union's finances. The certification officer can now require the production of documents relating to the union's financial affairs. The powers are comprehensive and are similar to those possessed by the Serious Fraud Office under the Criminal Justice Act 1987, with respect to investigating the financial dealings of companies. Clearly these powers are going to alter the role of the certification officer. Section 37C(8) of the 1992 Act states that any report, made under these powers which is certified by the certification officer, will be admissible in any legal proceedings as evidence.

Appeals from decisions of the CO are heard by the Employment Appeal Tribunal.

COMMISSIONER FOR THE RIGHTS OF TRADE UNION MEMBERS

20. Introduction

The Employment Act 1988 allowed the Secretary of State for Employment to appoint a Commissioner for the Rights of Trade Union Members. The functions of the Commissioner are now governed by the 1992 Act.

21. Functions

Section 109 of the 1992 Act, states that the Commissioner is empowered to 'assist' trade union members who wish to bring enforcement proceedings in relation to the following matters:

(a) A failure to hold a proper ballot before industrial action: s. 62 of the 1992 Act.

(b) The right to inspect a union's accounting records: s. 31 of the 1992 Act.

(c) The recovery of union funds used to indemnify unlawful conduct: s. 71 of the 1992 Act.

(d) The restraint of trustees from acting unlawfully: s. 16 of the 1992 Act.

(e) A failure to comply with the CO's rules for conducting a political fund ballot: s. 81 of the 1992 Act.

(f) A failure to comply with the provisions of the 1992 Act regulating election to a union's principal executive council: s. 56 of the 1992 Act.

Section 109(2) of the 1992 Act further extends the powers of the Commissioner to a number of proceedings or prospective proceedings in respect of an alleged or threatened breach of the rules of a trade union relating to the matters listed below:

(a) The appointment or election of a person to, or the removal of a person from, any office.

(b) Disciplinary proceedings by the union (including expulsion).

(c) The authorising or endorsing of industrial action.

(d) The balloting of members.

(e) The application of the union's funds or property.

(f) The imposition, collection or distribution of any levy for the purposes of industrial action.

(g) The constitution of proceedings of any committee, conference or other body.

Section 110(4) of the 1992 Act does, however, state that the Commissioner may only assist on the above matters where members of the union other than the applicant are affected, or similar breaches of the rules have been committed in relation to other members of the union.

The type of assistance which the Commissioner may provide includes the costs of legal advice and representation in proceedings relating to the above matters: s. 111(2) of the 1992 Act. The Commissioner has a discretion whether or not to provide assistance but where the application is refused reasons must be given for that decision: s. 110(5) of the 1992 Act. However, the Commissioner is under a duty to provide assistance where the complaint concerns the ballot for political funds or elections to the principal executive council: s. 110(3) of the 1992 Act.

The 1992 Act (as amended) now provides for the appointment of the Commissioner for Protection Against Unlawful Industrial Action. At the time of writing this post will be held by the Commissioner for the Rights of Trade Union Members. An individual considering taking action against a union because it is felt that the industrial action is unlawful can apply to the new Commissioner for assistance.

SECRETARY OF STATE FOR EMPLOYMENT

22. Introduction

With the increasing intervention of central government in employment and industrial relations, the Secretary of State for Employment has been given considerable powers and duties in relation to these matters.

23. Functions

The main functions of the Secretary of State are:

(a) Approving agreements making provision for payments to redundant persons.

(b) Approving Codes of Practice and seeking Parliamentary approval for them (*see* **15**).

(c) Approving dismissals procedure agreements.

(d) Receiving notification of proposed redundancies (*see* **14:19**).

(e) Approving guarantee payments agreements (*see* **7:15**).

(f) Reviewing various financial limits.

(g) Making regulations upon a wide range of matters.

(h) Issuing, after consultation with ACAS, Codes of Practice containing such practical guidance as he thinks fit for the purpose of promoting the improvement of industrial relations and keeping such Codes of Practice under review: Employment Act 1980, s. 3. As with Codes issued by ACAS, a failure to observe the provisions of such a Code of Practice does not of itself render a person liable to proceedings, but in any proceedings before a court, industrial tribunal or the CAC, a Code is admissible in evidence. The present position is that either the Secretary of State or ACAS can now issue Codes superseding the original 1972 Code or their own or each other's Codes. The Secretary of State has issued a number of Codes of Practice and these will be discussed where appropriate.

As has been stated above, the Codes are admissible in evidence in both tribunals and courts. The Code on Picketing (*see* **19:19**) was used by the High Court in *Thomas* v. *NUM* (1986) (*see* **19:19**) in order to justify an injunction limiting the number of pickets to six. It can be argued that such Codes are introducing law by back door methods in that they have not passed through a full Parliamentary procedure.

THE ORDINARY COURTS

24. Introduction

Despite the creation of the industrial tribunal system, the civil and criminal courts retain a number of areas of jurisdiction in relation to employment. Obviously the system of precedent applies as in any other area of law.

25. Jurisdiction

The most important matters with which the courts are concerned are:

(a) Actions by employees for damages following injury at work (*see* Chapter 16).

(b) Actions in tort arising from industrial action (*see* Chapter 19).

(c) Actions for breach of contract including breach of a covenant in restraint of trade (*see* 5:**21**).

(d) Prosecutions under the health and safety at work legislation (*see* Chapter 16).

EUROPEAN COURT OF JUSTICE

26. Introduction

By virtue of accession to the European Community (EC), Britain is bound by decisions of the European Court of Justice (the Court of the EC): European Communities Act 1972, s. 3. Clearly the decisions of the ECJ are only relevant when there is a conflict between British and European law.

27. Procedure

An industrial tribunal, employment appeal tribunal or any court may (by virtue of Article 177 of the Treaty of Rome) refer a case to the ECJ where there is a question of any conflict between the two sets of law. Recent decisions of the European Court of Justice which have been subsequently applied by the English courts show the primacy of European law. In *Factortame Ltd* v. *Secretary of State for Transport* (1989) the House of Lords in effect gave the courts a constitutional power of review over Acts of Parliament. The actual case concerned an injunction which was granted to suspend a section of a statute (The Merchant Shipping Act 1988) as it did not comply with EC law. Further in *Foster* v. *British Gas* (1991) it was held that a worker can rely on a Directive against not only the British Government but also against a body providing a public service under the control of the state. Finally, in *Marleasing* v. *La Comercial Internacional de Alimentación* (1992) the

ECJ now requires UK courts and tribunals to apply domestic law consistently with any Directive of the EC.

28. Recent developments

Two important principles stemming from decisions of the ECJ must be discussed. Firstly, in *Francovich* v. *Italian Republic* (1992) the ECJ held that where an individual suffers loss as a result of the failure of a Member State to implement a Directive which confers rights on an individual; then the individual can sue the State for that loss. The ECJ in *R.* v. *HM Treasury ex parte British Telecommunications plc* (1996) laid down criteria on the operation of the 'Francovich' principle. The two key elements seem to be that the non-conferment of the rights must have led to a serious breach. An example of a serious breach has been held to be the failure of a Member State to implement a Directive into national law within the time limit laid down: *Dillenkofer* v. *Federal Republic of Germany* (1997). Finally, in this regard, such a claim in our jurisdiction must be brought in the ordinary courts, not in an industrial tribunal: *Potter* v. *Secretary of State for Employment* (1997).

Secondly, the ECJ has held in *United Kingdom* v. *Council of the European Union* (1997) that the United Kingdom Government will have to implement the provisions of the Working Time Directive (for details *see* 6:**13** below). The Government had argued that this Directive required the unanimous agreement of all Member States of the EC in order to be implemented as it concerns rights of employed persons (Article 100 of the Treaty of Rome). The ECJ held that this was not the case as the Directive is concerned with health and safety issues as it involved the 'working environment' and therefore unanimous agreement was not needed. The effect of this decision may well mean that more legislation of a 'social' nature could become part of English domestic law.

The influence of ECJ decisions is clearly having an increasing effect on employment law.

EQUAL OPPORTUNITIES COMMISSION (EOC)

29. Creation and composition

The EOC was established by the Sex Discrimination Act 1975, s. 53. It consists of between eight and fifteen commissioners in addition to its full-time staff.

30. Functions

The three general duties of the EOC are:

(a) To work towards the elimination of discrimination in employment and elsewhere.

(b) To promote equality of opportunity between men and women.

(c) To keep under review the Equal Pay Act 1970 and the Sex Discrimination Act 1975.

The EOC produces an annual report for presentation to Parliament and is also empowered to produce Codes of Practice (*see* **15** above).

31. Powers

The main powers of the EOC in relation to employment are as follows:

(a) To carry out investigations during which it may require persons to produce documents or give evidence. If in the course of such an investigation the EOC is satisfied that a breach of the Sex Discrimination Act or Equal Pay Act has occurred, it may issue a non-discrimination notice against which there is a right of appeal to an industrial tribunal. The effect of such a notice, which is kept on a register, is that in the following five years the EOC may apply to a county court if it considers that a further breach of the legislation is likely: SDA 1975, ss. 67–70.

(b) To bring proceedings in respect of discriminatory advertisements or instruction or pressure to discriminate (*see* 10:**11**).

(c) To give assistance to aggrieved persons: SDA 1975, s. 74.

The substantive law in relation to equal pay and sex discrimination is considered in Chapters 9 and 10.

COMMISSION FOR RACIAL EQUALITY (CRE)

32. Creation and composition

The CRE was established by s. 43 of the Race Relations Act 1976 and replaces the former Race Relations Board and Community Relations Commission. It consists of between eight and fifteen commissioners in addition to its full-time staff.

33. Functions and powers

The function and powers of the CRE in relation to discrimination within the ambit of the Race Relations Act 1976 are similar to those exercised by the Equal Opportunities Commission in relation to discrimination dealt with by the Sex Discrimination Act 1975 (*see* **30** and **31** above).

HEALTH AND SAFETY COMMISSION (HSC)

34. Creation and composition

The HSC was established by s. 10 of the Health and Safety at Work etc. Act 1974. It has a chairman and between six and nine commissioners representing employers, trade unions and local government interests. The HSC is responsible to the Secretary of State and must adhere to directions from him.

35. Duties and powers

The HSC has a number of duties, the main ones being:

(a) To assist and encourage persons to further the general purposes of the 1974 Act.

(b) To make arrangements for research and the promotion of training and information connected with it.

(c) To act as an information and advisory service.

(d) To submit proposals for regulations.

(e) To approve and issue Codes of Practice (subject to the approval of the Secretary of State).

In pursuing these duties, the HSC has considerable powers, e.g. directing investigations and inquiries, appointing staff, publishing information etc.

HEALTH AND SAFETY EXECUTIVE (HSE)

36. Creation and composition

The HSE was established by s. 10 of the Health and Safety at Work etc. Act 1974. It consists of a director and two deputies in addition to the staff whom it controls. The HSE embraces an amalgamation of bodies which had existed for some time prior to 1974 including the Factories Inspectorate, the Mines and Quarries Inspectorate and the Explosives Inspectorate. The HSE is answerable to the Health and Safety Commission except as regards the enforcement of the health and safety at work legislation.

37. Functions and powers

The function of the HSE is to enforce the health and safety at work legislation by means of inspection of premises, the issuing of improvement and prohibition notices, prosecution etc. (*see* 16:**20–22**).

38. Fundamental social rights of workers

As a consequence of the May 1997 Election result, the Community Charter of the Fundamental Social Rights of Workers (1990) is now seemingly a potential source of law. The Labour Government has expressed its intention to sign the United Kingdom up to this Charter. Whilst the Charter is largely an enabling measure, currently the only provisions relate to employee representation and parental leave. However it may well become a fruitful source of employment rights in the future.

2

THE CONTRACT OF EMPLOYMENT (1): FORMATION

DEFINITION OF THE CONTRACT

1. General considerations

When the terms 'employee' or 'servant' are used, this assumes the existence of a contract of employment or a contract of service, as distinct from a contract for services under which a person (referred to as an 'independent contractor') performs services under contract for another person. Legally speaking, the independent contractor is self-employed and the distinction between an employee and an independent contractor is of considerable significance.

2. Reasons for the distinction

There are three main reasons for distinguishing between a contract of service (or employment) and a contract for services:

(a) *Legislative provisions*. Many Acts of Parliament and statutory regulations demand such a distinction. For example, Part XI of the Employment Rights Act 1996 (Redundancy Payments) extends only to persons who are 'employees'. This is also the case with Parts I and X of the same Act (Particulars of Terms of Employment and Unfair Dismissal). In these and other cases, persons who are not 'employees' are not covered by the statutory provisions. Furthermore, the system of taxation is different as between employed and self-employed persons. As a result of this (and other reasons), many employers, particularly in the construction industry, have deliberately chosen to engage workers on the basis that they are self-employed, thus avoiding the need to pay certain statutory levies payable in respect of employees and also eliminating a certain amount of administrative and legal responsibility: *see* **4** below.

(b) *Vicarious liability*. The concept of vicarious liability normally extends only to the employer/employee relationship. In other words an employer is responsible for the legal consequences of acts done by his employees during the course of their employment. This does not normally apply to the relationship between an independent contractor and the person for whom he is working. This is discussed in more detail later: *see* **10** below.

(c) *Implied terms.* There are certain rights, duties and obligations which are implied into every contract of employment, but they do not extend to the relationship between an independent contractor and the person for whom he is working: *see* Chapter 5.

3. Ways of distinguishing

It should be noted that many legislative provisions contain a definition of 'employee' and/or 'contract of employment' (e.g. s. 230 of the 1996 Act), but these are generally unhelpful and thus one must turn to the judicial interpretations of the terms.

It should be noted also that the question of whether the relationship of employer/employee exists is a matter for determination by the courts rather than relying solely on the description or label attached to the contract by the parties.

Young & Woods v. *West* (1980): the Court of Appeal stated that whether a person is to be regarded as self-employed or employed is a question of law, not of fact. The label which the parties attach to the relationship may be relevant to determining that relationship but it is not conclusive.

The label which the parties attach to the contract may be relevant where there has been a deliberate alteration in the basis of the employment relationship: *Massey* v. *Crown Life Insurance Co.* (1978). The fact that the worker pays his own income tax/social security contributions does not necessarily indicate that he is not an employee: *Davis* v. *New England College of Arundel* (1977).

The courts have developed several tests for distinguishing between employees and independent contractors. The checklist below whilst important should not be applied mechanistically (*Hall* v. *Lorrimer* (1994)). However the tests do still provide a useful guide as can be illustrated in the decision in *Lane* v. *Shire Roofing Co. Ltd* (1995). In this case L was a roofer who traded as a self-employed person and paid tax on that basis. The defendants contracted with L to undertake work on a 'payment by job' basis. L fell off a ladder whilst carrying out work for D. L suffered injuries. In order to be able to claim compensation L had to show he was employed by D. The Court of Appeal held that L was employed by D as D admitted in evidence that he was responsible for the safety of L.

(a) *The control test.* The first test developed by the courts was the 'control' test, i.e. did the person alleged to be the employer control the alleged employee both in respect of what work was done and as regards the manner of performance of that work? If the answer was in the affirmative the relationship of employer/employee was established. As Bramwell LJ said in *Yewens* v. *Noakes* (1880): 'A servant is a person subject to the command of his master as to the manner in which he shall do his work.'

Walker v. *Crystal Palace Football Club* (1910): the plaintiff was a professional footballer with the defendant club. The question arose as to whether the plaintiff was an employee of the club. Held: he was an employee of the club because he was subject to their overall control in respect of training, discipline and method of play.

However, it was soon recognised by the courts that this test was not satisfactory as a general method of explaining the distinction between an employee and an independent contractor in so far as certain persons with special skills (e.g. doctors, nurses, engineers etc.) were undoubtedly employed persons but they could hardly be said to be subject to the 'control' of their employers. To meet this difficulty the courts developed the 'integration' test. As stated the 'control' test is no longer the dominant one in this respect. However, it is still crucial in determining who is the employer where there is more than one possible employer: *Clifford* v. *Union of Democratic Mineworkers* (1991).

(b) *The integration test.* This test was first stated in precise terms by Denning LJ in *Stevenson, Jordan and Harrison* v. *Macdonald and Evans* (1952):

> 'One feature which seems to run through the instances is that, under a contract of service, a man is employed as part of the business, and his work is done as an integral part of the business; whereas, under a contract for services, his work, although done for the business, is not integrated into it, but is only accessory to it.'

This test has been used to explain professional, artistic and entertainment relationships and the position of doctors and nurses, for whom the control test was inappropriate.

Cassidy v. *Ministry of Health* (1951): a hospital patient was deprived of the use of a hand due to the negligence of full-time medical staff. He claimed that the defendants were vicariously liable for the negligence of the staff, as the staff were employees of the Hospital Board for whom the defendants were responsible. Held: the full-time staff were employees of the Board. Denning LJ said that the staff were employees because their work was integrated into that of the organisation.

A further illustration of this principle is the decision in *Clark* v. *Oxfordshire Health Authority* (1995) where a nurse who was retained by a health authority to fill vacancies on a casual basis was held to be an employee. Emphasis was placed on the need to recognise the increased flexibility of modern employment arrangements.

(c) *The economic reality test.* In recent years the courts have used a more flexible approach which incorporates both of the previous tests. This totality approach is variously referred to as the 'multiple', 'mixed' or 'economic reality' test. It means that factors such as control, integration and powers of selection etc. are simply issues which contribute to the decision which must be based on all the circumstances.

Ready Mixed Concrete (South-East) Ltd v. *Minister of Pensions and National Insurance* (1968): the worker to whom the case related was the driver of a lorry which he obtained on hire-purchase from the company. He was required to paint the lorry in the company's colours and had to obey instructions from the company's servants. On the other hand, he could use substitute drivers if he was ill or on holiday and the contract provided that he was not to be regarded as an employee (this is not conclusive in itself). In other words, certain terms of the contract tended to suggest that he was employed whilst others pointed to his being self-employed. The question arose as to whether he was an 'employee'. Held: there are three conditions which establish the existence of a contract of service:

(i) the employee agrees to provide his own work and skill

(ii) there must be some element of control exercisable by the employer; and

(iii) the other terms of the contract must not be inconsistent with a contract of service.

In this case, a consideration of point (iii) and particularly the question of the use of substitute drivers led to a finding that the driver was an independent contractor.

The tribunals and courts now tend to ask the single fundamental question posed by Cooke J in *Market Investigations Ltd* v. *Minister of Social Security* (1969): 'Is the person who has engaged himself to perform these services performing them as a person in business on his own account?', prior to an examination of all relevant indicia.

Young & Woods v. *West* (1980): W worked for the appellants as a skilled sheet metal worker. He chose to be treated as self-employed when engaged, making himself responsible for his own income tax liabilities, national insurance contributions etc. He had no holiday or sick pay entitlement from the company. Following termination of his contract he claimed to be an employee for the purposes of pursuing a remedy for unfair dismissal. The Court of Appeal said, applying the above test, that it was impossible to regard W as in business on his own account. Apart from receiving wages without deductions and having no holiday or sick pay, W's working conditions were exactly the same as those workers who were subject to PAYE.

See also *Construction Industry Training Board* v. *Labour Force Ltd* (1970); *Ferguson* v. *John Dawson and Partners (Contractors) Ltd* (1976); *Thames Television* v. *Wallis* (1979); *Withers* v. *Flackwell Heath Supporters Club* (1981); *Nethermere (St Neots) Ltd* v. *Gardiner & Taverna* (1983).

4. Labour-only sub-contracting

One of the many difficult problems arising out of the distinction between an employee and an independent contractor is that, particularly in the construction industry, workers are often engaged on the basis that they are self-employed although they may appear to all intents and purposes to be employed. The reasons why this system of 'labour-only sub-contracting' has developed are many and varied but perhaps the most basic reasons are as follows:

(a) From the 'employer's' point of view, he is relieved of the duty to pay certain statutory levies (e.g. social security contributions) which would be payable if the worker was an 'employee'; he avoids certain administrative work (e.g. in connection with the PAYE taxation system); and the worker is not eligible to receive a redundancy payment or present a complaint of unfair dismissal.

(b) From the worker's point of view, he is taxed in arrears as a self-employed person and, since he is usually outside the trade union system, he can negotiate a high lump-sum payment for completion of the work without adhering to agreed terms.

However, the real disadvantage of the system lies in the fact that such workers fall outside the protection of a number of the statutory and common law rules relating to safety at work and relatively few of the State benefits are available to a worker who is injured as a result of an accident at work. In addition, it is argued that the system of labour-only sub-contracting seriously undermines the industrial relations system in the construction industry. Furthermore, it is believed that considerable evasion of tax has occurred because of labour-only sub-contracting.

Since 1971, legislative provisions have existed whose purpose is to minimise the income tax evasion through use of a system of exempting certificates available only to genuine sub-contractors. By reducing the possibilities of tax evasion, it is thought that the system of labour-only sub-contracting may decline. *See Phelps* v. *Moore* (1980).

A good example in relation to labour-only sub-contracting is *Ferguson* v. *John Dawson and Partners (Contractors) Ltd* (1976): P worked for D as a labourer on a building site. He used a false name and no income tax or social security contributions were paid. The parties regarded him as self-employed for reasons which they considered to be to their mutual advantage. P was injured and brought an action for damages under the Construction (Working Places) Regulations 1966 on the basis that he was an 'employee'. D argued that P was not an 'employee'. The Court of Appeal held by a majority that P was an 'employee'. Megaw LJ cited with approval the view of the judge at first instance that 'I regard the concept of the 'lump' (i.e. labour-only sub-contracting) in the circumstances of the present case as being no more than a device which each side regarded as being capable of being put to his own advantage ... but which in reality did not affect the relationship of the parties'. The court considered that D, through its site agent, controlled the work of P. *See also Lane* v. *Shire Roofing Co. Ltd* (1995) in **3** above.

5. The borrowed employee

When an employee is lent or hired from one employer to another, the question arises as to which of them is to be regarded as his employer in law. The principle established in *Mersey Docks and Harbour Board* v. *Coggins and Griffith (Liverpool) Ltd* (1947) is that the first (or general) employer remains liable unless there has been an agreement to the contrary. It should be noted, however, that there can be no such transfer of an employee unless he consents to it.

The growth of employment agency workers has caused difficulties in this regard. In *McMeechan* v. *Secretary of State for Employment* (1995) the EAT held that there was no general rule of law that agency workers are not employees of the agency through which they obtain work. Each case must turn on its particular facts and any evidence must be looked at. On the facts of the case itself it was held that the documentation created a contract of employment between the parties.

FORM OF THE CONTRACT

6. General principle

With two exceptions (merchant seamen and apprentices), there is no requirement that a contract of employment be in writing. As Mackinnon LJ said in *O'Grady* v. *Saper Ltd* (1940), a contract of employment is 'usually concluded orally by people who rarely think out, and still more rarely express, any terms'. This position undoubtedly leads to a situation where proof of the terms of the contract can be difficult. To alleviate this difficulty the Contracts of Employment Act 1963 was passed (subsequently the 1972 Act) with the basic object of ensuring that most employees were provided with some written evidence of the main terms of employment. These provisions are now contained in Part I of the Employment Rights Act (ERA) 1996 which applies to all employees with the following major exceptions:

(a) Registered dock workers

(b) Where an employee works wholly or mainly outside Great Britain

(c) Part-time employees who do not have continuity of employment (*see* **16**)

(d) Crown employees (*see* 3:**5**).

7. The written statement

Section 1 of the ERA 1996 provides that employers must provide employees to whom this part of the Act applies with a written statement containing particulars of certain terms of the contract of employment. This statement must be supplied within two months of the commencement of employment.

The particulars which must be given are as follows:

(a) The names of the employer and employee;
(b) The date when the employment began and the date when the employee's period of continuous employment began;
(c) The scale or rate of remuneration, or method of calculating remuneration;
(d) The intervals at which remuneration is paid;
(e) Any terms and conditions relating to hours of work;
(f) Any terms and conditions relating to holiday entitlement (these must be sufficiently specific to allow the employee's holiday entitlement to be precisely calculated);
(g) Any terms and conditions relating to incapacity for work due to sickness or injury – including any provisions for sick pay;

(h) Any terms and conditions relating to pensions and pension schemes (although this does not apply to employees of any body or authority if the employee's pension rights are defined by statute and the employer is obliged by that statute to give new employees information concerning their pension rights);

(i) The length of notice which the employee is obliged to give and entitled to receive to terminate the contract of employment;

(j) The title of the job which the employee is employed to do;

(k) As an alternative to the job title, a brief description of the work for which the employee is employed;

(l) Where the employment is not intended to be permanent, the period for which it is expected to continue or, if it is for a fixed term, the date on which it is to end;

(m) Either the place of work or, where the employee is to work at various places, an indication of that and the address of the employer, and

(n) Any collective agreements which directly affect the terms and conditions of the employment including, where the employer is not a party, the persons with whom they are made.

The written statement may be given in instalments: s. 1 ERA 1996, provided the particulars listed above are given before the end of the two month period. However s. 2(4) ERA 1996 states the following, listed below, must be contained in a single document:

the names of the employer and employee;
the date of the beginning of the employee's employment under that contract and period of continuous employment with that employer;
the required particulars relating to remuneration and hours of work;
the particulars of terms relating to holidays;
the job title or description; and
details of the place of work.

All employees qualify for a written statement if they have worked for more than one month and the employment normally involves more than eight hours per week: s. 5 ERA 1996.

The above document is referred to as the 'principal statement'.

Any agreed changes in these particulars must be communicated to the employee in writing within one month.

The requirement to provide a note concerning the disciplinary procedure still remains. But there is an exemption from this right where the employer has fewer than 20 employees: s. 3 ERA 1996.

8. Reference to another document

Previously instead of giving an employee individual notification of the particulars, the employer could make reference to another document; s. 2 ERA 1996 now makes this the exception rather than the general rule. Section 2 now requires that the particulars must be notified in full but there are still two exceptions: terms and conditions relating to absence through sickness or injury and terms relating to pension schemes. In addition the written statement need not set out the terms relating to notice but may refer the employee instead either to the statutory provisions contained in s. 86 ERA 1996 or to the provisions in any collective agreement.

9. Significance of the written statement

It is quite clear that the written statement is not a contract but is merely evidence of certain terms of the contract of employment. As the EAT held in *System Floors (UK) Ltd* v. *Daniel* (1981): 'It seems to us, therefore, that in general the status of the statutory statement is this. It provides very strong prima facie evidence of what were the terms of the contract between the parties, but does not constitute a written contract between the parties. Nor are the statements of the terms finally conclusive: at most they place a heavy burden on the employer to show that the actual terms of the contract are different from those which he has set out in the statutory statement.' Therefore, if the written statement does not accurately reflect the terms of the contract as agreed by the parties, the agreed terms prevail over the written statement: *see Robertson & Jackson* v. *British Gas Corporation* (1983). An employee who is not given a written statement to which he is entitled, or who is given an incomplete or incorrect statement, may complain to an industrial tribunal for a determination of what particulars ought to have been included. In the case of an incomplete statement or where no statement has been given the tribunal can specify what ought to have been included and in the case of an incorrect statement the tribunal can amend or replace the particulars given. The Court of Appeal decision in *Eagland* v. *British Telecommunications plc* (1992) discussed this issue. It was held that an industrial tribunal has no power to invent particulars of terms of employment which the contract is not required to contain. However, it must be emphasised that the statute gives no power to rewrite what the parties have agreed or to make an agreement for the parties. A tribunal must simply ensure that the statutory statement records what the parties agreed: *see Mears* v. *Safecar Security* (1982). A tribunal has no power to enforce its decision (e.g. by awarding an employee back-pay). If an employee then wishes to complain of a breach of the terms of the contract of employment, he must at present use the ordinary courts, although when this jurisdiction is transferred to the industrial tribunals, the tribunal will be able to deal with both matters at the same time (*see* 1:3 *et seq*).

However, it is no doubt true to say that the fact that reference may be made to collective agreements as being the source of the terms of the contract enables the courts and tribunals to regard the collective agreement as incorporated into the individual contract of employment more easily than was formerly the case (*see* 4:9–11). As a matter of evidence, therefore, it is most important for both parties that the written statement be correct since it may be difficult to establish that the written statement does not accurately reflect the agreed contractual terms. Thus an employer might find it difficult to show that a dismissal was fair if he dismissed an employee for breach of a rule of which the employee had not been informed in the written statement: *see*, for example, *Meridan Ltd* v. *Gomersall* (1977) and *Meyer Dunmore International* v. *Rogers* (1978). As examples of the difficulties raised by inaccurate, incomplete or misleading written statements, see *Gascol Conversions Ltd* v. *Mercer* (1974) and *Burroughs Machines* v. *Timmoney* (1977).

VICARIOUS LIABILITY

10. General principle

The basic principle of vicarious liability is that an employer is liable in law for the torts committed by his employees whilst they are in the course of their employment. The reasoning behind this principle is two-fold:

(a) The tort is committed while the employee is engaged on the employer's business and therefore the employer should be liable.

(b) An employer is normally likely to be able to meet a damages claim (perhaps he is insured against such a risk) and therefore the injured person is in a better position to recover damages than if he could only claim against the employee.

11. In the course of employment

In order to be able to apply the concept of vicarious liability, it must be established that the employee was acting 'in the course of his employment' at the time of committing the tort. The precise meaning of this phrase is complicated but the following principles are suggested as a summary of the present law.

(a) An employee is regarded as being in the course of his employment if the act during which the tort is committed was expressly or implicitly authorised by the employer. For example, if a lorry driver is involved in a road accident while driving for the employer, any liability which may arise as a result of the accident falls on the driver's employer. This extends to acts which are necessarily incidental to the employment. As Lord Porter said in *Weaver* v. *Tredegar Iron and Coal Co. Ltd* (1940):

> 'The man's work does not consist solely in the task which he is employed to perform, it includes also matters incidental to that task. Times during which meals are taken, moments during which the man is proceeding towards his work from one portion of his employer's premises to another and periods of rest may all be included. Nor is his work necessarily confined to his employer's premises.'

In *Smith* v. *Stages* (1989) the House of Lords held that an employee who was paid wages by the employer to travel to and from his home, in order to carry out his job, was acting in the course of his employment.

(b) An employee may still be regarded as being in the course of his employment where he acts in a negligent manner or performs an act wrongly, provided that he is authorised to do that act by the employer, albeit properly. This may include several situations.

(*i*) Where the employee behaves in an extremely foolish manner. *Century Insurance Co.* v. *NIRTB* (1942): a lorry driver was transferring petrol from his tanker to a store in a garage. He was smoking while he did this and a fire resulted. Held by the House of Lords: the lorry driver's employer was vicariously liable because the driver was in the course of his employment.

(*ii*) Where the employee oversteps the limits of his contractual duties, provided that he is acting for the benefit of his employer. *Kay* v. *ITW* (1968): X was employed in a warehouse to drive small vans and trucks. As he was trying to drive one of the vehicles which he was authorised to drive into the warehouse, he found a large vehicle (which he was not authorised to drive) blocking the doors. He climbed into it but due to his failure to realise that it was in reverse gear, he knocked down the plaintiff who was at the rear of the vehicle unloading it. Held: the employer was vicariously liable for the actions of X because, although he was acting outside the basic obligations of his contract of employment, he was nevertheless acting for the overall benefit of his employer.

However, if an employee does something entirely for his own benefit, he is said to be 'on a frolic of his own' and is no longer regarded as being in the course of his employment. *Hilton* v. *Thomas Burton (Rhodes) Ltd* (1961): an employee (the plaintiff's husband) was killed while travelling in a van which was involved in an accident due to the negligence of a fellow employee. The men were returning from a public house some considerable distance away from their place of work. Held: the employer was not vicariously liable for the employee's negligence because, by going to a public house some distance away, they were 'on a frolic of their own'.

Two recent decisions of the EAT and the Court of Appeal have moved away from the more traditional approach outlined above. Both cases concern the need for employers to implement ethical employment practices, rather than hiding behind principles of control and vicarious liability. The first case, although not directly on the point, illustrates how an employer should act in a given situation. In *Burton and Rhule* v. *De Vere Hotels* (1996) the employer was held liable for subjecting two waitresses to racial harassment via a series of racial comments made by a comedian speaking at a dinner. This liability was imposed even though the employer was neither aware of at the time nor had suspected such actions would take place. The EAT held that good employment practice required such harassment to be prevented or, at the very least, reduced.

Similar reasoning was used by the Court of Appeal in *Jones* v. *Tower Boot Co. Ltd* (1997). J had been subjected to a number of incidents of racial harassment which were of a very serious nature. The Court held that to allow the employer to argue that it was not liable as these acts were outside the 'course of employment' would frustrate the purpose of anti-discrimination legislation.

These two cases seem to suggest than an employer may be held responsible for actions of its employees which the older law may not have done so.

(*iii*) Where the employee disobeys an express prohibition as regards the *manner* of performing an authorised act. *Limpus* v. *London General Omnibus Co.*

(1862): employees of the defendant company were forbidden to drive their vehicles in such a way as to cause an obstruction. On one occasion, an employee caused an accident by driving his vehicle in front of the plaintiff's vehicle. Held: the employer was vicariously liable because the prohibition was simply as to the *manner* of performing the authorised act of driving.

However, where there is an express prohibition as to what the employee should, or should not, do and the employee disobeys this, he is no longer regarded as being in the course of employment, despite the fact that the third party may be unaware of the prohibition: *see Twine* v. *Bean's Express Ltd* (1946); *Rose* v. *Plenty* (1975).

(*iv*) Where the employment gives rise to the opportunity to defraud. *Heasmans* v. *Clarity Cleaning Co.* (1987): Company C contracted with H to clean the offices of H. C agreed to provide all the necessary labour, insurance, cleaning materials and equipment in order to clean, in particular, the telephones. One of C's servants employed to carry out the work wrongfully used the telephones in order to make international calls. The telephone bill amounted to £1,450. Held: Purchas LJ stated 'that before the master can be held to be vicariously liable for the acts of the servant there must be established some nexus other than mere opportunity between the tortious or criminal act of the servant, and the circumstances of his employment.' Mere access to premises, in this case, was held not to be sufficient to make the employer vicariously liable.

12. Vicarious criminal liability

As a general rule an employer is not liable for the criminal offences committed by his employees in the course of employment. However, in modern times, a number of statutory exceptions have been created to the general rule, particularly as regards offences committed by the employees of corporate bodies, e.g. under the Trade Descriptions Act 1968 and the Health and Safety at Work etc. Act 1974 (*see* 16:**23**).

SELECTION OF EMPLOYEES

13. Introduction

A number of statutory restrictions have been introduced upon an employer's 'right' to select employees upon whatever basis he so chooses. The main ones are the Rehabilitation of Offenders Act 1974, the Sex Discrimination Act 1975 and the Race Relations Act 1976. The last two Acts are examined in Chapter 10. In addition the provisions of the Disability Discrimination Act 1995 will be dealt with in this chapter. The Act imposes new duties in the case of selecting a disabled person for work. Finally the question of an employee being discriminated on grounds of membership, or non-membership, of a trade union will be looked at in Chapter 17 (*see* s. 137 TULR(C) Act 1992).

14. Rehabilitation of Offenders Act 1974

The 1974 Act allows a person to 'live down' certain criminal convictions after a specified period. After a specified period of between six months and ten years (depending upon the sentence imposed), a conviction is deemed to be 'spent' provided no serious offence is committed during the 'rehabilitation period'. The Act provides that normally a spent conviction, or failure to disclose it, is no ground for refusing to employ or dismiss a person or discriminating against him in employment. However, it is only in respect of dismissal that a remedy is provided in that if the only reason for a dismissal was the employer's knowledge of a spent conviction, such a dismissal would, all other things being equal, almost certainly be regarded as unfair: *see Property Guards Ltd* v. *Taylor and Kershaw* (1982) (*see* Chapter 13). It should be noted that by virtue of regulations made under the 1974 Act, the Act does not apply to a number of kinds of employment including teaching, medicine, accountancy etc.

CONTINUOUS EMPLOYMENT

15. Introduction

The concept of 'continuous employment' is most important in that nearly all of the various statutory rights of employees are dependent upon the acquisition by the employee of a minimum period of continuous employment, e.g. two years before a claim alleging unfair dismissal may be presented. At the time of writing, the statutory provisions governing this area are under review in the courts: *see* **17** below. In addition, if such a claim (and others) is successful, the amount of compensation awarded will be partly dependent upon the length of continuous employment of the employee.

16. Current trends

The current trends in employment mean that an increasing number of people are working on a temporary and part-time basis. Employers are also increasingly using fixed-term contracts (*see* 3:**16–18**) for a set length of time rather than employing a person on a permanent basis. This so-called 'enterprise' culture has meant that the question of continuity is of increased importance as employees may be working for two or more years with an employer but without necessarily satisfying the basic rules.

17. Basic rules

The rules for computing the period of continuous employment are contained in Part XIV of ERA 1996.

(a) Employment is presumed to be continuous unless the contrary is shown.

(b) Any week in which an employee is employed counts towards computing the period of employment. Hours for which a person is employed do not include hours 'on call' (*see Suffolk CC* v. *Secretary of State for the Environment* (1985)).

(c) A week counts even though an employee does not actually work if he/she would normally have done so but did not because of absence due to holiday, sickness, injury, pregnancy or confinement.

(d) Can separate concurrent contracts, with the same employer, be aggregated in order to give a person continuity of employment? (*See* 3:**16** below for fixed-term contracts.) In *Lewis* v. *Surrey County Council* (1987) L had worked for S since 1969 as a photography teacher on courses in three art college departments. L had separate contracts for each college term and for each of the three courses. Each contract was confined to the particular department concerned. The contracts merely specified the total number of hours to be worked. The House of Lords held that the contracts could not be aggregated as the legislation referred only to one single contractual obligation. On the facts it was said that L worked under a series of contracts. The House of Lords did however indicate that L should have pleaded that in fact the separate contracts amounted to one single contractual obligation.

(e) Any week in which an employee is absent on account of a 'temporary cessation of work' counts in the calculation of a period of continuous employment. A wide interpretation was given to these words in *Ford* v. *Warwickshire County Council* (1983). F had been employed by the respondents as a part-time teacher between 1971 and 1979 on a series of fixed-term contracts which ran from September to July each year. During the summer vacation F was not employed by the respondents. F's claim for compensation for unfair dismissal and redundancy was contested by the respondents on the basis that she did not have a long enough period of continuous employment. The House of Lords held that F was entitled to pursue her claim as the breaks between the fixed-term contracts could be characterised as periods where there was absence from work 'on account of a temporary cessation of work'. Accordingly her continuity of employment, and period of continuous employment, was preserved.

The courts will not take a strict mathematical approach to this issue. In *Flack* v. *Kodak Ltd* (1986) the Court of Appeal, approving the EAT, stated that all the circumstances must be taken into account and the tribunal or court should not merely limit itself to looking at the percentage that the cessation of work bore in relation to the periods of work. The relevance of the whole period of intermittent employment was shown by *Boast* v. *Willerby Caravan Ltd* (1987).

B started work as a labourer for W.C. Ltd on 10.12.84. After 14 weeks B was made redundant. Two weeks later B was re-employed for a period of 13 weeks, before being dismissed again. Following a gap of 12 weeks he was taken back into employment on 13.9.85. The employment continued unbroken until 2.6.87. B was then summarily dismissed for alleged misconduct. Held: looking at the employment history as a whole B had continuity. Any gaps did not break continuity because of the cyclical nature of the industry.

(f) Any week during which an employee is absent counts towards continuous employment if, by arrangement or custom, the employment is regarded as continuous.

(g) Any week in which an employee is on strike, or absent from work because of a lock-out, does not count in computing the period of employment but does not break continuity.

(h) Previously an employee had to work more than sixteen hours per week for a period of two years in order to be continuously employed. Alternatively if an employee had been employed for more than eight hours a week, but less than sixteen hours, that employee would have to have worked for more than five years in order to be regarded as having been continuously employed for that period. The above has changed as a result of the recent landmark decision of the House of Lords in R. v. *Secretary of State for Employment ex parte Equal Opportunities Commission* (1994). The narrow effect of the decision is to abolish the different qualifying periods based on the number of hours worked per week. The basis of the decision was that the provisions were incompatible with Article 119 of the Treaty of Rome and EEC Equal Pay Directive 7511 (see generally Chapter 9), and the different conditions in respect of rights to compensation for unfair dismissal were incompatible with the EEC Equal Treatment Directive 76/207; the reasoning being that the majority of employees who work less than 16 hours are female.

As a result of the decision in the case above the Government introduced the Employment Protection (Part-Time Employees) Regulations 1995. The effect of these Regulations is to abolish the qualifying hours thresholds for statutory employment rights. Under the Regulations all employees may now claim unfair dismissal and statutory redundancy pay after two years' continuous employment regardless of their hours of work.

The issue has not stopped there, as the ability of the Government to impose any form of qualifying period has been challenged in the courts in the case of *R. v. Secretary of State for Employment ex p. Seymour-Smith* (1995). The case concerned a challenge to the Unfair Dismissal (variation of qualifying period) Order 1985 which extended the qualifying period from one to two years. The basis of the challenge was similar to the *ex parte EOC* case above; that is, such a provision was discriminatory and contravened Article 119 of the EC Treaty. The Court of Appeal held that the applicants, at the time of their dismissal, were able to demonstrate that the effect of the two-year qualification period was incompatible with the principle of equal treatment enshrined in EC legislation. Further the Secretary of State was not able to objectively justify the discriminatory impact of the two-year qualifying period. The Court of Appeal emphasised that the decision was dependent on the facts of the particular case.

The House of Lords gave its judgment in the Seymour-Smith case in 1997. Unfortunately, as we shall see below, the legal position has not been clarified as numerous matters have been referred to the European Court of Justice. The House did, however, discharge a declaration granted by the Court of Appeal that the qualifying period was unlawful at the date of the applicant's dismissals in 1991. A number of reasons were given for this decision, the most notable of which was that the Equal Treatment Directive does not assist private sector employees. The Directive has not been implemented into United Kingdom domestic law; therefore, no rights could be given in this case. The House of Lords said it would be wrong to have piecemeal rights given to individuals by way of individual challenges in the courts.

The House of Lords then referred a number of issues to the ECJ, before it felt able to rule on the question as to whether a qualifying period is discriminatory. Amongst the questions referred are:

(*i*) does an award of compensation for breach of the right not to be unfairly dismissed constitute pay within the meaning of Article 119

(*ii*) if the answer in (i) above is correct then does the right not to be unfairly dismissed fall within the provisions of Article 119; and

(*iii*) what is the legal test to be used to establish whether a provision is indirectly discriminatory as between men and women. If so how, if at all, can it be objectively justified.

The definitions of 'pay' in Article 119 is discussed in more detail in Chapter 9. The case is unsatisfactory in that no decision has been made. Consequently there are numerous cases pending which can only be resolved after the ECJ has made a ruling and the House of Lords has delivered its final judgment.

A number of cases have arisen as a result of this litigation with the most notable being that of *Biggs* v. *Somerset County Council* (1996). The case concerned a retrospective application for unfair dismissal from 1976, the basis of the claim being that the decision in *Seymour-Smith* had changed the qualifying period requirement. The Court of Appeal disallowed the application as it had not been brought within three months of the original dismissal as required by legislation. The Court of Appeal emphasised that it would be contrary to the principle of legal certainty to allow past cases to be re-opened when the existing law at the time was misunderstood.

3

THE CONTRACT OF EMPLOYMENT (2): SPECIAL PROBLEMS

A number of groups of employees are, for different reasons, in a special position and some of the problems relating to such special positions are considered in this chapter.

DIRECTORS AND PARTNERS

1. Directors

A company director is regarded as an 'employee' for most of the statutory purposes if he has a written service contract with the company, but a non-executive director will not normally be regarded as an 'employee'. Whether such a service contract exists is a matter of law, to be determined by reference to the facts of the particular case (*see Albert J. Parsons and Sons Ltd* v. *Parsons* (1979)). Thus even a director of a 'one-man business' may be an 'employee' and, as such, be entitled to a redundancy payment from the company, as employer, if it goes into liquidation (*see Robinson* v. *George Sorbey Ltd* (1967) and, as to other such rights, *see Folami* v. *Nigerline (UK) Ltd* (1978)).

However, as has been stated, it is a question of law whether or not a contract of service exists. In *Eaton* v. *Robert Eaton and Secretary of State for Employment* (1988), E was the managing director of RE Ltd. When the company ceased trading, he applied to the tribunal for a redundancy payment. No payment was granted as there was nothing in writing to indicate that E was an 'employee' of the company and since 1981 E had not received any financial remuneration from the company because of its financial position. The EAT supported the decision of the tribunal as the facts could not rebut the presumption that E was an 'office holder' and therefore not an 'employee'. In *Buchan* v. *Secretary of State for Employment* (1997) it was held that two company directors who owned a controlling interesting in their company were not employees. The essence of the reasoning in the EAT appears to be that it would be wrong to confer rights on such individuals, under the ERA 1996, when the decision to dismiss could only be taken with their consent.

There are two statutory provisions governing directors' service agreements. Firstly, s. 318 of the Companies Act 1985, requires a company to keep a copy of every written service agreement. Secondly, a company cannot give its directors a contract of employment for more than five years unless the company approves it by resolution in a general meeting (s. 319 CA 1985).

2. Partners

A partner in a firm is self-employed. If a person is employed by partners, the relationship of employer/employee exists.

APPRENTICES

3. Nature of apprenticeship

A contract of apprenticeship is an agreement whereby the apprentice binds himself to the master in order to learn a trade, in return for the master's agreement to teach and instruct him. Such a contract must be in writing: Apprentices Act 1814, s. 2. Apprentices are now included in most statutory definitions of employment: s. 230(1) ERA 1996. The contract may only be terminated by the master if the apprentice evinces an intention not to learn (e.g. by persistent absenteeism) or for gross misconduct. Conversely, the apprentice may only terminate the contract if the master fails to provide instruction. The contract may be frustrated (*see* 11:**14–15**).

4. Unfair dismissal and redundancy

It would seem that although apprentices are entitled to claim statutory rights of unfair dismissal and/or redundancy (*see*, for example, *Finch* v. *Betabake (Anglia) Ltd* (1977)), the expiry of an apprenticeship contract is not, of itself, either an unfair dismissal or redundancy: *North East Coast Ship Repairers Ltd* v. *Secretary of State for Employment* (1978). As stated above apprenticeship contracts are to be treated as contracts of employment for certain rights. However the common law rules are still applicable in certain situations and this is illustrated by the decision in *Wallace* v. *CA Roofing Services Ltd* (1996). An apprentice was dismissed for redundancy before his training period was completed. The High Court held that an employer could not dismiss for redundancy before the training was complete unless there was a closure or fundamental change in the nature of the business carried on by the employer.

PUBLIC SECTOR EMPLOYEES

5. Crown servants

The precise legal status of Crown servants has long been the subject of controversy although, in practice, this has not given rise to many problems. The prevailing view now seems to be that the Crown and its servants enjoy a relationship analogous to a contract of employment, subject to an implied right on the part of the Crown to dismiss it at pleasure, i.e. without notice: *A-G for Guyana* v. *Norbrega* (1969). It should be noted that the employees of the nationalised industries and local authorities are not Crown servants.

6. Statutory rights

Irrespective of the common law position, a number of modern employment law provisions have expressly been extended to cover Crown employees, notably the unfair dismissals provisions: *see* s. 191 ERA 1996. It should be noted that unless an Act expressly so provides it does not bind the Crown: *Wood* v. *Leeds Area Health Authority (Teaching)* (1974).

7. Police

The police are excluded from many of the statutory rights to which other employees are entitled, e.g. the right to present a complaint of unfair dismissal: s. 200(1) ERA 1996. The definition of 'police service' in the 1996 Act is wide enough to include prison officers, who also lose the relevant statutory rights: *Home Office* v. *Robinson and The Prison Officers' Association* (1981). In addition, the rights of members of the police force to be members of trade unions and to engage in industrial action are severely limited. Nevertheless, as 'office holders', police officers cannot be dismissed without a hearing and have a right to reinstatement in the event of a dismissal being found to be wrongful: *see Ridge* v. *Baldwin* (1964).

8. The armed forces

The armed forces are excluded from the various statutory rights enjoyed by employees.

9. Remedies

One of the questions which has recently been raised is whether or not a public sector employee is able to have the decision of his/her dismissal reviewed by a court through the judicial review procedure. The essence of this procedure is that if the court holds that a decision has been made in an *ultra vires* fashion, whether procedurally or substantively, then the decision is void. In the context of dismissal the effect will be to reinstate the employee, as it is as if the decision had never been made.

How does the law decide whether a public sector employee is able to use the judicial review procedure as opposed to claiming unfair dismissal in an industrial tribunal? In *R.* v. *East Berkshire Health Authority ex p. Walsh* (1985) it was held that as the employee, a nurse, had a contract of employment, any claim concerning his dismissal should be pursued in an industrial tribunal for unfair dismissal.

The 'normal' route for claiming a remedy cannot be followed where the person is an 'office-holder' e.g. a police officer (*see* **7** above) or a prison officer. In this case there is no contract of employment and therefore judicial review will be the appropriate procedure to obtain a remedy as there is no alternative: *R.* v. *Home Secretary ex p. Benwell* (1985). The distinction between public and private law was recently re-affirmed in *Doyle* v. *Northumbria Probation Committee* (1992). Here it was held that the court should not permit a genuine private law action based on contract to be defeated by the introduction of a public law issue.

It should be noted, however, that the mere existence of a contract of employment will never preclude the courts from reviewing the decision of a public sector employer where the employment conditions of the employee are affected. In *McGoldrick* v. *London Borough of Brent* (1987), the Court of Appeal indicated that if the statutory underpinning of, in this case, a teacher, was adversely affected by the decision of a public authority then the courts would be willing to review such a decision.

MINORS

10. Common law principle

The ordinary rule of the law of contract is to the effect that a minor (i.e. a person under the age of eighteen) is bound by a contract of employment if the agreement, taken as a whole, is 'substantially for his benefit'. In *Doyle* v. *White City Stadium Ltd and BBBC* (1935) an infant boxer held a British Boxing Board of Control (BBBC) licence to box. After one contest, he was disqualified and in accordance with the rules of the BBBC his 'purse' was withheld. He claimed that this could not be done because he said the contract with the BBBC was not binding on him. Held: the contract was substantially for his benefit because the other terms of the agreement were clearly beneficial to him, e.g. those which regulated the conduct of contests. Therefore the contract was binding on him and the retention of the 'purse' was not wrongful.

11. Statutory restrictions

The Children and Young Persons Act 1933 and the Employment of Children Act 1973 regulate the employment of those minors below school-leaving age (16). These Acts, and regulations made thereunder, prevent, with limited exceptions, the employment of any person under the age of 13. Between the ages of 13 and 16, a minor may be employed in part-time work subject to restrictions as to the number of hours which may be worked and as to the time of such work. In addition, there are restrictions upon employment in certain kinds of work, e.g. in factories and mines.

Between the ages of sixteen and eighteen, minors are classed as 'young persons' and in various legislative provisions (e.g. Part VI of the Factories Act 1961), restrictions are imposed upon the kind of work and the number of hours which such persons may do. It should be mentioned at this stage that the Sex Discrimination Act, 1986, s. 7 removes most of the existing statutory provisions restricting women's hours of work. It is the piecemeal nature of the legislation which causes problems in this area.

Sections 3–6 of the Employment Act 1989 modify the differences between working conditions for women. Of more fundamental importance is s. 10 of the Employment Act 1989, which seeks to repeal the majority of restrictions relating to employment of 'young persons'. The aim of these repeals is to remove restrictions on hours and holidays.

The Health and Safety (Young Persons) Regulations 1997 impose new obligations on employers to protect under 18 years old from dangerous practices in the workplace. For the purpose of these regulations a 'child' and a 'young person' have the same meanings as above.

The Regulations fall into two broad categories: firstly assessment of and information about risks; secondly protection of young persons. An employer is not allowed to employ anyone under 18 without first making or reviewing an assessment of that person's ability to work. The Regulations list factors to be taken into account, including the experience of young persons generally and the way in which equipment is to be used. Further there is an obligation placed on existing employers of young persons to review the assessment 'forthwith'. The Regulations further require that an employer, before employing a 'child', must provide a parent with information on any risks identified of the assessment on Health and Safety issues and the preventive and protective measures taken by the employer. The Regulations provide two exceptions to the requirement of assessment when the employment is of an 'occasional or short-term' nature in a private household or work within a family undertaking which is not harmful to young people.

Secondly the Regulations provide an express requirement for employers to ensure that all under 18 year olds are protected at work from risks to their Health and Safety arising from their lack of experience or immaturity. This requirement may prevent certain work from being undertaken without specific training and supervision being provided.

TEMPORARY EMPLOYEES

12. General principle

The mere fact that an employee has been engaged expressly on the basis that he is 'temporary' does not, of itself, give the employer an automatic ground for terminating the employment fairly: *Terry* v. *East Sussex County Council* (1976). Once an employee has completed the appropriate period of continuous employment (notably two years for unfair dismissal), he is eligible to claim the various statutory rights. Consequently, the fact that he is regarded as 'temporary' does not automatically make a dismissal fair although this may constitute 'some other substantial reason' for dismissing the employee and as such, provided that the employer acted reasonably (e.g. possibly considered the availability of other employment), the dismissal might not be unfair (*see* Chapter 13). In *North Yorkshire County Council* v. *Fay* (1985) the Court of Appeal held that the non-renewal of a series of fixed term contracts amounted to dismissal for 'some other substantial reason'. On the facts of the case the fixed term contract was for a specific purpose, i.e. the replacement of other teachers on secondment, and as that purpose had been made known to F then any subsequent dismissal was fair. In *Brown* v. *Adjudication Officer* (1997) a casual worker who had worked on a series of day-to-day contracts for a period of three months was deemed (by what is now s. 86 ERA 1996) to be employed under a contract for an indefinite period and was therefore entitled to statutory minimum notice (see above) and, on the facts, statutory sick pay (see above).

13. Special cases

By virtue of s. 106 ERA 1996, an employee who is engaged expressly as a temporary employee to replace someone suspended on medical grounds or absent on maternity leave is not normally to be regarded as unfairly dismissed if the employment is terminated when the absent employee returns (*see* 7:**24**).

PROBATIONARY EMPLOYEES

14. General principle

An employee may be engaged subject to a probationary period, the employer thus reserving the right to terminate or confirm the employment within, or at the end of, a specified period of time. As with temporary employees (*see* **12** above), it must be stated that once the employee has achieved the necessary period of continuous employment, he is eligible to present a complaint of unfair dismissal.

15. Dismissal

As with any other dismissal which is alleged to be unfair the employer must show that he acted 'reasonably' (*see* 13:**11**). It seems that in determining whether the dismissal of a probationary employee is unfair, an industrial tribunal will normally require the employer to establish that he took reasonable steps to maintain appraisal of the probationer, that he gave appropriate guidance to the employee, that he made an honest effort to determine whether the probationer came up to the required standard and that he kept himself informed of the relevant facts (*see Post Office* v. *Mughal* (1977); *White* v. *London Transport Executive* (1981)). Many employers recognise special obligations to probationers in their terms of employment and a failure to meet these obligations may render a dismissal unfair: *ILEA* v. *Lloyd* (1981).

EMPLOYEES ON FIXED-TERM CONTRACTS

16. Rights of employees

Under such contracts employment rights depend on whether or not the contracts can be aggregated in order to give the employee 'continuous employment' of two or more years (*see* 2:**17**).

17. Of one year or more

It should be noted that the expiry of a fixed-term contract without renewal is a 'dismissal' for the purposes of unfair dismissal and redundancy (*see* 13:**6**, 14:**3**). However, by virtue of s. 197 ERA 1996 if before a fixed-term contract of one year or more expires, the employee agrees in writing to exclude any claim in respect of unfair dismissal/redundancy, such an undertaking is binding. The waiver only applies to dismissal 'on the expiry of the terms' i.e. at the end of the fixed-term period, therefore dismissal on grounds of discrimination during the course of the contract cannot be excluded. A further difficulty is where there is a series of fixed-term contracts, of less than a year, which when aggregated are of a year or more. It has been decided, albeit at industrial tribunal level, that the relevant contract was the final contract and if this was less than a year any waiver could not apply (*McKee* v. *Tyne & Wear Passenger Transport Executive* (1987)).

18. Meaning of 'fixed-term contract'

There is no statutory definition, but, following *British Broadcasting Corporation* v. *Dixon* (1979), it is now clear that a fixed-term contract is not 'fixed' if it contains a clause for early termination. A fixed-term contract is one which expires on a particular date, rather than on the performance of a task or the happening of an event: *Wiltshire County Council* v. *NATFHE* (1980). This view is further supported by the decision in *Brown* v. *Knowsley Borough Council* (1986) where the contract was expressed to last only so long as sufficient funds are provided by the MSC or by other firms or sponsors.

GOVERNMENT TRAINING SCHEMES

19. Introduction

In recent years the number of Government Training Schemes has proliferated. The status of a person on such a scheme depends very much on its nature; e.g. the presumption is that if the scheme is essentially one of training then the person is not an employee. Further the question of continuity needs to be discussed.

20. Youth Training Scheme

By analogy with its predecessor, the Youth Opportunities Programme, the YTS is aimed primarily at training as its objects are those of work experience and learning. Therefore a person on such a scheme is not an employee: *Daley* v. *Allied Suppliers* (1983). However, a person on such a scheme does have the protection of the Health and Safety at Work Act, as well as the Race and Sex Discrimination Legislation (*see* Chapters 10 and 16).

21. Community Programme

(as replaced by the Employment Training Scheme). The aim of the Community Programme was to provide temporary work for long-term unemployed adults. In *Dyson* v. *Pontefract and District Council CP Scheme* (1988), the EAT decided that participants in the Community Programme were employees. It will be interesting to see whether the same decision is made about participants on the Employment Training Scheme.

22. Continuity of employment and training schemes

Clearly, if the person is an employee under the scheme then this period of training will count when aggregating length of employment (*see* 2:**17**). However, in schemes where the person is not an employee, previous training will not count towards continuity: *Kennett* v. *Syme-Rumsby* (1974). A person who is taken on after a YTS will not be able therefore to count that period of training towards his continuity of employment.

PERSONS OVER RETIRING AGE

23. Introduction

The law in this area was determined by the European Court of Justice (ECJ) decision in *Marshall* v. *Southampton and South West Hampshire Area Health Authority* (1986). The decision meant that the Equal Treatment Directive (76/1207/ EEC) was directly applicable to State employees, but legislation was required to provide a remedy for private sector employees. The decision concerned men and women being required to retire at different ages which the ECJ held to be discriminatory. The response of the Government was to pass the Sex Discrimination Act 1986 which gave effect to the decision in *Marshall* but also made other amendments.

24. Unfair dismissal

Section 109(1) ERA 1996 equalised the age at which men and women cease to be eligible to claim unfair dismissal. If the contract states the normal retirement age then there is a strong presumption that this age applies. However, this may be rebutted if evidence shows that this age is regularly departed from in practice and has been superseded by some definite higher age. The House of Lords in *Waite* v. *GCHQ* (1983) established the principles outlined above. The issue arose in *Bratko* v. *Beloit Walmsley Ltd* (1995) where it was held that an employer who had failed to get the consent of the employees for the reduction in contractual retirement age could not unilaterally reduce the normal retirement for the purpose of s. 109(1) to an age below the contractually agreed age. This is governed by s. 156(1) ERA 1996 which states that it is a maximum age of 65 irrespective of practice

4

THE CONTRACT OF EMPLOYMENT (3): TERMS OF THE CONTRACT

INTRODUCTION

1. Significance of the terms

In any dispute between an employer and employee, the terms of the contract are of considerable significance in that one party may have a right to take legal action against the other in respect of any breach of contract. Of perhaps more general importance, however, is the significance of the terms of the contract when an action for unfair dismissal is brought. In such a case, although the question of whether one or more or both parties has broken the contract is of considerable importance, other considerations arise—notably whether the employer acted reasonably in dismissing the employee (*see* 13:**17**). Prior to the introduction of the remedy of unfair dismissal, an employer could always terminate the contract (without the employee having any recourse in law) provided that he gave proper notice (*see* 11:**2**), even if the employee was merely trying to assert his contractual rights. For example, if the employee was employed in Bristol and the contract made no provision for his being moved to another place, if the employer then ordered the employee to move his place of work to London and the employee refused, at common law the employer could quite lawfully terminate the employment by giving proper notice; but such a dismissal might now be considered to be unfair: *see Little* v. *Charterhouse Magna Assurance Co. Ltd* (1980). In addition, an employee may be able to assert his contractual rights through the notion of 'constructive dismissal' (*see* 13:**7**).

2. Sources of the terms of the contract

The terms of the contract of employment may be derived from a number of sources:

(a) Minimum statutory standards

(b) Express statements of the parties

(c) Collective agreements

(d) Works' rule-books

(e) Custom

(f) Duties of employees (*see* Chapter 5)

(g) Duties of employers (*see* Chapter 6).

3. Written statement

It should be noted that, by virtue of s. 1 of the 1996 Act, an employer is under an obligation to supply his employees with a written statement containing information as to certain terms of the contract of employment (*see* 2:7). It is important to appreciate that this statement is not the contract of employment—it is merely written evidence of certain parts of the contract, but may be regarded as important if no contradictory evidence is available.

MINIMUM STATUTORY STANDARDS

4. General principle

In effect all those statutory rights and duties which apply to the employer/employee relationship may be said to form part of every contract of employment except those to which the statutory provisions do not apply. With very few exceptions, it is not possible for the parties to contract out of the statutory provisions. The statutory rights can only be improved upon by the contract of employment.

5. Present trends

Traditionally our Labour Law has had very limited minimum provisions laid down to regulate certain rights. An exception used to be Wages Councils which had the ability to make wages orders which laid down minimum rates of pay in certain industries. Wages Councils and their abilities were abolished in 1993. The new Labour Government is committed, through its manifesto, to introduce minimum wage provisions. At the time of writing there are no details.

EXPRESS STATEMENTS OF THE PARTIES

6. Nature of express statements

An express statement, in this context, is a statement, either oral or written, made by the employer to the employee (or vice versa) concerning the terms of the contract. Such statements may include letters of appointment, formal contracts drawn up by the employer, verbal statements as to the terms and conditions of employment upon which the person is to be employed (as to wages, hours, holidays etc.) or other statements, e.g. a memorandum from one party to the other.

7. Pre-contractual statements

If an express statement is made before the parties enter into the contract of employment, it forms part of the contract and may not be subsequently altered without the mutual consent of the parties. If one party deviates from the agreed pre-contractual terms, that party is in breach of contract unless the other consents to the deviation either expressly or by implication, e.g. by continuing to employ, or work for, the other party after becoming aware of the breach.

The whole of the question of variation will be dealt with in more detail subsequently: *see*, generally, Chapter 12.

8. Post-contractual statements

Post-contractual statements do not form part of the contract of employment unless the parties expressly or implicitly agree that such a statement does become part of the contract. If an employee is employed upon certain terms which are stated prior to the commencement of the contract and he is subsequently given a written statement (under the provisions of s. 1 of the 1996 Act) which differs from the original terms as stated, the written statement does not supersede the agreed terms because, as stated at **3** above, the written statement is not to be regarded as contractual but merely as evidence of the contract, and in such a situation the employee ought to press his employer to give him an accurate written statement. If he is unable to do this, he may seek assistance from the industrial tribunals. If he fails to obtain a correct version of his written statement the presumption may arise that he has impliedly accepted the written statement as being a mutually agreed variation of the terms of the contract of employment and he may be stopped from denying that the statement represents the actual terms of the contract.

COLLECTIVE AGREEMENTS

9. General principle

The term 'collective agreement' has a particular definition in s. 178 of the Trade Union and Labour Relations Act 1992, but in general terms it may be described as an agreement between a trade union(s) and an employer(s) or employers' association which deals, amongst other things, with the terms and conditions of employment of employees of the employer(s) who is a party to the agreement. A collective agreement must be considered at two levels:

(a) Its effect as between the parties to it (*see* 18:3).

(b) Its effect upon the individual contracts of employment of the employees who are the object of the agreement. This second aspect is considered in this section.

A substantial proportion of all employees have their terms and conditions of employment determined by collective agreements and it is therefore important to know the extent to which, as a matter of law, such agreements form part of the individual contract of employment. This is sometimes referred to as the 'normative' effect of collective agreements. Several arguments have been advanced to suggest that a collective agreement must automatically be regarded as forming part of the contracts of employment of those employees to whom the agreement refers; but these arguments (e.g. that the trade union negotiates as agent of the employees) have generally been refuted by the courts: *see Edwards v. Skyways* (1964).

The correctness of this view has been put under pressure by the Court of Appeal decision in *Marley v. Forward Trust Group Ltd* (1986). M was employed as a field supervisor in F's Bristol office. His terms and conditions of employment incorporated the terms of a collective agreement with ASTMS, and included both a mobility and redundancy clause, the latter allowing a six months trial period. However, the final clause of the agreement stated that the agreement 'is binding in honour only'. F closed their Bristol office and M worked in London, under the terms of the agreement, for a trial period. He found the job unsuitable and sought a redundancy payment. Both the IT and the EAT rejected his claim on the ground that the agreement was stated to be 'binding in honour only' and was accordingly unenforceable. The Court of Appeal rejected this and held that the terms of an unenforceable collective agreement can be incorporated into contracts of employment and are then enforceable by the individual employee. The unenforceable nature of the agreement was limited to the parties to the agreement, in this case the employer and the union.

10. Express incorporation

It is fairly well established that it is possible to incorporate a collective agreement into an individual contract of employment if the contract expressly provides that this is to be the case. In *National Coal Board v. Galley* (1958) it was held that a clause of a collective agreement which stated that colliery deputies would work 'such days or part days in each week as may reasonably be required by the employer' could be regarded as being part of the individual contracts of employment because the contracts of the deputies referred to that collective agreement as being the source of the terms of their contracts.

It should be noted that the written statement supplied pursuant to s. 1 of the 1996 Act permits the employer to refer an employee to a document, such as a collective agreement, as being the source of certain terms of the contract of employment. The leading case on this issue is *Robertson and Jackson v. British Gas Corporation* (1983). Two employees appointed as gas meter readers were told, by letter, that incentive bonus scheme conditions would apply to the work. The employees were also given a written statement of terms of employment which stated that the provisions of the collective agreement would apply to their remuneration—and that any bonuses 'will be calculated in accordance with the rules of the scheme in force at the time'. The employers gave notice terminating the scheme on the ground that it had no legal force. No new scheme was negotiated and no bonus payments were received. The employees sued for loss of wages. Held: although the collective agreement was not binding between the union and the employers, it had been incorporated into the contracts of employment. The employers could not unilaterally alter the scheme and therefore the employees were entitled to the bonus payments.

The importance of the case is that the letter of appointment was the contract and not the written statement. Therefore, all the relevant documents are pertinent in determining this issue and it is clear that a s. 1 statement is not necessarily conclusive. *See* also *Gibbons* v. *Associated British Ports* (1985); *Cadoux* v. *Central Regional Council* (1986).

A collective agreement may also expressly become part of a contract of employment by virtue of statutory provisions. There are a number of situations where this is possible:

(a) Under s. 110 of the 1996 Act, provision is made for application to be made to the Secretary of State for the approval of dismissals procedures agreements. Such agreements, which replace the right to claim unfair dismissal for those employees covered, form part of the terms of employment of those employees within their ambit.

(b) Under s. 157 of the 1996 Act, a collective agreement may be made which substitutes for the right to claim a redundancy payment under the provisions of the 1996 Act, a right to claim under the collective agreement. If such an agreement is approved by the Secretary of State, it forms part of the terms of employment of those employees to whom it applies.

(c) Under s. 35 of the 1996 Act a collective agreement may be made which substitutes for the right to a guarantee payment under the provisions of the 1996 Act, a right to claim under the collective agreement. If approved by the Secretary of State the agreement forms part of the terms of employment (*see* 7:**10**). It should be noted that where the terms of a collective agreement are expressly incorporated and varied by consent between the union(s) and employer(s) the new terms become incorporated into the individual contracts of employment; however, unilateral variation or abrogation of the agreement by one party does not have a corresponding effect on individual employment contracts: *Robertson & Jackson* v. *British Gas Corporation* (1983).

Two recent decisions show the continued importance of collective agreements in regulating the contracts of employment of individuals. In *Adams* v. *British Airways plc* (1996) a dispute arose regarding the terms of contracts of pilots who had joined British Airways as the result of a take-over of another airline. The collective agreement provided that 'new entrants' to employment as pilots should be appointed at the bottom of the seniority scale irrespective of experience. The Court of Appeal held that this provision applied only to pilots who had left other airlines to join British Airways and not to pilots who had joined as the result of a take-over.

Secondly the Court of Session in *R. v. The Robert Gordon University ex p. the Educational Institute of Scotland* (1996) held, despite the fact that the Statutory Authority which had established the collective agreement had been abolished, the collective agreement itself remained effective. Therefore it still applied to both prospective and current employees alike.

11. Implied incorporation

On occasions, the courts have been prepared to permit the implied incorporation of collective agreements.

Sagar v. Ridehalgh and Son Ltd (1931). Held: employees entered employment in a Lancashire mill on whatever terms were normally observed there including the terms of relevant collective agreements. (*See also Brand v. London County Council* (1967).)

However, the general trend of the cases has been against the principle of implied incorporation.

Young v. Canadian Northern Railway Co. (1931): the plaintiff had been employed by the defendants. It was alleged by him that a collective agreement requiring that workers should be laid off in order of seniority was incorporated into his individual contract of employment. Held by the Privy Council: this agreement had not become incorporated into the contract of employment of the plaintiff despite the fact that this agreement had been normally observed as a matter of practice.

The decision in *Young's* case was apparently followed in *Dudfield v. Ministry of Works* (1964), *Faithful v. Admiralty* (1964).

However, it is possible that the terms of a collective agreement may be incorporated into a contract of employment by virtue of long observance (*see* Custom at **16** *below*).

Maclea v. Essex Line Ltd (1933): the terms of a collective agreement had been observed as a matter of practice for a number of years. Held: this agreement was incorporated into individual contracts of employment.

The House of Lords decision in *Scally v. Southern Health and Social Services Board* (1992) imposes an obligation on an employer to take reasonable steps to draw to the attention of workers terms which have not been negotiated with them personally, but have been negotiated with trade unions or other representatives. This obligation is of particular importance when the rights created are of a complex nature and the worker cannot be reasonably expected to be aware of them.

WORKS' RULE-BOOKS

12. Meaning of the term

A 'works' rule-book' can take a variety of forms in so far as it may consist of an actual book given to each employee when he enters employment or at some subsequent date; alternatively it may be a book of rules which is not given to each employee but which is known to exist and which is kept in the works' office; or it may simply be a list of rules pinned on a notice-board at the place of work. The rules in such a rule-book are often laid down by the employer without consultation and normally consist of rules relating to disciplinary action, suspension, dismissal for misconduct, bad time-keeping etc. It may also contain rules as to safety procedures to be adopted at the place of work. Note that as regards disciplinary rules, these must be referred to in the written statement (*see* 2:7).

13. The effect of the rule-book on the contract

The question of whether a works' rule-book forms part of the individual contract of employment of the employees who work in that place depends upon the particular circumstances, but the following principles have emerged.

(a) If the employer gives the employee a copy of the rule-book or expressly refers the employee to it before the contract is formed and the employee agrees that it is part of the contract (e.g. by signing an acknowledgment to that effect), then it is to be regarded as part of the contract of employment.

(b) It may be regarded as part of the individual contract if the employee is otherwise given notice of the fact that the rule-book has contractual force, e.g. by a notice posted on the wall of the place of work which can be clearly seen. This will almost certainly be the case if the employee's attention is drawn to that fact before employment commences. If he only sees the notice after he has entered into the contract, then it is a matter of custom and practice (*see* **14** below).

In *Petrie* v. *Macfisheries Ltd* (1940) a notice was posted on the wall of the work-place stating the circumstances in which sick pay would be paid. The plaintiff claimed that the notice did not form part of his contract of employment. Held: the rule as to sick pay had been incorporated into his contract of employment by virtue of his continued working in that place. This case is also illustrative of the principle that rules which are contained in the written statement will be terms of the contract. *See* also *Dal* v. *A S Orr* (1980).

(c) However not all works' rules will be terms of the contract of employment. This will be particularly so when there are numerous rules contained in the relevant documentation; some, for example, may have become out of date and therefore inappropriate. This principle is well illustrated by the decision in *Secretary of State for Employment* v. *ASLEF (No. 2)* (1972), a case concerning the rule book of British Rail, where Lord Denning said 'Each man signs a form saying that he will abide by the rules, but these rules are in no way terms of the contract of employment. They are only instructions to a man as to how he is to do his work'. The effect of this judgment is undoubtedly to increase the scope of managerial prerogative.

CUSTOM

14. Different kinds of custom

Custom plays a significant part in employment law, both from the practical aspect of industrial relations where emphasis is laid upon 'custom and practice', and in the courts when they are called upon to decide what are the terms of a particular contract of employment. This topic is somewhat nebulous but it seems that there are four different categories of custom which may form part of a contract of employment:

1. Custom of a particular place of work.
2. Custom of an industry or trade.
3. Custom of a specific geographical locality.
4. Customary conduct of the parties to the contract of employment.

15. Custom of a particular place of work

When an employee has been employed in a place of work for some length of time, there may be implied into his contract of employment terms based upon the custom of that place and he may not be able to contend that he never agreed to those terms. This may be particularly true where it is shown that the employee was aware of the existence of such customs and practices. As Lord Goddard said in *Marshall* v. *English Electric Co. Ltd* (1945):

'. . . an established practice at a particular factory may be incorporated into a workman's contract of service, and whether he knew it or not, it must be presumed that he accepted employment on the same terms as applied to other workers in that factory'.

The kind of customs which may arise under this head are those relating to breaks, suspension, dismissals procedures etc.

16. Custom of an industry or trade

Many industries and trades have their own particular customs applicable in a variety of situations. If a person agrees to be bound by the customs of the industry or trade when he enters employment or he continues to be employed in that industry, it may be said that those customs have become part of his contract of employment.

In *Sagar* v. *Ridehalgh and Son Ltd* (1931) it was held that the customs of the Lancashire weaving trade were incorporated into the contract of employment of a Lancashire weaver and therefore customary deductions for faulty workmanship were lawfully deductible. As Lawrence LJ said: 'A Lancashire weaver knows and has known for very many years past precisely what his position was as regards deductions for bad work in accepting employment in a Lancashire mill'. It was also stated that the weaver's knowledge of this practice was irrelevant since he accepted employment in accordance with the usual terms.

In *Davson* v. *France* (1959) a musician was given one week's notice to terminate his engagement. He claimed that this was wrongful dismissal on the basis that it was an implied term of his contract, by virtue of a custom of the music trade, that he should receive fourteen days' notice. Held: this was wrongful dismissal because there had been a breach of an implied term.

17. Custom of specific geographical locality

Certain areas of the country have customary practices which apply to persons employed in that area or to persons employed in certain work in that area. Such customs often concern holidays, e.g. it is customary in certain parts of England for a particular day to be a holiday. If this is implied into a contract of employment, it is a breach of contract for the employer to prevent an employee from having that day as a holiday. Note that in *Sagar* v. *Ridehalgh* (*see* **16** above) there was a geographical element involved.

18. Customary conduct of the parties

The courts may be prepared to regard the conduct of the parties as an aid to the interpretation of a contract of employment. In *Mears* v. *Safecar Security Ltd* (1982) a security guard who had been absent from work for two periods totalling seven months out of an employment period of fourteen months and who had not requested nor received any sick pay during the periods of absence, applied to an industrial tribunal under s. 11(1) of the 1996 Act (complaint relating to the failure of an employer to provide an adequate written statement of the main terms of the contract; *see* 2:**9**) for a determination of what particulars relating to sick pay ought to have been included. The Court of Appeal held that where there was no express agreement on the matter, the tribunal is entitled to consider all the facts and circumstances of the relationship between the employer and employee, including their subsequent acts and conduct under the contract. Accordingly it was held that no sick pay was payable. *See* also *O'Grady* v. *M. Saper Ltd* (1940).

> *Note*: in all these cases, the longer the person has been employed in that particular work, the stronger the presumption that a custom has become part of his contract of employment.

5

THE CONTRACT OF EMPLOYMENT (4): IMPLIED DUTIES OF EMPLOYEES

GENERAL CONSIDERATIONS

1. Significance of the implied duties

Into every contract of employment are implied a number of obligations in so far as these are not inconsistent with the express terms of the individual contract of employment. These duties are based upon principles developed by the courts in the decided cases. However, the mere existence of these obligations is not, in itself, important—the important question is as to the consequences which may follow from a breach of one of the duties. The answer will vary according to which of the duties is broken and the gravity of such breach.

On occasions, the employer may be justified in dismissing the employee without notice (*see* 11:6), or with notice in circumstances which are not deemed to be 'unfair' within the meaning of the 1996 Act, s. 94 (*see* 13:10).

Alternatively, the employer may be able to obtain an injunction to prevent an employee from benefiting from a breach of one of the duties, or levy a fine on, or suspend, the employee without pay. Of course, it is also important to note that if an employer chooses to ignore a breach of one of the duties, that is the end of the matter.

2. The implied duties

The implied duties may be classified as follows:

(a) to be ready and willing to work

(b) to use reasonable care and skill

(c) to obey lawful orders

(d) to take care of the employer's property

(e) to act in good faith.

TO BE READY AND WILLING TO WORK

3. The basic obligation of employment

The fundamental duty which an employee owes to his employer is the duty to present himself at work, in accordance with the contract of employment, and to work at the direction of the employer in return for the implied obligation of the employer to pay wages as agreed (*see* 6:2)

4. Absence of employee

Therefore, if an employee is absent from work without excuse, that constitutes a breach of contract and the employer may act accordingly.

5. Taking of industrial action by an employee

An interesting issue in this area of being ready and willing to work concerns an employee taking industrial action (*see* generally Chapter 19). What happens if the employee is only ready and willing to do a proportion of his work? Two cases need to be discussed in this context. In *Miles* v. *Wakefield Metropolitan District Council* (1987) M was a superintendent registrar of births, deaths and marriages. He normally worked 37 hours per week, three of which were on Saturday mornings. As part of industrial action M refused to carry out marriages on Saturday mornings, although he was willing to do his other work. The council made it clear that unless he was willing to perform all his duties then it would deduct his wages for that period. M did perform other work on Saturdays but the council withheld 3/37 of his wages. M sued for the lost wages. It was held by the House of Lords that where an employee refuses to perform the full range of his duties and had been told that he would not be paid if he did not, then the employers were entitled to withhold the whole of his remuneration, although he attended for work and carried out a substantial part of his duties.

The above case can be compared with the decision in *Wiluszynski* v. *London Borough of Tower Hamlets* (1989). W was employed as an estates officer. W took part in limited industrial action which took the form of refusing to answer members' inquiries. This was part of the contractual duties of W, but did not take up much of his time. The industrial action had been taking place for a two week period before the council did anything about it and then no action was taken as W agreed to work normally. The action then continued for a five week period in total. W cleared the back-log of members' inquiries within three hours. He had satisfactorily performed all his other work during this period. The council refused to pay him any wages for this five week period. W sued for payment. Held: the council was entitled to withhold the wages as W had to perform all his contractual obligations during this period to be entitled to his contractual remuneration.

A similar line of reasoning was adopted by the Court of Appeal in *Ticehurst* v. *British Telecommunications plc* (1992). The employee was involved in a 'rolling campaign of strategic strikes'. The employer insisted that when the employee returned to work she signed an undertaking to work normally. When she refused to do so, she was again told to leave the work premises. It was held that where an employee took part in industrial action the employer was entitled, without terminating the contract, to refuse for all of them to remain at work. Hence the employer was under no obligation to pay wages.

It should be noted that the Court of Appeal did reject the employer's argument to extend this principle to the intention to become involved in industrial action. Consequently the employee must be actually involved in industrial action for a breach of contract to arise.

6. Withholding of pay without due cause

Employers, however, cannot unilaterally withhold or deduct pay without just cause. If the employers decide to reduce pay unilaterally, then such an action will be seen as a fundamental breach of contract giving the employee the option to repudiate the contract. However, it should be noted that such a breach does not automatically bring the contract to an end: *see Rigby* v. *Ferodo Ltd* (1988).

TO USE REASONABLE CARE AND SKILL

7. Extent of the duty

The duty to use reasonable care and skill in the performance of the duties under the contract has two aspects:

(a) The duty not to be unduly negligent.

(b) The duty to be reasonably competent.

8. Not to be unduly negligent

If an employee is negligent in the performance of his work, he may be regarded as being in breach of contract. This is particularly true if there has been a pattern of negligent conduct by that employee or if the single act of negligence is especially serious. In *Lister* v. *Romford Ice and Cold Storage Co. Ltd* (1957) a lorry driver, employed by the company, carelessly reversed his lorry and injured a fellow employee, who was in fact his father. The employers paid damages to the father but claimed an indemnity from the son on the grounds that he had broken an implied term of the contract of employment, i.e. the duty not to be negligent in the performance of the work. Held: the employee would be liable because of the breach of the implied duty.

Another example of the application of the *Lister* principle is to be found in *Janata Bank* v. *Ahmed* (1981), where a bank employee, A, was successfully sued by his employers for losses caused by his negligence in authorising the overdrafts of non-creditworthy customers.

However, it is clear that if the principle of *Lister's* case is extended to its potential limits, this would seriously affect the doctrine of vicarious liability in so far as employers would be able to seek an indemnity from employees for whom they were vicariously liable. The notion of this implied duty must therefore be approached with caution. For example, in *Jones* v. *Manchester Corporation* (1952), the court held that the employers remained liable for the negligence of their employees because they had allowed inexperienced employees to perform a difficult job without proper supervision.

It should be noted that there are few cases where an employer has sued an employee for breach of the contractual duty of care. In practice an employer is much more likely simply to dismiss the employee.

9. Duty to be reasonably competent

If an employee is incompetent this in itself may constitute a breach of the contract of employment, particularly if the employee has professed his ability to do that particular work. As Willes J said in *Harmer* v. *Cornelius* (1858):

> 'It may be, that, if there is no general and no particular representation of ability and skill, the workman undertakes no responsibility. If a gentleman, for example, should employ a man who is known to have never done anything but sweep a crossing, to clean or mend his watch, the employer probably would be held to have incurred all risks himself'.

By implication, therefore, if an employee states that he can do a particular job and he is not, in fact, competent to do that work, the employer may regard the incompetence as a breach of contract.

Other forms of misconduct (e.g. drunkenness or fighting) may also amount to a breach of the overall obligation to use reasonable care and skill in doing his work. However, the employee must be shown to have acted unreasonably since he is not expected to be above reproach in everything he does. As to the extent to which lack of competence may be used to justify a dismissal as fair, *see* 13:**14**.

TO OBEY LAWFUL ORDERS

10. Disobedience may justify summary dismissal

An employee is under a duty to obey all the lawful orders of his employer, i.e. those which are within the scope of the contract. A failure to do this is a breach of the contract of employment and may, in certain circumstances, justify summary dismissal (*see* 11:6). However, it must be established that the order was one which is within the scope of the contract of employment. In *Price* v. *Mouat* (1862) a lace-salesman was ordered to 'card' (pack) lace but he refused and was dismissed without notice. He claimed that this was wrongful dismissal. Held: the dismissal was wrongful because the order was not one which was within the scope of the contract.

An employee is not, therefore, obliged to do any act which is deemed to fall outside the ambit of his individual contract of employment. The question of the introduction of new technology has caused problems here and must be linked to the scope of managerial prerogative in introducing new work techniques. In *Cresswell* v. *Board of Inland Revenue* (1984), the Revenue wished to introduce a computer system to assist with the PAYE system. The majority of the work associated with the system had previously been done manually. Did the employers have the ability to change the nature of the working system? Held: employees were expected to adopt the new methods and techniques in performing their contracts if the employer provided the necessary training in the new skills. It should be mentioned that the judge added the caveat that the nature should not change 'radically' as a result of the changes; clearly this is a question of degree based on the facts of individual cases.

11. Justifiable refusal to obey an order

The only circumstances in which an employee may be justified in refusing to obey an order which is apparently within the scope of his contract are:

(a) Where such an order involves exceptional danger for which the employee is not given extra payment. In *Robson* v. *Sykes* (1938) a merchant seaman was ordered to sail on a ship which was to call at Spanish ports. He refused on the grounds that serious danger was involved on account of the Civil War. He was dismissed for his refusal but he claimed that the dismissal was wrongful. Held: his action succeeded because, while the order was prima facie within the scope of the contract, it involved unreasonable danger to the employee.

(b) Where the employer orders the employee to do something which would constitute a criminal offence; *see Morrish* v. *Henleys (Folkestone) Ltd* (1973) and *Gregory* v. *Ford* (1951).

12. Disobedience and unfair dismissal

In practice, claims under the statutory procedures for unfair dismissal are much more numerous than the common law action for wrongful dismissal. Although there are circumstances where an employer may still be entitled to dismiss summarily in respect of a refusal to obey an order (e.g. where the refusal amounts to grave misconduct), the usual position will be that the employers' reasonableness in treating the refusal as a ground for dismissal will have to stand up to scrutiny before a tribunal, even though the refusal has amounted in law to breach of contract. *See* generally Chapter 13.

TO TAKE CARE OF EMPLOYER'S PROPERTY

13. Extent of the duty

An employee is under an obligation to take reasonable care of his employer's property. In *Superflux* v. *Plaisted* (1958) the defendant had been in charge of a team of vacuum cleaner salesmen and had negligently allowed fourteen cleaners to be stolen from his van. Held: he was in breach of his contract of employment.

14. Indemnity

In such circumstances an employee is under an obligation to indemnify his employer for the loss sustained.

TO ACT IN GOOD FAITH

15. Several aspects

The implied duty of the employee to act in good faith towards his employer has several different aspects which together form the basis of what is regarded as a relationship of trust by the law.

16. Duty not to make a secret profit

An employee must not abuse his position by making a secret profit, e.g. by accepting a bribe to ensure that a person obtains a contract with the employer. This principle is clear from the case of *Reading* v. *A.G.* (1951), which concerned a member of the armed forces, in which Lord Normand said:

'. . . though the relation of a member of His Majesty's forces is not accurately described as that of a servant under a contract of service . . . he owes to the Crown a duty as fully fiduciary as the duty of a servant to his master . . . and in consequence . . . all profits and advantages gained by the use of his military status are to be for the benefit of the Crown'.

17. Duty to disclose certain information

There appears to be no general duty on an employee to inform his employer of his misconduct or deficiencies: *Bell* v. *Lever Brothers* (1932). However, to that general principle there is one important exception, namely where the employment of that particular person is made more hazardous by virtue of an undisclosed defect on the part of the employee. In *Cork* v. *Kirby Maclean Ltd* (1952) an epileptic employee was engaged by an employer but he did not disclose the fact of his epilepsy. He fell while working at some height above the ground and was killed. His widow brought an action for damages on behalf of her husband. Held: damages must be reduced because of the fact that her husband had failed to inform his employer of his condition. Singleton LJ:

'A man who knew himself to be in the conditions in which Mr Cork knew that he was ought to have told his employers. However anxious he was to get work, he owed a duty to himself and his fellow workmen and failure to inform the employers, followed by instructions to work at some height above the ground, involved risk to the other workman as well as himself'.

There is no general duty to inform an employer of the misconduct or deficiencies of a fellow employee. However, such a duty can arise where the employee has expressly contracted to serve the best interests of the employer: *Swain* v. *West (Butchers) Ltd* (1936). The position of an employee in the hierarchy of a company may also be relevant to the existence of the duty. Thus where an employee has managerial responsibilities over a complete section of the employer's business, then a duty to report the misdeeds of subordinates may arise: *Sybron Corporation* v. *Rochem Ltd* (1983).

18. Duty not to act to detriment of employer

There is, apparently, a duty on an employee not to act in such a way as to harm the interests of the employer. For example, if an employee works in a position of financial trust, it may be a breach of his contract of employment if he is found guilty of dishonesty not connected with his employment in so far as such conduct reflects on his employer. The same may be true of gross immorality or drunkenness: *Clouston & Co.* v. *Corry* (1906).

Such conduct may justify summary dismissal, but it is probably more likely that it would be regarded as conduct which would justify dismissal that would not be regarded as 'unfair' within the meaning of s. 94 of the 1996 Act (*see* 13:2). Of course, similar conduct occurring in connection with employment would probably constitute a breach of the duty to use reasonable care and skill (*see* 7–8 above).

19. Duty not to disclose confidential information

Persons who work under a contract of employment owe a general duty to their employers not to disclose confidential information relating to them. As Lynskey J said in *Bent's Brewery* v. *Hogan* (1945): 'In my view, it is quite clear that an employee is under an obligation to his employers not to disclose confidential information obtained by him in the course of and as a result of his employment'. This duty applies both during employment and afterwards if the employee seeks to use such information to the detriment of the employer. The remedy available to an employer for breach of this duty is to seek an injunction restraining the employee (or any other person) from using the information. The basis of this implied duty is that the information is in the nature of a property right which cannot be taken from the employer without his consent. The courts take the view that employers would not allow their employees to have access to such information unless they thought that the law would protect them against the misuse of it.

20. Meaning of 'confidential information'

It is difficult to state in general terms what may be regarded as confidential information or a trade secret, but in *Thomas Marshall (Exports) Ltd* v. *Guinle* (1978) a number of factors were identified as being relevant:

(a) The information must be information the release of which the owner believes would be injurious to him or advantageous to his rivals.

(b) The owner must believe that the information is confidential or secret, i.e. not already public knowledge.

(c) The owner's belief under the above two heads must be reasonable.

(d) The information must be judged in the light of the usage and practice of the particular industry or trade concerned.

Therefore, information which is public knowledge is not protected by this implied duty. If an employer wishes to prevent an employee from utilising non-confidential information, or information which is not personal to the employer, he can only do so by using an express covenant (*see* **21** below).

'Confidential information' relates to such matters as manufacturing processes of a secret nature, designs, customer lists, accounts etc., and *see* the *Faccenda Chicken* case below. In *Thomas Marshall (Exports) Ltd* v. *Guinle* (1978) the managing director of a company (which was in business purchasing clothing from manufacturers in the Far East and Eastern Europe for resale to large mail order and multiple stores) secretly set up a rival company. He was prevented by injunction from using or disclosing confidential information relating to such matters as names and telex addresses of manufacturers and suppliers, prices paid by his employers for goods and details of the employers' new ranges and prices paid by customers to the employer.

However, this duty does not extend to the employee's general skill and knowledge as to the method and manner of performing his work, often referred to as 'know-how'. The scope of this duty was discussed by the Court of Appeal in the important case of *Faccenda Chicken Ltd* v. *Fowler* (1986) where the company sought an injunction to restrain F, and other former employees who had formed a rival company, from using 'confidential' information which they had acquired whilst working for the company. The information included purchasing requirements of customers, pricing structure and marketing strategy. There was no express term limiting the disclosure of information, therefore the question was whether a term could be implied to that effect. The Court of Appeal made a number of general observations from which it appears that while an employee remains in the employment of an employer, the duty of confidentiality forms part of a more general duty of good faith and fidelity. The duty does extend to ex-employees, but in a more limited form and it only covers trade secrets, designs, special methods of construction and other information which is of a 'sufficiently high degree of confidentiality as to amount to a secret'.

The Court of Appeal then laid down four criteria to distinguish between 'confidential' information (which is protected) and 'know-how' (which is not).

(a) *The nature of the employment.* If secret information is 'habitually handled', an employee will be aware of the sensitivity of the information.

(b) *The nature of the information itself.* Such information must 'in all the circumstances be of such a highly confidential nature as to require the same protection as a trade secret'.

(c) *Confidential nature of the information emphasised by the employer.* For the application of this criterion, it is essential to establish whether the employer impressed on the employee that the information was confidential.

(d) *The 'detached' nature of the information.* For information to be classified as 'confidential', it would need to be shown whether the information could easily be isolated from other information which the employee is free to disclose.

Applying these principles, the Court of Appeal decided that neither the information about prices by itself, nor when taken together with the other sales information, had the degree of confidentiality to warrant an injunction being granted. The court took account of the following facts in making its decision:

(a) Some of the information was clearly not secret, e.g. van routes.

(b) The information about prices could not be severed from the rest.

(c) The information had been acquired in order to allow the employees to do their work and could have been memorised anyway.

(d) The information available was not restricted to senior staff.

See further application of these principles in *Roger Bullivant Ltd* v. *Ellis* (1987) and *Johnson and Bloy (Holdings) Ltd* v. *Wolstenholme Rink plc* (1987).

The principles from the *Faccenda Chicken Case* (above) were applied by the Court of Appeal in *Lancashire Fires Ltd* v. *SA Lyons & Co. Ltd* (1997). The case concerned information which an ex-employee cannot disclose due to its confidential nature. The Court held that it was not for the employer to state the precise limits relating to the disclosure of such information. The information, on the facts of the case, related to the manufacturing process. The ex-employee used this information in order to hire equipment and gain financial assistance for the new business. The requirements to protect such information were satisfied as it put the ex-employee 'on the wrong side of the line' as to what he could do.

In *Hivac Ltd* v. *Park Royal Scientific Instruments Ltd* (1946) five employees of the appellant company were employed to assemble hearing aids, which was a highly specialised form of work. On Sundays they did similar work for a rival company. There was no evidence to show that they had actually transmitted trade secrets. Held: because of the particular nature of the work and the possibility that information could be passed, there was justification for an order restraining the respondents from employing the five men.

COVENANTS IN RESTRAINT OF TRADE

21. Meaning of the term

A covenant in restraint of trade is a clause in a contract which purports to limit an employee's right to seek employment where and when he chooses upon leaving his employment. An employer may wish to insert such a covenant into a contract of employment for one of two reasons:

(a) He wishes to prevent an employee from using general information which is not covered by the implied duty of non-disclosure of confidential information (*see* **19** above); or

(b) He does not wish to rely solely on that implied duty, even in respect of matters which might be covered by it, e.g. customer lists and manufacturing processes.

22. General attitude of the courts

The general attitude of the courts to such covenants is to regard them as prima facie void as being a restraint upon the right to seek employment freely. However, if an employer can establish that such a covenant is reasonable, it may be enforceable. To prove that such a clause is reasonable, it must be shown that it is necessary to protect the employer's proprietary interests and that it is not an undue restriction upon the employee's right to seek employment elsewhere. Furthermore, the covenant must not be contrary to the public interest.

An example of the legal meaning of a proprietary right is provided by the decision in *Cantor Fitzgerald (UK) Ltd. v. Wallace* (1992). D had been employed by P Company as a broker in Eurobonds, subject to a clause in his contract preventing him from working for a competition business for six months after terminations of employment. D left P and went to work for another firm of brokers in competition with P. P sought an injunction to prevent D from working for its competition. The alleged proprietary interest to be protected concerned existing customers of P which D tried to take with him. It was held that no injunction could be granted as the customer connection which arises as a result of the employee's personality qualities could not be said to be a proprietary interest and, therefore, could not be protected.

The above decision can be compared with that in *Euro Brokers Ltd v. Rabey* (1995). An injunction was granted to prevent an employee from working for a competitor when he was on so-called 'garden leave' for a six months period. The term means he was working out his period of notice, in this case six months. The justification was that this was to prevent the employee using his customer connections which had been built up through his employer over a period of time. Clearly each case turns on its own particular facts and therefore it is often difficult to make hard and fast decisions.

23. Factors to be considered

In determining whether a particular covenant is reasonable and therefore enforceable, the courts make reference to certain factors:

(a) *Time.* The court must be satisfied that the time for which the covenant is to run is not excessive. In general terms, it must be for no longer than is strictly necessary to prevent the employer's proprietary interests from being prejudiced. For example in *Roger Bullivant Ltd v. Ellis* (1987) an injunction was granted restraining an ex-employee from using a card index containing confidential information for a year after his employment ended. Similarly in *Credit Suisse Asset Management Ltd* v. *Armstrong* (1996) in effect a year long restraint was upheld. What is interesting with this decision is that this was split into two six-month periods, one of these periods relating to 'garden leave' and the other being a six-month restraint which was held to be valid.

(b) *Area*. The geographical area to which the covenant extends must normally be limited to the area within which the employee formerly worked. This may be countrywide if the business of the employer is a national concern (this is more likely to be a manufacturing rather than a service industry), but in certain circumstances, the limits must be very narrow. In *Mason* v. *Provident Clothing and Supply Co.* (1913) it was held that an employer could not rely on a clause which sought to obtain protection from competition from a former employee within twenty-five miles of London because the former employee's work had only brought him into contact with customers in a small area of London. In *Dewes* v. *Fitch* (1921) the contract of employment of a solicitor's clerk provided that he should not enter into employment with any other solicitor within a radius of seven miles of his former employer. Held: this was reasonable and therefore valid.

Where the clause seeks to prevent an employee from depriving his former employer of customers, the clause must normally be restricted not only to a particular geographical area but also to customers or former customers in that area: *Gledhow Autoparts* v. *Delaney* (1965); *Financial Collection Agencies (UK) Ltd* v. *Batey* (1973); *Marley Tile Co.* v. *Johnson* (1982).

(c) *Similarity of business*. The covenant must be restricted to employment in a similar kind of business as that in which the employee was formerly engaged. In *Attwood* v. *Lamont* (1920) a clause in the contract of employment of a tailor employed in a department store stated that the employee must not subsequently enter into employment with any employer whose business competed with that of the store. Held: the clause was unenforceable since it should have been limited to business which competed with that of the tailoring department.

(d) *Public interest*. The public interest in these circumstances is that society ought not to be deprived of the services of a skilled man and it seems that this virtually corresponds with the employee's interests: *Wyatt* v. *Kreglinger and Fernau* (1933); *Eastham* v. *Newcastle United FC* (1964); *Bull* v. *Pitney-Bowes Ltd* (1967).

24. Severance

If the covenant is found to be unreasonable, the contract as a whole is not necessarily to be regarded as void, unless it is impossible to distinguish the covenant from the rest of the contract. If the covenant can be severed from the rest of the contract, without altering the nature of the agreement, the unreasonable clause may be struck out: *see Commercial Plastics Ltd* v. *Vincent* (1965).

25. Effect of wrongful dismissal

If an employer breaks the contract of employment by wrongfully dismissing an employee (*see* 11:5), the employee may disregard any covenant in the contract which purports to limit his right to seek employment elsewhere: *General Billposting Co.* v. *Atkinson* (1909). There has been a clarification regarding the operation of the application of the above principle. Modern restraint clauses, as a result of their wording, purport to apply even after a repudiatory breach of contract by the employer. Such wording would include phrases such as 'howsoever caused' as to why the contract had been terminated. The correct approach to these clauses was finalised in the Court of Appeal decision in *Rock Refrigeration Ltd* v. *Jones and Seward* (1996) where it was held that the correct approach is to determine whether the employer has committed a repudiatory breach. If the answer is yes, then the clause is unenforceable for that reason under the General Bill Posting principle (above). The issue as to whether a clause is reasonable, or not, only applies when the covenant is enforceable.

26. Effect of breach of covenant

If an employee acts in breach of a covenant in restraint of trade, his former employer may seek an injunction to prevent the former employee from continuing to act in breach. However, as a matter of practice, such covenants are often inserted into contracts of employment as a deterrent rather than with any real intention of enforcing them. The Court of Appeal has, however, extended the scope of injunctions to enforce restraint of trade covenants. In *PSM International* v. *Whitehouse* (1992) an injunction was granted against an ex-employee preventing him from fulfilling a commercial contract already made with a third party, as opposed to entering into a future contract. It must be emphasised that it will only be in rare circumstances that such an injunction will be granted.

Covenants in a contract which prevent an employee from working for a rival during employment will normally be upheld, although, if the effect of such a covenant is to enforce performance of the existing contract, the court may be unwilling to issue an injunction (*see* 12:7).

The increased use of 'non-poaching' clauses is worth noting. The purpose of such clauses is to prevent ex-employees from taking former colleagues with them. The justification of this approach is to protect the employer in allowing him to maintain a stable workforce. A recent example of this is the decision in *Alliance Paper Group plc* v. *Prestwich* (1996) where, amongst other things, a 12-month non-poaching clause was upheld for these reasons.

PATENTS

27. Common law position

At common law, unless the contract dealt with the matter, an employee would not normally be entitled to the benefit of any invention made by him if to allow him to do so would be a contravention of the implied duty of the employee to act in good faith.

28. Patents Act 1977

The 1977 Act (ss. 39–47) gives ownership of an invention to the employee inventor unless the invention was made in the course of the duties for which he was employed. This exception applies where either an invention should have been reasonably expected to result from carrying out his duties or, because of the nature of the employee's duties, he had a special obligation towards the employer. In addition, even if the employer is entitled to an invention made by an employee who has patented it, the employee may claim compensation from the employer if the patent has been of outstanding benefit to him. Disputes are dealt with by the Patents Court.

6

THE CONTRACT OF EMPLOYMENT (5): DUTIES OF THE EMPLOYER

INTRODUCTION

1. Obligations

By virtue of the common law and a variety of statutory provisions, employers have a considerable number of obligations towards employees. The main examples of these duties are:

(a) to pay contractually agreed remuneration

(b) to observe provisions relating to sick pay

(c) to treat employees with trust and confidence

(d) to observe provisions relating to holidays

(e) to observe provisions relating to hours of work

(f) to permit employees time off work for public duties

(g) to indemnify employees

(h) to provide references

(i) to insure employees and other duties.

> *Note*: Other duties are dealt with elsewhere, e.g. in relation to safety. *See* Chapter 16.

TO PAY REMUNERATION

2. General principle

The amount of remuneration to which an employee is entitled is determined by the contract, often arising as a result of collective bargaining.

The basic obligation of the employer arising from the contract is to pay the contractually agreed remuneration, and a failure to do so constitutes a breach of contract which, depending upon the circumstances, might be such as to constitute a constructive dismissal (*see* 13:**6**). Traditionally it has been assumed that, subject to two well-established exceptions and one more recent exception, an employer is under no duty to provide work so long as he pays the contractually agreed remuneration. As Asquith LJ said in *Collier* v. *Sunday Referee Publishing Co. Ltd* (1940): 'Provided I pay my cook her wages regularly she cannot complain if I choose to take any or all of my meals out'. However, in addition to the three exceptions dealt with in **3** below, in recent times the general principle that an employer has no duty to provide work has been questioned, particularly in relation to skilled employees. Lord Denning said in *Langston* v. *AUEW* (1973): 'In these days an employer, when employing a skilled man, is bound to provide him with work. By which I mean that the man should be given the opportunity of doing his work when it is available and when he is ready and willing to do it.' If such a view is generally accepted by the courts, a failure on the part of an employer to provide an employee with work of the kind which he is contractually employed to do might be regarded as a constructive dismissal (*see* 13:**6**): *see Breach* v. *Epsylon Industries Ltd* (1976).

3. Exceptions

Three exceptions to the general principle are well-established:

(a) Where the employee is employed wholly or mainly on piece-work or on a commission basis, he is entitled to receive wages which are equivalent to what he would have received had he been given work to do. This right continues for as long as the contract subsists unless there is a contrary agreement in the contract itself. In *Devonald* v. *Rosser and Sons* (1906) an employer closed his factory because of a trade recession and gave his piece-work employees one month's notice to terminate their contracts. They were given no work to do during this period and could therefore earn no wages. Held: by the Court of Appeal: there was an implied term of their contracts that they would be able to earn wages during the period of notice and they were therefore entitled to damages based upon the average of their weekly earnings during the last six weeks of their normal employment.

In practice many piece-workers are now covered by collective agreements which provide a contractual right to minimum earnings and, in addition, note the provisions of ss. 28–35 of the 1996 Act in relation to guarantee payments (*see* 7:**10**). Note also that ss. 88–91 of the 1996 Act sets out the rights of the employee during a period of notice to terminate employment.

(b) Where the nature of the employment is such that the actual performance of the work forms part of the consideration supplied by the employer, the employee may be entitled to compensation over and above the contractual wages. These situations are sometimes referred to as 'name in lights' clauses and if the employer fails to give the employee work to do, he may be obliged to compensate the employee for the loss sustained in not being able to enhance his reputation or advance his experience in that particular kind of work. In *Clayton etc.* v. *Oliver* (1930) it was held that an actor who had been promised a leading role in a play, and who was not given such a part, was entitled to compensation for loss of the chance to enhance his public reputation and for the fact that his name would not be advertised as it would otherwise have been.

(c) When an employee is taking part in limited industrial action (*see* 5:5).

SICK PAY

4. General principle

An employer may have an obligation by virtue of a term in the contract of employment to pay sick pay to employees when they are unable to work because of illness. Such an obligation may arise under an express term (it has been officially calculated that at least 80 per cent of all employees are covered by occupational sick pay schemes); or an obligation may arise under an implied term. The principles governing the implication of terms relating to sick pay were discussed by the Court of Appeal in *Mears* v. *Safecar Security Ltd* (1982) where it was held that there is no general presumption of an implied right to sick pay. The job of the tribunal or court is to ascertain what was agreed expressly or impliedly and in performing this task the court '. . . should consider all the facts and circumstances of the relationship between the employer and employee concerned including the way in which they had worked the particular contract since it was made in order to imply and determine the missing term . . .'

The presumption relating to sick pay is a strictly neutral one, and an industrial tribunal should approach the matter with an open mind unprejudiced by any preconception: *see Houman & Son* v. *Blyth* (1983). The written statement ought to specify the right of the employee, if any, to payment during absence from work due to sickness (*see* 2:7).

5. Statutory sick pay (SSP)

Since April 1983 all employers have had a statutory obligation to pay SSP to their employees. The obligations in this area are now governed by the Social Security Contributions and Benefits Act (SSCBA) 1992. The basic principle is that an employer is required to pay SSP to any employee who is away ill (s. 151 of the 1992 Act). The employee cannot claim for the first three days of absence, but thereafter the employer must pay SSP up to the equivalent of twenty-eight weeks (s. 155 of the 1992 Act).

For these purposes an employee is defined as a person over the age of sixteen who is 'gainfully employed in Great Britain either under a contract of service or in an office (including elective office) with emoluments chargeable to income tax under Schedule E': s. 163. Before an employee can become entitled to SSP three conditions must be met: there must be a period of incapacity for work (PIW); the

PIW must fall within a period of entitlement; the day(s) of absence must be a qualifying day(s).

(a) *Period of Incapacity for Work.* A PIW is any period of four or more consecutive calendar days (including days on which the employee would not be required to be available for work, e.g. bank holidays, weekends). The employee must be deemed incapable of working; this will normally mean that the employee must be suffering from physical or mental illness.

(b) *Period of Entitlement.* A period of entitlement is the period commencing with a PIW and which ends on the occurrence of one of the following events:

(*i*) the termination of the PIW; *or*
(*ii*) the employee's entitlement for SSP being exhausted; *or*
(*iii*) the end of the employee's contract of employment.

(c) *Qualifying days.* SSP is payable only in respect of 'qualifying days' in any PIW. Qualifying days must be agreed between employer and employee and usually these agreed days will reflect the normal pattern of the working week. SSP is paid from the fourth qualifying day and onwards of any PIW.

(d) *Rates of SSP.* At the time of writing SSP is payable at the following single rate:

Weekly Earnings	Weekly SSP
more than £62	£55–70
less than £62	nil

Many part-time employees earn over £62 per week and thus qualify for SSP.

(e) *Employer refuses to pay SSP.* If an employer refuses to pay SSP (e.g. because he does not believe that the employee has been genuinely ill) he is obliged on receipt of a reasonable request from the employee to give him written reasons within a reasonable time. The employee is entitled to refer the matter in writing within six months to an adjudication officer who will give a written decision on the reference. Either employer or employee can appeal against his decision to the local DSS office within 28 days and the appeal will be heard by a Social Security Appeals Tribunal, with a further appeal to a Social Security Commissioner.

(f) *Entitlement where employee 'directly interested' in a trade dispute.* Under Schedule 1 of SSCBA 1992, an employee has no entitlement to SSP where he is directly interested in a trade dispute. Such a situation can arise where in one work place an employer deals with a number of trade unions, one of which becomes involved in a trade dispute with the employer. If the consequence of that trade dispute is that groups of workers other than those in the trade union with which the employer is in dispute are laid off, those other groups of workers are 'directly interested' provided two conditions are met. First, whatever the outcome of the dispute, it must be applied to all groups of workers (and not just to those belonging to the union participating in the dispute). Second, this application of the outcome of the dispute 'across the board' should come about automatically

65

as a result of (*i*) a legally binding collective agreement, or (*ii*) a collective agreement which is not legally binding, or (*iii*) established industrial custom and practice at the place of work concerned: *see Presho* v. *DHSS* (1984).

6. Effect of sickness

The effect of sickness on the employment relationship varies with the circumstances. Sickness on the part of an employee may justify an employer in terminating the employment: *see*, for example, *East Lindsey District Council* v. *Daubney* (1977). In addition, long-term sickness may have the effect of frustrating the contract (*see* 11:**13**).

7. Effect of health insurance

The position of health insurance needs to be mentioned in this respect. The High Court in *Aspden* v. *Webb Poultry & Meat Group (Holdings) Ltd* (1996) held that employees were able to benefit from the terms of a permanent health insurance scheme which provided for the payment of three quarters of salary until their death, retirement or dismissal. The Court came to this decision despite an express term in the contract of employment which allowed the employers to terminate by reason of prolonged incapacity alone

TO TREAT EMPLOYEES WITH TRUST AND CONFIDENCE

8. General principle

In recent years the tribunals and courts have developed a wide and somewhat indefinite mutual obligation upon each party to a contract of employment to treat the other with trust and confidence. The impetus for this development has come from the evolution of legal principles surrounding the doctrine of constructive dismissal following the decision of the Court of Appeal in *Western Excavating* v. *Sharp* (1978) (*see* 13:**7**). The limits of the duty are still expanding and have been variously described as below. What is important to note is the development of this concept in modern employment law.

In *Courtaulds Northern Textiles Ltd* v. *Andrew* (1979) the EAT held: '. . . there is an implied term in a contract of employment that employers will not, without reasonable and proper cause, conduct themselves in a manner calculated or likely to destroy or seriously damage the relationship of trust and confidence between the parties'. In *Woods* v. *W.M. Car Services (Peterborough) Ltd* (1982) Lord Denning said: '. . . It is the duty of the employer to be good and considerate to his servants. Sometimes it is formulated as an implied term not to do anything likely to destroy the relationship of confidence between them'.

The existence of such a term has again been approved by the Court of Appeal in *Bliss* v. *South East Thames Regional Health Authority* (1985) and *Lewis* v. *Motorworld Garages Ltd* (1985).

The EAT has considered the nature of this implied term in the context of express mobility clauses in an employee's contract of employment. In *White* v. *Reflecting Road Studs Ltd.* (1991), it was stated that the employer should not exercise his discretion in such a way as to prevent the employee from being able to carry out his part of the contract. The EAT deliberately did not say that the employer must act 'reasonably' and limited the scope of such a term to that of trust and confidence.

HOLIDAYS

9. Contractual position

The written statement supplied to employees under s. 1 (as amended) of the 1996 Act ought to state the holidays to which the employee is entitled, and whether the employee is entitled to holiday pay (and if so, how much) by virtue of his contract of employment. If an employee is not entitled to a written statement or he does not receive one from his employer, the questions of holidays and holiday pay still rest upon the contract of employment but it may be more difficult to produce evidence of these rights.

Further, as a general principle, there is no implied term to the effect that if the employment is terminated without the employee having taken his holiday entitlement then payment would be made in lieu of this: *Morley* v. *Heritage plc* (1993).

10. Statutory provisions

The few statutory provisions governing this area have now been repealed.

HOURS OF WORK

11. Contractual position

The hours which an employee is required to work are determined by reference to his individual contract of employment and it should again be noted that the written statement supplied under s. 1 (as amended) of the 1996 Act ought to state the position in respect of hours of work. The number of hours that may be contractually agreed is, however, limited by certain statutory provisions (*see* **12** below).

12. Statutory limits

Section 7 of the Sex Discrimination Act 1986 removes the majority of limitations imposed concerning the hours to be worked by women. Section 10 of the Employment Act 1989 similarly removes restrictions relating to the employment of young persons.

There are no general limitations on persons over the age of 18, but there are a number of specific restrictions imposed in respect of particular work, e.g. coach and lorry driving. Breach of these regulations is a criminal offence punishable by fine.

13. Working Time Directive (1993)

In 1:27 above the implementation of this Directive was discussed. The essence of the Directive is to ensure that employees should not exceed an average working week of 48 hours unless employees consent to this period. Preference may be made to a four-month period to calculate this. There are numerous exceptions to this general principle; in particular where the work time cannot be measured or predetermined. The latter would include managers and those with autonomous decision making ability. At the time of writing it is not clear how these particular requirements will be implemented.

Additionally the Directive includes provisions relating to minimum periods of daily rest, annual leave and breaks. For example there must be a rest break where the working day is more than six hours. The Directive also imposes restrictions on 'night time' work. Night time work is between 12.00 – 5.00 am and must not be for a period of not less than seven hours. Normal hours for night time work must not exceed an average of eight hours in any 24 hour period. Further, employees should be given four weeks paid annual leave; note that there is a three-year transition period for this provision and its implementation will be progressive. The Government, at the time of writing, has started a consultation process on the question of implementation. A number of industries are exempt from these provisions, for example numerous transport industries. The EC is currently reviewing these exemptions.

TIME OFF WORK

14. For public duties

Section 50 of the 1996 Act provides that an employer must permit an employee to have time off work for the purpose of carrying out duties as:

(a) a Justice of the Peace

(b) a member of a local authority

(c) a member of a statutory tribunal

(d) a member of a Regional Health Authority or an Area or District Health Authority

(e) a member of the governing body of a local authority maintained educational establishment

(f) a member of a water authority.

The amount of time off (which is without pay unless the contrary is agreed) to which the employee is entitled is such as is 'reasonable in all the circumstances' having regard to certain specified factors.

A number of categories of employees are excluded from this right: ss. 199 and 200 of the 1996 Act. An employee who considers that his right has been infringed may present a complaint to an industrial tribunal normally within three months. A tribunal has the power to make a declaration and award compensation: *see Corner* v. *Bucks CC* (1978).

15. For ante-natal care

Under ss. 55–57 of the 1996 Act a pregnant employee has the right not to be unreasonably refused time off work with pay in order that she may keep appointments for receiving ante-natal care. Evidence of pregnancy and of the appointment must be produced if requested by the employer. An employee who considers that this right has been infringed may present a complaint to an industrial tribunal (normally within three months of the appointment in question). If the tribunal finds the complaint well-founded it will make a declaration to that effect and award compensation: *see Gregory* v. *Tudsbury Ltd* (1982).

TO INDEMNIFY EMPLOYEES

16. General principle

An employer is under an obligation to indemnify his employees in respect of any expenses incurred in performing their duties under the contract of employment, e.g. travelling expenses and liability incurred as a result of wrongs committed by employees for which the employer is vicariously liable.

17. Indemnity by employee

In certain circumstances, however, an employee may be under an obligation to indemnify the employer for the loss sustained: *Lister* v. *Romford Ice and Cold Storage Co. Ltd* (1957) (*see* 5:8).

TO PROVIDE REFERENCES

18. No duty to provide one

There is no obligation on an employer to supply character references for employees although, in practice, employers normally supply them since failure to provide one speaks for itself. In *Spring* v. *Guardian Assurance* (1994) it was suggested by the House of Lords that a duty to provide a reference may arise where an employee could not enter the new employment without a reference being provided.

19. Legal effect of references

If an employer does provide a reference it ought to be correct for two specific reasons.

(a) *Defamation*. If a reference is defamatory, the defamed employee may bring an action against the employer, although the defence of qualified privilege is available to the employer, i.e. the employer may show that the statements were made without malice.

(b) *Negligent misstatement*. A person who acts in reliance on a reference which has been issued negligently may apparently bring an action to recover any loss sustained as a consequence: *Hedley Byrne and Co.* v. *Heller and Partners* (1964). However, the person issuing the reference may avoid liability if he disclaims legal responsibility for the reference, subject, of course, to the test of 'reasonableness' contained in s. 2(2) Unfair Contract Terms Act 1977 being satisfied.

The most interesting development in this area concerns the issue and to whether a duty of care is owed by an employer when providing a reference for a current or former employee. In *Spring* v. *Guardian Assurance plc* (1994) the House of Lords held that a duty was owed in these circumstances and an employer would be liable in damages if the reference contained inaccurate information. Further two members of the House of Lords held that there was an implied term in the contract of employment to the effect that there is a duty on the employer to take due care and skill in the preparation of references.

7

STATUTORY REGULATION OF REMUNERATION

A number of legislative provisions exist affecting the amount of remuneration and the way in which it is paid. In addition, a number of relatively recent provisions provide for an employee to be paid by his employer when, for various reasons, the employee is unable to work. These different provisions are considered in this chapter.

WAGES PROVISIONS

1. Introduction

Part I of the Wages Act 1986 repealed the Truck Acts 1831–1940 and other enactments imposing restrictions on the payment of wages. The Wages Act 1986 replaced them with a new regulatory system, based on the contract of employment. Redress, under the 1986 Act, was to an industrial tribunal whereas under the previous legislation any breach of regulations was a criminal offence. The provisions of the Act are now consolidated in the ERA 1996.

2. Who is covered by the provision?

The scope of the provisions is wide. Sections 27(4), 230(3–5) and 235(1) state that a worker means an individual who has entered or works under a contract. Section 230(3) defines contracts as ones of service, apprenticeship and those under which a person undertakes to perform any work personally for the other party. Therefore, the Act is not limited to people working under a contract of employment.

3. What is meant by wages?

Section 27 defines wages in very broad terms. Wages means 'any sums payable to a worker by his employer in connection with his employment and includes any fee, bonus, commission, holiday pay or other emolument referable to his employment, whether payable under his contract or otherwise. . . .' However a number of payments are specifically excluded and these include expenses and redundancy payments. The definition is by no means clear and two cases illustrate this fact. Firstly, the House of Lords in *Delaney* v. *Staples* (1992) finally clarified the question as to whether 'payment in lieu of notice was covered by the definition of wages as contained in s. 27'.

Delaney, who had been dismissed, sought to recover £82 as a payment in lieu of notice. The House of Lords held that such a payment did not constitute 'wages' for the purposes of the Act. The reasoning being that wages related to consideration for work done, or to be done, under the contract whereas any payment in relation to the period after the employment had terminated was not wages. Therefore, Delaney had to pursue her claim through the County Court as a breach of contract. (But *see* **4** below.)

The second decision concerns the potential breadth of s. 27. The issue in question is whether discretionary or ex-gratia payments could amount to wages. The EAT decided in *Kent Management Services Ltd.* v. *Butterfield* (1992) that such non-contractual payments are recoverable under the Act as 'wages' if the employee can show that through a course of conduct they would normally be expected.

The definition has led to further case law in recent years and shows the difficulty faced by the tribunals. In *London Borough of Southwark* v. *O'Brien* (1994) expenses are excluded from the definition of wages, even though they may include profit elements. Similar reasoning to the *Kent Management Services Ltd* (above) was adopted in *Blackstone Franks Management Ltd* v. *Robertson* (1996) where the EAT held that an ascertainable commission payable on the termination of the employee's contract was still wages.

4. Mode of payment

One of the effects of the Wages Act 1986 was to abolish the requirement that workers be paid in the 'coin of the realm'. Therefore, we now have the concept of 'cashless' pay. It may well be that an employee has the right – predating the Act – to be paid in cash and if this were unilaterally taken away then a claim for constructive dismissal may arise (*see* 13:7). However consensual variation of contracts has dealt with this problem.

5. Deductions

Section 13(1) of the 1996 Act allows a deduction from wages if it is made either by virtue of a statutory provision (for example income tax and national insurance contributions) or by a provision of the worker's contract, or if the worker has previously indicated his agreement in writing to it. Any written agreement must be clear as to the fact that the deduction is to be made from the employee's wages: *Potter* v. *Hunt Contracts Ltd* (1992). *Kerr* v. *The Sweater Shop (Scotland) Ltd* (1996) held that the mere placing of a notice on a notice board was not sufficient to comply with this requirement. Written notice has to be provided to each employee individually. The Act makes no provision as to whether the deduction should be fair or reasonable and the only limitation in amount applies to retail workers (*see* below). It should be noted in this context that the Act does not provide for deductions in respect of industrial action: *see Miles* v. *Wakefield MDC* (1987). Similarly the Act does not apply to deductions to recover overpayment of wages. However, the Act does still require that the deduction must be lawful in the first place. In *Home Office* v. *Ayres* (1992), Ayres, a prison officer, had been wrongly paid sick pay at full rather than half rate, after a serious operation. He did not know the mistake and was given no pay slips. The employers could not recover the overpayment as it had been received in good faith and he had spent it all on normal living expenses. In *Sunderland Polytechnic* v. *Evans* (1993) the EAT held that an industrial tribunal has no jurisdiction under the Wages Act to determine the lawfulness of deduction made from wages due to the involvement of an employee in industrial action. Such matters must be dealt with by the courts and not by a tribunal.

Sections 17–21 of the 1996 Act introduce much stricter controls on retail workers who are defined as being workers who carry out retail transactions directly with members of the public or with fellow workers. The definition includes collection of money in respect of retail transactions. Under the Act any deduction in respect of cash shortages or stock deficiencies must not exceed one-tenth of the gross amount of wages payable on that day. Also, any sum demanded of such a worker in respect of these losses shall not exceed the 10% figure. The limit only applies to deductions for the two reasons above, i.e. cash shortages or stock deficiencies.

WAGES COUNCILS

6. Abolition

Wages councils have been abolished by s. 35 of the Trade Union Reform and Employment Rights Act 1993, and consequently all wages orders cease to have effect. Therefore, there is now no statutory regulation of a minimum wage for any employees. The Labour Government elected on 1 May 1997 has a commitment to introduce a minimum wage. Details, at the time of writing, are too unclear as to how this commitment will be implemented.

GUARANTEE PAYMENTS

7. Introduction

Unless a contract of employment expressly or implicitly allows for it, an employee who is laid off (i.e. sent home because there is no work to do) is entitled to be paid during the period of such lay-off. In recent times a number of collective agreements have made provision for guaranteed minimum earnings for employees in the event of a lay-off. In 1975, provisions were introduced whereby there is a minimum entitlement to pay during the time an employee is laid off. These provisions are now contained in ss. 28–35 of the 1996 Act.

8. Basic provision

An employee is entitled to a guarantee payment in respect of any day during which he is not provided with work (a 'workless day') due to **(a)** a diminution in the requirements of the employer's business for work of the kind which he is employed to do; or **(b)** any other occurrence affecting the normal working of the employer's business in relation to work of that kind.

9. Eligibility

To be eligible to receive such a payment, an employee must:

(a) have been continuously employed for at least one month when the lay-off occurs (note that those engaged on a fixed-term contract for three months or less are excluded); and

(b) have been laid off for the whole of his normal working hours on a day he is normally required to work in accordance with the contract of employment: *see Mailway (Southern) Ltd* v. *Willsher* (1978); and

(c) not have unreasonably refused an offer of alternative employment which was suitable in all the circumstances; and

(d) have complied with any reasonable requirements imposed by the employer with a view to ensuring that his services are available; and

(e) not have been laid off because of a strike, lock-out or other industrial action involving any employee of the employer or of any associated employer; and

(f) have been available for employment on that day.

10. Amount of payment

An employee who is entitled to a guarantee payment is entitled to be paid at the guaranteed hourly rate (a week's pay divided by the normal weekly working hours) for the number of normal working hours for the day he is laid off subject to a maximum limit for any one day (£14.50 at the time of writing). There is a maximum entitlement of five guarantee payments in any period of three months (at the time of writing this is £72.50 in respect of five days in any period of three months).

> *Note*: The relationship between the statutory provisions and any provisions in a contract of employment or collective agreement must be fully considered since each must be set off against the other.

11. Enforcement

If an employer fails to pay a guarantee payment, the employee may complain to an industrial tribunal, normally within three months. If the tribunal finds the complaint well-founded, it will order the employer to pay the employee the amount due.

12. Exemption

The Secretary of State may exempt from the operation of the above provisions those employees covered by a collective agreement or wages order containing provisions as to guaranteed remuneration. At the time of writing some twenty exemption orders have been made.

Note also that by virtue of s. 199 of the 1996 Act a number of categories of employees are excluded from the operation of the guarantee payments provisions.

SUSPENSION FROM WORK ON MEDICAL GROUNDS

For the legislation governing suspension from work on medical grounds, *see* ss. 64 and 65 of the 1996 Act.

13. Basic provision

Sections 64 and 65 of the 1996 Act provide that an employee who is suspended from work is entitled to be paid by his employer if that suspension is in consequence of a requirement imposed under certain statutory provisions or a recommendation made in a Code of Practice issued or approved under s. 16 of the Health and Safety at Work etc. Act 1974. For example, under Regulation 6 of the Lead Paint Regulations 1927, an inspector must give notice to an employer requiring the suspension of employees if he is satisfied that the incidence of lead poisoning among a group of employees involved in painting is excessive. An employee suspended in consequence of such a notice is entitled to be paid during the period of suspension.

14. Eligibility

To be eligible for payment during such suspension, an employee must:

(a) have been continuously employed for at least one month by that employer (note that those engaged on a fixed-term contract for three months or less are excluded); and

(b) not be incapable of work due to sickness; and

(c) not have unreasonably refused suitable alternative work; and

(d) not have refused to comply with reasonable requirements imposed by his employer with a view to ensuring that his services are available.

15. Payment

An employee is entitled to be paid for up to twenty-six weeks of such suspension. Contractual payments to which the employee is entitled are set off against the statutory right to payment and vice versa. If the employer fails to pay the employee, a complaint may be presented to an industrial tribunal normally within three months. If the tribunal finds the complaint well-founded, it will order the employer to pay the employee the amount due.

16. Additional

Two additional points should be noted.

(a) If, instead of being suspended, an employee is dismissed on medical grounds of the kind specified in **13** above, the qualifying period for presenting a complaint of unfair dismissal is reduced to one month from two years (*see* generally Chapter 13).

(b) If the employer wishes to engage a temporary employee to replace the suspended employee, then provided the replacement employee is informed in writing that his employment will be terminated when the suspension has ended, the dismissal of the temporary employee in order to allow the suspended employee to return to work will be regarded as for a 'substantial reason' and, provided the employer acted reasonably, the dismissal will not be unfair: s. 106 of the 1996 Act.

Note also that by virtue of ss. 199 and 200 of the 1996 Act, a number of categories of employees are excluded from the above provisions.

MATERNITY PAY AND LEAVE

All provisions relating to these rights are now governed by the Employment Rights Act 1996 with the exception of maternity pay which is by the Social Security Contributions and Benefit Act (SSCBA) 1992 and the Statutory Maternity Pay (General) Regulations 1986 (SI 1986/1960) (as amended).

17. Basic provisions

An employee who is absent from work due to pregnancy or confinement is entitled to receive maternity pay from her employer. In addition, there is an *independent* right to return to work following confinement and a right not to be dismissed on grounds of pregnancy (*see* 13:**19**).

It should be noted that the drafting of the statutory provisions relating to maternity is exceedingly complex. In *Lavery* v. *Plessey Telecommunications Ltd.* (1983) the Court of Appeal agreed with remarks made in the EAT that the provisions are of 'inordinate complexity, exceeding the worst excesses of a taxing statute; we find that especially regrettable bearing in mind that they are regulating the everyday rights of ordinary employers and employees'.

18. Eligibility for maternity pay

To be eligible for maternity pay an employee must (ss. 164 and 165 SSCBA):

(a) still be pregnant at the eleventh week before her expected week of confinement, or have had the baby at that time; and
(*Note*: It is thought that it does not matter that the employee has actually stopped working, for whatever reason, before the eleventh week provided the contract of employment subsists until the eleventh week. The current regulations mirror the previous legislation to this effect.)

(b) have been continuously employed for at least 26 weeks ending with the week immediately preceding the fourteenth week before the expected week when the baby is due; and

(c) have normal weekly earnings for the period of 8 weeks ending with the qualifying week of not less than the lower earnings limit in force at the time for the payment of national insurance contributions; and

(d) have stopped working for the employer.

19. Amount of maternity pay

An employee who fulfils the conditions in **18** above is entitled to maternity pay for a maximum of eighteen weeks at the appropriate rate. The maternity pay period cannot start earlier than the eleventh week before the expected week of confinement, but subject to this, there is some flexibility. There is a central core period of 13 weeks commencing with the sixth week before the expected week of confinement. The remaining five weeks can be taken before or after this period.

There are two rates of maternity pay: the higher and lower rate (s. 166 SSCBA). The higher rate is a weekly rate equivalent to 90% of a week's pay less the appropriate deductions as it is treated as earnings. The higher rate is payable for six weeks in the case of employees who have been continuously employed for a period of two years (or its equivalent) until immediately before the qualifying week. The amount of maternity pay in this higher rate bracket was the subject of a reference to the European Court of Justice in the case of *Gillespie* v. *Northern Health and Social Services* (1996). The first issue was whether European principles of equal pay and treatment (Article 119) demanded that women receive full pay during maternity leave. The ECJ held that this is not the position as women taking maternity leave were in a special position and the protection that they were being currently afforded could be justified as it was not comparable to a woman being actually at work. However the ECJ did rule that any payments that are made must reflect any pay rise awarded between the period used to calculate maternity pay and the end of maternity leave. As a result of this decision the Statutory Maternity Pay (General) Amendment Regulations (1996) were introduced. The effect of these Regulations means that if there is a pay rise back-dated to the eight-week period on which the calculation is based, then this must be reflected in the amount of maternity pay given, even though it may not be actually received until after that period.

The lower rate, which is prescribed by regulation and is currently £55.70, is payable for the remaining 12 weeks. The lower rate only will be payable to employees who have been continuously employed for 26 weeks before the qualifying week, but do not satisfy the service requirements for the higher rate. In all cases the employee's average weekly earnings must be above the lower earnings limit for the purpose of National Insurance Contributions.

In the case of a dispute concerning maternity pay the matter is now dealt with by s. 20 of the Social Security Administration Act 1992. The initial complaint is to an Adjudication Officer with an appeal to the Social Security Appeals Tribunal.

20. What is recoverable by the employer?

The employer can recover payments of maternity pay in accordance with the Statutory Maternity Pay (Compensation of Employers) Regulations 1987 (SI 1987/9) as amended. Small employers, whose NI contributions were £20,000 or less in the previous tax year, are entitled to an additional refund of 6.5%. All other employers are entitled to receive 92% of the total costs of maternity pay.

21. Eligibility for the right to return to work

To be eligible to exercise the right to return to work following pregnancy or confinement, an employee must inform her employer in writing at least twenty-one days prior to her absence, or as soon as reasonably practicable thereafter:

(a) that she will be absent from work wholly or partly because of pregnancy or confinement

(b) that she intends to return to work, and

(c) of the expected week of confinement.

In addition the employer may write to the employee not earlier than forty-nine days after the beginning of her expected week of confinement (or the date of confinement) asking her to provide written confirmation of her intention to return and informing her that failure to reply will result in the loss of her right to return. The employee must reply to the request within fourteen days or, if that is not reasonably practicable, as soon as reasonably practicable. It is thought that the inability of the employee to make up her mind as to whether or not she wished to return to work is not a sufficient reason for failure to reply within fourteen days: *see Nu-Swift International Ltd v. Mallison* (1978).

22. The right to return

An employee who has been absent from work because of pregnancy or confinement is entitled to return to work in the job in which she was employed under the original contract of employment on terms and conditions no less favourable than would have been applicable had she not been absent. The right can be exercised at any time before the end of twenty-nine weeks from the *actual* week of confinement, and not the expected week of confinement previously notified to the employer: *Lavery* v. *Plessey Telecommunications Ltd* (1983). If it is not practicable for the employer to permit her to return because of redundancy she is entitled to be offered, if available, suitable alternative employment (i.e. of a kind which is suitable for her in relation to the nature and place of employment on terms and conditions not substantially less favourable than the previous employment). If the employer can show that there was no suitable vacancy for the woman whose job has disappeared because of redundancy, she will be entitled to a redundancy payment (*see*14:**14**). If she refuses a suitable vacancy, she has no such entitlement: *see Community Task Force* v. *Rimmer* (1986) and s. 78 of ERA 1996.

If it is not reasonably practicable for a reason other than redundancy for the employer to permit her to return in accordance with these provisions but the employer offers her suitable alternative employment (as defined above) which she either accepts or unreasonably refuses, there is deemed to be no 'dismissal' in such circumstances and consequently no action will lie. In addition, if the number of employees employed by that employer (and associated employers) did not exceed six at the time her absence began and for any reason it is not reasonably practicable for the employer to permit her to return to work or to offer suitable alternative employment (as defined above), there is deemed to be no 'dismissal' and consequently no action for unfair dismissal or a redundancy payment will lie: s. 96 of ERA 1996.

If she is not allowed to return to work in breach of her right to do so, or if she is redundant and not offered a suitable vacancy, that is treated as an unfair dismissal (*see* generally Chapter 13) unless the employer acted reasonably in so doing because of something that had happened during the employee's absence. It should be noted that if there is also a contractual right to return to work following maternity leave, the employee may exercise that right but the employee is not entitled to combine the statutory and contractual rights and take the most advantageous parts of each: *see Bovey* v. *Board of Governors of the Hospital for Sick Children* (1978), now contained in s. 77 of ERA 1996. During the period of maternity leave the employee is entitled to the benefit of all those contractual terms that she would have enjoyed had she not been on leave. The only exception to this relates to remuneration.

A number of recent cases have focused on the issue of a woman who is returning after maternity leave wanting to do so on different terms, for example on a job-share basis. In *British Telecommunication plc* v. *Roberts* (1996) two women had their request to return on a job-share basis turned down. The EAT held that they were not directly discriminated against (*see* Chapter 9) as being a parent with child-care responsibilities was not unique to women. The refusal would only be directly discriminatory if a man were treated differently. However the EAT left open the possibility for an indirect discrimination claim in that a requirement to work full-time could be complied with by a smaller proportion of women than men. It would then be for the employer to justify this requirement.

An employer may postpone an employee's return to work for up to four weeks for any specified reason, as long as he notifies her, before the day on which she had proposed to return, of the reasons and the day on which she may return.

23. Delaying the return

An employee may delay her return beyond the twenty-ninth week after the actual date of confinement in two situations:

(a) Where she is ill and unable to recommence employment. The postponement of the return can be for up to four weeks and can be exercised once only. In *Crees* v. *Royal London Insurance* (1997) C had taken advantage of this four-week period but was ill on her extended date of return. The EAT held that as C had not physically returned to work she had forfeited her right to return to work. The contract was terminated as a result.

(b) Where there is an interruption of work (because of industrial action or some other reason) which renders it unreasonable to expect the employee to return on the notified day. Her return is to be delayed until the interruption has ceased.

24. Temporary replacements

By virtue of s. 106 of the 1996 Act, if an employer engages a temporary employee to replace an employee on maternity leave, then, provided that the replacement employee is informed in writing that the employment will be terminated when the woman returns, the dismissal of the temporary employee in order to allow the woman to return will be regarded as for a 'substantial reason' and, provided that the employer acted reasonably, the dismissal will not be unfair.

25. Importance of 'continuous' employment

The EPCA (as amended) gives a right to 14 weeks maternity leave to all employees, irrespective of their length of service or hours of work. However the previous requirement of two years continuous service is still applicable with regard to the right to return at any time up to 29 weeks from the week in which child birth occurs: s. 79 ERA 1996.

ITEMISED PAY STATEMENTS

26. Basic provision

Every employee who works for more than eight hours has the right to an itemised pay statement giving particulars of:

(a) the gross amount of pay

(b) the amount of variable deductions and their purpose, e.g. income tax

(c) the amount of any fixed deductions, e.g. trade union contributions

(d) the net amount of pay and, where different parts of the net pay are paid in different ways, the amount and method of each part payment: s. 8 of the 1996 Act.

However, the employer need not provide an itemised list of fixed deductions if he has issued the employee with a standing statement of fixed deductions containing all relevant information. In this case, provided the standing statement is kept up-to-date and reissued at least once a year, the pay statement need only include the aggregate amount of fixed deductions. Further, the provision does not apply to employers with 20 employees or less.

27. Complaint to industrial tribunal

If an employer fails to provide a complete and accurate pay statement, an employee may complain to an industrial tribunal, normally within three months. The tribunal, if it finds the complaint well-founded, may issue a declaration as to the particulars which ought to be included and award the employee the amount of any unnotified deductions which have been made within the thirteen weeks preceding the date of application to the tribunal: *see Milsom* v. *Leicestershire County Council* (1978) and *Scott* v. *Creager* (1979). By virtue of s. 99 of ERA 1996, certain categories of employees are excluded from these provisions.

INSOLVENCY OF EMPLOYER

For the legislation governing the insolvency of an employer, *see* ss. 182–189 of the 1996 Act. *See* also s. 175 and Schedule 6 of the Insolvency Act 1986 (as amended by the Insolvency Act 1994).

28. Basic provisions

If an employer becomes insolvent an employee acquires certain rights.

(a) He becomes a preferential creditor in respect of up to four months' unpaid wages or a maximum set by the Secretary of State.

(b) Certain other payments are also deemed to be preferential debts including guarantee payments, payment for time off for trade union activities and payment for ante-natal care. *Clark* v. *Secretary of State for Employment* (1995) that payment in lieu of notice was pay for the purposes of Article 119 of the Treaty of Rome and may be recoverable by a woman made redundant during her maternity leave from this fund. The current legislation has been amended to take account of this decision.

(c) The employee is entitled to claim payment of certain amounts due to him from his employer from the Secretary of State who will pay them out of the Redundancy Fund. The Secretary of State needs to be satisfied that the employer is insolvent and that the employee was entitled to these debts. The relationship between European and domestic law regarding the definition of redundancy was clarified in *Francovich* v. *Italian Republic (No. 2)* (1996). The ECJ held that it was for national law to define insolvency and, therefore, any relevant provisions would only become effective at that stage. The situation in UK domestic law was clarified in *Secretary of State for Employment* v. *McGlone* (1996) where the EAT held that there was no conflict between British and European law. The consequence of the decision is that the Secretary of State is not obliged to pay statutorily guaranteed insolvency payments to employees unless an employer is deemed to be insolvent under UK law. The classes of debt for which payment may be made include arrears of wages (up to a maximum of 8 weeks), holiday pay (up to a maximum of 6 weeks) and wages during the statutory minimum notice period.

(d) The employee has the right to ask the Secretary of State to make up any contributions to an occupational pension scheme which have not been paid because of the employer's insolvency.

> *Note*: Depending on the circumstances of the case, any social security benefits received by an ex-employee while unemployed following the insolvency of an employer may be taken into account when determining certain classes of payment from the Redundancy Fund: *see Westwood* v. *Secretary of State for Employment* (1982).

29. Complaint to an industrial tribunal

If an employee has been refused a payment, or received less than the due sum from the Secretary of State, he may complain to an industrial tribunal, normally within three months of the communication of the decision of the Secretary of State. Where the tribunal finds that the Secretary of State ought to have made a payment, it will issue a declaration to that effect stating the amount of any payment which it finds ought to have been made. By virtue of s. 199 of the 1996 Act, certain categories of employees are excluded from these provisions.

8

RIGHTS OF EMPLOYEES REGARDING TRADE UNIONS

In this chapter, references are made to two consolidating statutes: the Trade Union and Labour Relations (Consolidation) Act 1992 and the Employment Rights Act 1996.

INTRODUCTION

1. General

The 1992 Act contains a number of rights as regards trade union membership and activities. These may be classified as follows:

(a) The right not to be refused access to employment on grounds of membership/non-membership of an independent trade union.

(b) The right to be a member of an independent trade union.

(c) The right not to be a member of a trade union, whether independent or not.

(d) The right to participate in the activities of an independent trade union.

(e) The right to time off work for trade union duties.

(f) The right to time off work for trade union activities.

2. Independent trade union

The rights dealt with in this chapter largely depend upon whether the trade union in question is 'independent' and in certain cases as to whether the trade union is 'recognised'. These terms are considered at 17:**6** and 18:**5** respectively.

ACCESS TO EMPLOYMENT

3. Basic principle

Section 137 of the 1992 Act sets out the basic right. It is unlawful to refuse a person employment **(a)** because he is, or is not, a member of a trade union or **(b)** because

83

he is unwilling to accept a requirement (i) to take steps or become or cease to be, or to remain or not to become, a member of a trade union or (ii) to make payments or suffer deductions in the event of his not being a member of a trade union.

It should be noted that the legislation does not prohibit discrimination on the grounds of trade union activities.

The case of *Fitzpatrick* v. *British Railways Board* (1991) which concerns s. 152 of the 1992 Act (*see* below) raises an interesting point about the possible operation of s. 137. An employer who refuses to hire a prospective employee on the grounds that the individual has concealed his (non)-membership of a trade union, is not acting in breach of s. 137. The rationale being that the reason not to hire is because of dishonesty or deception.

Finally, there is a presumption of discrimination in s. 137(3). The sub-section states that where a job advertisement indicates, or might reasonably be understood as indicating, that (amongst other things) the employment advertised is open only to union members or non-members, then there is a presumption in favour of the applicant. Therefore if the applicant seeks and is refused employment to which the advertisement relates, then he is conclusively presumed to have been refused employment on the grounds set out in s. 137(1) above.

In *Harrison* v. *Kent County Council* (1995) the EAT ruled for the first time on these provisions. Harrison was refused employment due to his record of trade union activities in his previous employment. The EAT ruled that it was not possible to separate the fact of union membership from the incidents of membership, for example trade union activities. Therefore if employment was refused for these reasons it is open for a tribunal to conclude that an employer had contravened s. 137(1)(2). As we shall see below (**11**) the decision in Harrison must be put doubtful given the decision of the House of Lords in *Associated Newspapers Ltd* v. *Wilson and Associated British Ports* v. *Palmer* (1995).

4. Union vetting and pressure

Where there is an arrangement or practice under which employment is offered only to union members approved or put forward by a trade union, a non-union member who is refused employment in pursuance of that arrangement 'shall be taken to have been refused employment because he is not a member of the trade union' (s. 137(4) of the 1992 Act). The section is directed at the exclusive union-only labour supply arrangements which operate between trade unions and employers.

The above provisions also apply to an employment agency acting on an employer's behalf (s. 137(7) of the 1992 Act). Indeed by s. 138 of the 1992 Act the provisions outlined in s. 137(1) and (3) above apply to employment agencies.

5. Refusal of employment

The Act contains an extended definition of refusal of employment as it is wider than merely a simple refusal. Section 137(5) of the 1992 Act lists the situations when a refusal can occur and these include refusing or deliberately omitting to entertain and process the person's application or enquiry; causing him to withdraw or cease to pursue the application; refusing or deliberately omitting to offer him employment; making him an offer of employment on terms which no reasonable employer would offer and which is not accepted; making him an offer of such employment but withdrawing it or causing him not to accept it.

6. Remedies

Sections 139–140 of the 1992 Act set out the enforcement proceedings and remedies. Complaints should be taken to an industrial tribunal within the normal three-month time-limit. The limit starts to run when the conduct arose which is being complained of.

When a complaint succeeds an industrial tribunal shall make a declaration to that effect and it may make **(a)** an order requiring the respondent to pay compensation, or **(b)** a recommendation that the respondent takes specified action for the purpose of obviating or reducing the adverse effect on the complainant.

Compensation is assessed on the same basis as damages for breach of statutory duty and may include compensation for injury to feelings. The maximum is set at the limit for compensation for unfair dismissal (*see* 13:**30** below).

RIGHT TO BE A MEMBER

7. Basic principle

The dismissal of an employee will be regarded as unfair if the reason for the dismissal is that he is or proposes to become a member of an independent trade union: s. 152 of the 1992 Act (*see* 13:**20**). In addition, every employee has the right not to have action short of dismissal taken against him by his employer for the purpose of 'preventing or deterring him from being or seeking to become a member of an independent trade union, or penalising him for doing so': s. 146 of the 1992 Act. Thus in *Carlson* v. *The Post Office* (1981) it was held that the refusal of an employer to issue a parking permit to a member of an independent, but unrecognised, trade union was enough to 'penalise' the employee.

In *Discount Tobacco and Confectionery Ltd* v. *Armitage* (1995) the EAT held that the provisions of s. 152 are not limited to dismissals based on the mere act of trade union membership but it also covers employees dismissed because they have made use of the services of the union. The decision in Armitage was questioned in the *Associated Newspapers* case, below, where the House of Lords held that the decision did not establish a general principle of law that membership of a union was to be equated with using the union's essential services.

The current position remains unclear as the EAT in *Speciality Care plc* v. *Pachela* (1996) held that statements made by the House of Lords on the Armitage decision were merely obiter and therefore not binding on it. Consequently a tribunal must find as a fact whether or not the principal reason for the dismissal related to the applicant's trade union membership. Reference must not only be made to the mere fact of union membership but also by reference to whether the introduction of union representation into the employment relationship led the employer to dismiss the employee.

8. Complaint to industrial tribunal

A complaint may be presented to an industrial tribunal normally within three months by an employee alleging that his employer has infringed the right under s. 146. If the tribunal finds the complaint well-founded (no account being taken of any pressure exerted on the employer), the tribunal may issue a declaration and award such compensation as is 'just and equitable' having regard to certain specified factors: *see Brassington* v. *Cauldon Wholesale Ltd*. (1978) and *Cheall* v. *Vauxhall Motors Ltd* (1979). There is no qualifying period of continuous employment necessary to support a complaint under these provisions.

Once an employee has become a member of a trade union the membership subscription may be deducted at source by the employer; this is often referred to as the 'check-off' system. Section 15 of the Trade Union Reform and Employment Rights Act 1993 introduces a new s. 68 into the TULR(C) Act 1992 which regulates the operation of this system. A duty is placed on employers to ensure that no deductions are made without written authorisation from the employee in question and that the amount deducted does not exceed what has been authorised. The authorisation from the employee must be in writing and lasts only three years. At the end of this three-year period further authorisation must be given in order for the arrangement to be lawful.

RIGHT NOT TO BE A MEMBER

9. Basic principle

If an employee is dismissed because he is not a member of a trade union (whether independent or not), or because he refuses to become a member, such dismissal is unfair: s. 152(1)(c) of the 1992 Act (*see* 13:**20**). Similarly he has the right not to have action short of dismissal taken against him for the purpose of compelling him to become a member of a trade union (whether independent or not): s. 146 of the 1992 Act. Where a union membership agreement as defined by the legislation (*see* 13:**21**) is in existence, the above rights are modified. Section 146 (1)(b) of the 1992 Act makes it automatically unfair to take action short of dismissal against a person because of their refusal to join a union in accordance with a union membership agreement. The remedy is by way of complaint to an industrial tribunal.

10. Union membership agreements and the right not to join

Section 152(1)(b) makes it automatically unfair to dismiss an employee for a reason relating to non-membership of a union, irrespective of whether the closed shop is supported by a ballot (*see* 13:**21**).

RIGHT TO TAKE PART IN TRADE UNION ACTIVITIES

11. Basic principle

The dismissal of an employee will be regarded as unfair if the reason for the dismissal is that he wishes to take part in the activities of an independent trade union at an appropriate time: s. 152 of the 1992 Act (*see* 13:**20**). In addition every employee has the right not to have action short of dismissal taken against him by his employer for the purpose of 'preventing or deterring him from taking part in the activities of an independent trade union at any appropriate time, or penalising him for doing so': s. 146(1)(b) of the 1992 Act. Although 'activities' are not defined in the statute, such activities as voting in union elections and attending union meetings are clearly included. There is an important distinction between the individual activities of an employee as a trade unionist and the activities of a trade union which affect individual employees. In *Therm A Stor Ltd* v. *Atkins* (1983) the Court of Appeal held that employees who were dismissed in retaliation for attempts by a trade union to be recognised for collective bargaining purposes were not protected by s. 152. That provision is concerned solely with the dismissal of an employee for his activities, not with the dismissal of an employee for the activities of the union itself.

The courts have interpreted the meaning of s. 146 in *Ridgway and Fairbrother* v. *National Coal Board* (1987). In this case the two applicants complained that they did not receive a pay increase because of their membership of the National Union of Mineworkers, when members of the Union of Democratic Mineworkers had received increased pay. The Court of Appeal held that (*i*) the action had affected the two members as individuals as they had been directly affected, i.e. they had lost pay; (*ii*) s. 146 outlaws not only action to deter trade union membership in general but also membership of a particular union.

The decision, above, must be contrasted with that in *Associated Newspapers Ltd.* v. *Wilson* (1992). The EAT held that where an employer de-recognised a union and negotiated individual contracts (with pay rises), an employee who refused to negotiate and received no such rise did not come within the protection of the section. The Court of Appeal, however, reversed the decision of the EAT. The Court of Appeal held that the purpose of the pay rise was to end collective bargaining and this had the same purpose as the de-recognition of the union and the change of the employment terms and conditions. Consequently the underlying purpose was to deter employees from being union members.

The decision in the Court of Appeal was overruled by the House of Lords. We have already mentioned the likely effects of the decision in other areas above. The actual decision itself was based on the grounds that the purpose of the employer was simply to encourage employees to sign personal contracts. The House of Lords thought that deterring employees from making use of the collective bargaining powers of a union was not the same as hindering an employee's ability to take part in the activities of a union.

Section 148 of the 1992 Act provides that where the tribunal finds that the employer had two or more purposes, one of which falls within s. 146, then the tribunal must disregard the s. 146 purpose. There is a limit on this, however, in that the disregarding should not place where no reasonable employer would have taken this action in the context of the employment relationship. Clearly this places a trade union member at a disadvantage.

The term 'appropriate time' in s. 152 of the 1992 Act refers to time which is outside working hours or inside working hours if, by arrangement agreed or consent given, it is permissible for the employee to take part in the activities at that time: *see Robb* v. *Leon Motor Services Ltd* (1978) and *Dixon* v. *West Ella Developments Ltd* (1978).

> *Note*: Although in a proper case consent may be implied, an employer's consent is not to be deduced from mere silence: *Marley Tile Co. Ltd.* v. *Shaw* (1980).

In *Burgess* v. *Bass Taverns* (1995) the principle illustrated is that an employee who is given permission by the employer to undertake activities within working hours is protected. An employee giving a union presentation to a trainee manager could not be dismissed if some of the comments made were critical of the employer. There was no implied limitation on such a presentation.

As regards use of the employer's facilities for participating in activities, if there is a 'union membership agreement' in force (*see* 13:**20**), the employees covered by it only have the right to take part in trade union activities on the employer's premises if the trade union in question is a party to, or specified in, the agreement. However, an employer should allow trade union members to hold a meeting on his premises unless this would cause undue inconvenience: *Carter* v. *Wiltshire County Council* (1979).

12. Complaint to industrial tribunal

In the event of an employee alleging that the employer has infringed his right to participate in trade union activities, a complaint may be made to an industrial tribunal in respect of action short of dismissal and dealt with as in **8** above.

TIME OFF WORK FOR TRADE UNION DUTIES AND ACTIVITIES

13. Trade union duties

The original provisions relating to time off for trade union duties was contained in s. 17 of the 1978 Act. The subject is governed by s. 168 of the 1992 Act.

Section 168 states that an employer shall permit an employee who is an official of an independent trade union recognised by the employer to take time off during working hours for the purpose of carrying out duties concerned with **(a)** negotiations with the employer related to or connected with matters of collective bargaining in relation to which the trade union is recognised by the employer and **(b)** the performance on behalf of employees of the employer of functions related to collective bargaining which the employer has agreed may be performed by the trade union.

In order to aid the understanding of these provisions ACAS have issued a Code of Practice on Time Off (SI 1991/1968) which emphasises that it is preferable for such rights to be negotiated by the parties against the background of statutory rights.

The previous decisions are now of little value as to the operation of this section. The EAT has, however, provided some guidance in the case of *London Ambulance Service* v. *Charlton* (1992). The EAT held that an official is not necessarily entitled to time off to attend a meeting simply because it is in connection with collective bargaining. The employer, in considering whether or not the request is reasonable, can take into account factors such as the overall history, time and agenda of the meeting concerned.

14. Trade union activities

An employer must permit an employee who is a member of a recognised independent trade union (i.e. recognised for collective bargaining purposes) to have 'reasonable' time off, not necessarily with pay, during working hours for the purpose of taking part in the activities of that trade union, e.g. attendance at meetings, regard being had to the ACAS Code of Practice (*see* **13** above). This provision expressly excludes time off for taking industrial action: s. 170 of the 1992 Act. Further there must be a genuine link between the activity and the employment relationship between the employer, the employee and the trade union. In *Luce* v. *Bexley London Borough Council* (1990) it was held that the attendance at a TUC rally in connection with proposed legislation affecting the teaching profession was not within the right to time off.

15. Complaint to an industrial tribunal

Failure to permit an employee time off under ss. 169–170 gives rise to a right to complain to an industrial tribunal, normally within three months. If the tribunal finds the complaint well-founded, it may make a declaration and award compensation.

9

EQUAL PAY

1. Scope of the chapter

In this chapter the principal statute which is considered is the Equal Pay Act 1970, as amended by the Sex Discrimination Act 1975 and the Equal Pay (Amendment) Regulations 1983. The relationship between the Equal Pay Act and the Sex Discrimination Act is also considered.

THE EQUAL PAY ACT 1970

2. The Equal Pay Act 1970 and the Sex Discrimination Act 1975

In broad terms, the Equal Pay Act 1970 is concerned with less favourable treatment of a person of one sex as compared to the other in respect of matters (pay and other terms and conditions) governed by the contract under which a person is employed whereas the Sex Discrimination Act 1975 deals with less favourable treatment in matters not governed by the contract (e.g. selection, training, promotion, dismissal, etc.) on grounds of sex and/or marital status. Thus the two Acts are designed to be mutually exclusive but complementary.

Some appreciation of the policies underpinning the above enactments is of assistance in appreciating how they operate. In the case of equal pay the growing number of women in the nation's workforce, and the fact that historically women's earnings are, on average, considerably lower than those of men, have provided the twin pressures leading to our equal pay legislation (although it must be remembered that the Act applies to men and women). In the case of discrimination on grounds of sex, traditional stereotyping has always worked to the disadvantage of women in employment. Undoubtedly some progress has been made as a result of the Equal Pay Act 1970 and the Sex Discrimination Act 1975. It is also true that such progress has been much more limited than many would have hoped for and that a number of difficulties remain.

3. The Equal Pay Act 1970 and the Treaty of Rome

The influence of the Treaty of Rome and the effect of certain European Community Directives have been considerable in this area and have significant practical consequences for any applicant contemplating bringing an action alleging breach of the 1970 Act. Article 119 of the Treaty of Rome provides that:

> Each Member State shall . . . maintain the application of the principle that men and women should receive equal pay for equal work. For the purpose of this Article, pay means the ordinary basic or minimum wage or salary and any other consideration, whether in cash or kind, which the worker receives, directly or indirectly, in respect of his employment from his employer.'

The approach taken by the Employment Appeal Tribunal in determining what is meant by pay was clearly set out in *Manor Bakeries* v. *Nazir* (1996). N worked part-time; she attended the annual conference of her trade union as a delegate and, in accordance with the relevant collective agreement, she was paid 'in respect of the hours worked by the employee. . . .' On this basis N was paid for a total of 18 hours for the four-day conference. A colleague of N's, who worked full-time, was paid his full salary for the same period while attending the conference. N claimed equal pay with her colleague, but the EAT rejected an argument that under Article 119 she was entitled to equal pay. The EAT held that attendance at a trade union conference was not 'work' and therefore the pay which the delegates received under the collective agreement for attending the conference did not fall within the scope of the right to equal pay for equal work under Article 119. The EAT found that N was being paid for time off rather than for work.

The Article is directly enforceable by individuals in the courts of member states of the EC: *see Defrenne* v. *Société Anonyme Belge de Navigation Aérienne (SABENA)* (1976). Accordingly, if the domestic legislation of a member state in relation to equal pay falls short of the standards required by Article 119, an individual may be able to plead the Article: *see*, for example, *Macarthys Ltd* v. *Smith* (1980). An interesting illustration of this principle was provided by the decision of the EAT in *Diocese of Hallam Trustee* v. *Connaughton* (1996). The applicant had been the first Director of Music in the Roman Catholic Diocese of Hallam. Following her resignation a male successor was appointed at a considerably enhanced salary. She brought a claim for equality of pay and the EAT held that although the 1970 Act applied only to comparisons with a male who was employed contemporaneously in the same employment as a female applicant, the tribunal was able to hear a complaint based on Article 119 on the basis that the male successor's contract was so proximate to her own as to render him an effective comparator. However, it is important to realise that the relationship between Article 119 and our own domestic law is complex, and a detailed survey of the problematic issues is beyond the scope of this book.

The prevailing uncertainty in this area is perhaps best demonstrated by the different reasoning adopted in achieving the same result in the Court of Appeal and House of Lords in *Pickstone* v. *Freemans plc* (1988). The Court of Appeal in that case ruled that, because of the detailed drafting of the amended 1970 Act, the applicant was not entitled to succeed under the Act, but *was* entitled to succeed in her claim under Article 119. One effect of this ruling was that it seemed that s. 1(2)(c) of the Act failed to meet the UK's obligations under Article 119. The House of Lords, however, interpreted s. 1(2)(c) in such a way as to allow the applicant to succeed, thus ensuring that the UK's treaty obligations were met. In other words, the relationship between the two systems of law still contains some uncertainty in this area. However, it suffices to say that in any case where the interpretation of the Equal Pay Act (or, in some circumstances, the Sex Discrimination Act 1975) falls to be decided, the courts and tribunals will endeavour to interpret the domestic statutes so as to give effect to Article 119: *see Garland* v. *British Rail Engineering* (1982) and *Pickstone* v. *Freemans plc* (1988).

The application of Article 119 in conjunction with an EC Directive of 1975 (the Equal Pay Directive), which clarified the obligations under Article 119, in *Commission of European Communities* v. *The United Kingdom* (1982) led directly to parliamentary approval of the Equal Pay (Amendment) Regulations 1983 which amended the Equal Pay Act to bring UK law into line with its European obligations.

4. Scope of the Act

Despite its short title, the 1970 Act is designed to secure equal treatment as between men and women not only as regards pay but also as regards other terms and conditions, e.g. sick pay, mortgage schemes: *Sun Alliance and London Insurance Ltd* v. *Dudman* (1978).

Certain terms are, however, excluded from the operation of the Act:

(a) Terms 'affected by compliance with the laws regulating the employment of women': s. 6(1)(a). It should be noted, however, that the effect of s. 7 of the Sex Discrimination Act 1986 is to repeal parts of the Hours of Employment (Conventions) Act 1936, the Mines and Quarries Act 1954 and the Baking Industry (Hours of Work) Act 1954 which contained discriminatory provisions in relation to women. The consequence is that s. 6(1)(a) of the 1970 Act is unlikely to be used significantly in the future.

(b) Terms 'affording special treatment to women in connection with pregnancy or childbirth': s. 6(1)(b) *Coyne* v. *Exports Credits Guarantee Department* (1981). Thus, for example, a man cannot claim paternity leave if a woman's contract allows for maternity leave.

(c) Terms 'related to death or retirement, or to provision made in connection with death or retirement': s. 6(1A)(b). It should be noted, however, that under s. 6(1A)(a) it is provided that an equality clause 'shall operate in relation to terms relating to membership of an occupational pensions scheme'.

Some tension has arisen over the relationship between Article 119 of the Treaty of Rome and s. 6(1A). Article 119 requires that: 'Each Member State shall ... maintain the application of the principle that men and women should receive equal pay for equal work.' In *Worringham* v. *Lloyds Bank* (1982) male and female staff were required to join occupational pension schemes; once over the age of 25 the treatment of men and women was the same, but below that age men, but not women, were required to contribute five per cent of their salary to the pension scheme. To compensate for this difference men under the age of 25 received a five per cent addition to their gross pay; this had the consequence that men under 25 had a higher gross salary for the purpose of calculating certain benefits, such as redundancy payments and mortgage facilities. Also, if a male employee left Lloyds Bank his contributions were returned, whereas if a woman left under the age of 25 there was no refund. Following a reference by the Court of Appeal the European Court of Justice held that a contribution to a retirement benefits scheme which is paid by the employer in the name of the employees by means of an addition to the gross salary, and which helps to determine the amount of that salary, is 'pay' under Article 119. The Court of Appeal subsequently gave effect to the judgment of the European Court of Justice in the instant case, by declaring that on terminating their employment with the Bank female employees were entitled to be paid a sum equal to the refund of pension contributions they would have received had they been male employees.

Note that the operation of the Act includes employees, the self-employed and those in Crown employment but not the armed forces. While the Act is expressed in the female, it applies equally to men: s. 1(13). It covers persons of all ages: s. 11(2).

5. How the Act works

The Act uses the device of the 'equality clause': 'if the terms of a contract under which a woman is employed at an establishment in Great Britain do not include (directly or by reference to a collective agreement or otherwise) an equality clause they shall be deemed to include one': s. 1(1).

The effect of the equality clause is to give a woman the right to equal pay with a man when:

(a) the woman is employed on 'like work' with a man in the same employment: s. 1(2)(a); or

(b) the work she is doing is 'work rated as equivalent' with that of a man following a job evaluation study: s. 1(2)(b); s. 1(5). However, there is no requirement that a job evaluation study be carried out where an employer did not consent; or

(c) the work the woman is doing is of 'equal value', in terms of the demands made upon her, to that of a man in the same employment: s. 1(2)(c).

Inclusion of the deemed equality clause based on 'like' work and 'work rated as equivalent' has been in the Equal Pay Act 1970 from its inception, but a clause based on work of 'equal value' is more recent in origin and has an interesting history. In 1975 the Council of the EC issued a Directive on equal pay which had the effect of clarifying the obligations owed by member states under Article 119 of the Treaty of Rome. Article 1 of the Directive states: 'The principle of equal pay for men and women outlined in Article 119 of the Treaty . . . means, for the same work or for work to which equal value is attributed, the elimination of all discrimination on grounds of sex with regard to all aspects and conditions of remuneration.' The effect of the Directive was to require all member states to introduce suitable legislation to give effect to the requirements of the Directive.

In *Commission of European Communities* v. *The United Kingdom* (1982) enforcement proceedings were brought before the European Court of Justice alleging that the UK had failed to fulfil its obligations under the Directive. The Commission argued that the Directive required that a woman receive equal pay for work which, although different from that of a man, is of equal value, even where no job evaluation study had been carried out. The Court held that the UK had failed in its obligations in that no compulsory procedures existed to ensure equal pay where work of equal value was being done. Accordingly, in the Equal Pay (Amendment) Regulations 1983 the third strand to the equality clause, based on work of equal value, was introduced. This is considered further at **8** below.

In order to bring a successful application under the Act the applicant must identify a male comparator in the same employment who is doing like work, work rated as equivalent or work of equal value. This covers male comparators who are working at another establishment but for the same or an associated employer where common terms and conditions of employment are observed either generally or for employees of the relevant classes: s. 1(6). In *British Coal Corporation* v. *Smith* (1996) the House of Lords held that in this context 'common' does not mean 'identical' or 'the same' but simply means sufficiently similar so as to enable a fair comparison to be made.

EQUAL PAY AND WORK RATING

6. Like work

Under s. 1(2)(a) a woman is entitled to equal pay as a man 'where the woman is employed on like work with a man in the same employment'. Section 1(4) defines 'like work' in the following terms: 'A woman is to be regarded as employed in like work with men if, but only if, her work and theirs is of the same or a broadly similar nature and the differences (if any) between the things she does and the things they do are not of practical importance in relation to terms and conditions of employment: and accordingly in comparing her work and theirs regard shall be had to the frequency or otherwise with which any such differences occur in practice as well as to the nature and extent of the differences.'

The wording of s. 1(4) is intended to prevent irrelevant or insignificant differences being used to justify not paying equal pay. Alleged 'additional responsibilities' which are said to justify different pay rates must be real. In interpreting s. 1(4) the courts and tribunals have adopted a fairly broad approach.

Capper Pass Ltd v. *Lawton* (1977): L was a cook in the kitchen from which the directors of the company were served. She worked a forty-hour week cooking lunches for a small number of people. She sought equal pay with an assistant chef who worked a forty-five hour week in the company's canteen preparing different meals on a large scale. Held: she was entitled to an equal hourly rate of pay because the differences were 'peripheral'. The Employment Appeal Tribunal said that the correct approach to s. 1(4) was to ask the following:

(a) Is the work of the same or a broadly similar nature? This must be answered by a general consideration of the two kinds of work.

(b) Are any differences which do exist of 'practical importance'? If the answer to this is 'no', it is 'like work'.

Phillips J said that the industrial tribunals should disregard 'trivial differences' and should not undertake too minute an examination or be constrained to find that work is not like merely because of 'insubstantial differences'.

Dugdale v. *Kraft Foods Ltd* (1976). Held: the time at which work is performed should be disregarded when considering whether there is 'like work' and thus a woman's claim for equal pay with a male quality control inspector succeeded even though the men were required to work shifts. The fact that the men worked shifts could be dealt with by paying a shift premium when shifts were actually worked.

Coombes (Holdings) v. *Shields* (1978): a female counter-hand employed in a betting shop claimed equal pay with a man doing the same work. The employer said that the man was paid more because he was required to deal with any trouble which arose. Held: on the facts, this did not justify a finding that the man and the woman were not doing 'like work' and hence the woman was entitled to equal pay. *See also Eaton* v. *Nuttall* (1977).

The following general points should also be noted:

(a) A woman may compare herself with any man employed by the employer at that establishment if she is doing 'like work' (or 'work rated as equivalent') and not merely the man with whom the employer says she should compare herself: *Ainsworth* v. *Glass Tubes and Components Ltd* (1977). It is clearly sensible for the woman to choose a reasonably typical comparator. If the chosen comparator is untypical the employer may be able to rely on the 'genuine material difference' defence: *see* **9** below; but it must be emphasised that the chosen comparator has to be representative of a number of other workers: *see Thomas* v. *National Coal Board* (1987).

(b) Comparison may be made with an ex-employee whom the woman has replaced provided the interval between the employments was short: *Macarthys Ltd* v. *Smith (No. 1)* (1978). But note that a change in the volume of work which leads to the dismissal of a male predecessor may provide the employer with a defence: *Albion Shipping Agency* v. *Arnold* (1981).

(c) The doctrine of *res judicata* applies to equal pay applications, i.e. unless it can be shown that there has been some appreciable change in the facts, a woman cannot bring a second application for equal pay if an industrial tribunal has decided against it: *McLoughlin* v. *Gordons (Stockport) Ltd* (1978).

7. 'Work rated as equivalent'

There is no obligation upon an employer to carry out a job evaluation or work rating exercise but if he does do so within the definition of s. 1(5), he is obliged to pay equal pay etc. if a woman's work is rated as equivalent with that of a man employed at the same establishment. Section 1(5) states that:

'A woman is to be regarded as employed on work rated as equivalent with that of any men if, but only if, her job and their job have been given an equal value, in terms of the demand made on a worker under various headings (for instance effort, skill, decision) . . . or would have been given an equal value but for the evaluation being made on a system setting different values for men and women on the same demand under any heading.'

Where such a claim is made by a woman, she must establish that it satisfies the requirements of s. 1(5): *England* v. *Bromley London Borough Council* (1978). The industrial tribunal must then apply it unless it is shown that there was a fundamental error or a plain mistake on the face of the record: *Green* v. *Broxstowe District Council* (1977).

Once a job evaluation study has been carried out it will be regarded as binding on the employer for the purposes of the Equal Pay Act, even though he has not implemented it: *O'Brien* v. *Sim Chem Ltd* (1980). But *see also Arnold* v. *Beecham Group Ltd* (1982).

A useful example of the principle to be applied following a job evaluation study is found in *Springboard Sunderland Trust* v. *Robson* (1992), where the employer operated a grading scheme based on points. Following a job evaluation study the points totals of the respondent in this case and her male comparator were different, but fell within the same scale on the employer's grading scheme. The EAT found that in these circumstances the respondent was employed on work rated as equivalent with that of the male comparator within the terms of s. 1(5) and accordingly was entitled to equal pay with him.

8. 'Work . . . of equal value to that of a man in the same employment.'

Under s. 1(2)(c) of the 1970 Act (added by the Equal Pay (Amendment) Regulations 1983: *see* 5 above) an equality clause is to be implied into a contract of employment: 'Where a woman is employed on work which . . . is, in terms of the demands made on her (for instance under such headings as effort, skill and decision), of equal value to that of a man in the same employment . . .' This clause applies only where the provisions relating to 'like work' and 'work rated as equivalent' do not apply.

The procedure which an industrial tribunal must follow where a reference has been made under s. 1(2)(c) is governed by s. 2A of the 1970 Act (added by the 1983 Regulations and subsequently amended by the Sex Discrimination and Equal Pay (Miscellaneous Amendments) Regulations 1996). The tribunal may either proceed to determine the question as to whether the work is of equal value or, unless it is satisfied that there are no reasonable grounds for determining that the work is of equal value, require a member of a panel of independent experts to prepare a report with respect to that question. This panel is designated by ACAS. An example of the kind of situation where there will be no reasonable grounds for determining that the work is of equal value is where there has already been a job evaluation study which has demonstrated that the work of the applicant is not of equal value. It should also be noted that the right of a tribunal to strike out an application in these circumstances is separate from the right which the tribunal has to strike out proceedings which are scandalous, frivolous or vexatious by virtue of the Industrial Tribunals (Constitution and Rules of Procedure) Regulations 1993 as subsequently amended: *see Ashmore* v. *British Coal Corporation* (1990).

Where the tribunal has required a report to be prepared by the independent expert, that report becomes evidence in the case, but it does not have the effect of removing or shifting the burden of proof, which rests on the applicant and is in no sense conclusive in the proceedings: *see Aldridge* v. *British Telecommunications plc* (1990).

A leading authority on work of equal value, and a most instructive case, is *Hayward* v. *Cammell Laird Shipbuilders Ltd* (1988). The applicant was employed as a cook in a shipyard canteen. She claimed, under s. 1(2)(c) of the Act, that she was doing work of equal value to male shipyard workers who were being paid at a higher rate. An evaluation by an independent expert was followed by a finding by an industrial tribunal that she was doing work of equal value to the male comparators. However, at a subsequent hearing, the industrial tribunal found that *all* her terms and conditions of employment should be compared with the male employees and not just the terms relating to basic pay and overtime. Accordingly, her claim for equal pay was dismissed. On appeal, ultimately to the House of Lords, it was held, overturning the decision of the industrial tribunal, that on its true construction s. 1(2) of the Act referred to the specific term or terms of the contract (i.e. those relating to pay in this case) about which complaint had been made. This meant that even though the contract of employment taken as a whole was not less favourable than those of the male comparators, the specific term on pay was to be compared with those of the male employees. Accordingly, the case was remitted to the industrial tribunal for a decision on the applicant's specific pay entitlement. *See* also *Pickstone* v. *Freemans plc* (1988) and *Leverton* v. *Clwyd County Council* (1989).

9. Defences available to the employer

Under s. 1(3) of the 1970 Act (as substituted by the 1983 Regulations) it is provided that an equality clause shall not operate where the employer proves that the variation is genuinely due to a material factor which is not the difference of sex and that factor:

(a) (in the case of an equality clause implied through 'like work' and 'work rated as equivalent') must be a material difference between the woman's case and the man's: and

(b) (in the case of an equality clause implied through work of 'equal value') may be such a material difference.

There is some uncertainty over the precise scope and meaning of this rather complex provision, but it is important to distinguish the ways in which 'like work' and 'work rated as equivalent' on the one hand, and 'work of equal value' on the other, are treated. In the case of like work and work rated as equivalent, an employer will not be obliged to pay equal pay if there is a genuine material factor which differentiates between the woman's case and the man's, as long as that factor is a material difference between the two cases. The burden rests on the employer to prove this defence, i.e. that there is a material difference between the employees who are being compared and that their differential treatment is due to that difference: *Financial Times* v. *Byrne (No 2)* (1992). In *Calder* v. *Rowntree Mackintosh Confectionery Ltd.* (1993), although the employer conceded that the work of the women applicants and the male comparator was of equal value, but sought to justify differences in pay by reference to a shift premium paid to the male comparator for working rotating rather than fixed shifts, the Court of Appeal held that the fact that some indeterminate part of the shift premium represented compensation for working unsocial hours (which the applicants also worked) did not preclude a finding that the payment of the shift premium was genuinely due to working on rotating shifts.

Under the legislative predecessor of s. 1(3) such factors as length of service, academic qualifications and the place of employment (e.g. London, as opposed to Blackburn) have been held, in appropriate circumstances, to constitute genuine material differences: *see*, for example, *Snoxell* v. *Vauxhall Motors* (1977).

It used to be thought that the genuine material difference defence relating to 'like work' and 'work rated as equivalent' rested on factors personal to the employees concerned, but in *Rainey* v. *Greater Glasgow Health Board* (1987) the House of Lords took a broader approach and stated that the employer's defence is not limited to personal differences, but can apply where the employer can show economic factors affecting the efficient carrying on of the business, as long as those factors are not based on intentional sex discrimination. Accordingly, the employer in this case, who was paying newly-recruited prosthetists higher rates of pay than existing employees in order to attract recruits from the private sector, was not obliged to raise the pay of the female applicant to the rate being paid to the new recruits. In *Barber* v. *NCR (Manufacturing) Ltd* (1993) the EAT held that the economic forces used by the employer to support his defence must go further than simply being an historical justification but must objectively support that defence. *See also Tyldesley* v. *TML Plastics Ltd* (1996).

In the case of 'work of equal value', the employer's defence is slightly different. Here the employer must show that the variation is genuinely due to a material factor which *may* be a material difference – in other words it is not mandatory that it *is* a material difference. The purpose of this different approach seems to be to allow the employer to plead economic arguments as justifying differential rates of pay more readily than was thought to be the case, at least before the decision in *Rainey*, in relation to like work and work rated as equivalent.

An important recent decision of the European Court of Justice has marked a significant development in this area. In *Enderby* v. *Frenchay Health Authority and Secretary of State for Health* (1993) a test case brought by a senior speech therapist was based on an equal value claim. The essence of the employer's defence was that the higher pay enjoyed by the male comparators was as a consequence of separate collective bargaining machinery and pay negotiations for the two groups, and that this constituted a genuine material factor distinguishing the cases. The Court of Appeal referred to the ECJ the question of whether an employer could defend the allegations made on the basis that the differences resulted from separate collective bargaining processes which were not internally discriminatory. The ECJ held that the fact that the respective rates of pay of two jobs of equal value, one carried out almost exclusively by women and the other predominantly by men, were arrived at by collective bargaining processes is not a sufficient objective justification for the difference in pay between the two jobs. It would be too easy for an employer to circumvent the principles of equal pay if he were able to point to separate collective bargaining processes, which were themselves non-discriminatory.

A further example which illustrates the way in which the defences open to the employer have been narrowed by the courts is afforded by the decision of the House of Lords in *North Yorkshire County Council* v. *Ratcliffe* (1995). The applicants were female school catering assistants who had originally been employed by the respondent county council on nationally negotiated rates of pay and conditions of employment. Their work had previously been rated as of equal value to that of men employed by the council at various establishments. Following the introduction of compulsory competitive tendering the applicants were dismissed as redundant and then re-employed through a direct service organisation at rates of pay below the nationally agreed rates. The applicants sought equal pay with male comparators, working at similar grades, who were all still employed on broadly the same terms and conditions as under the national agreement. The House of Lords held that the fact that the female applicants were paid less than the male comparators was to enable the direct service organisation to be competitive, but that this was not a material factor other than the difference of sex. It took the view that it is inescapable that when an evaluation has shown that the women were being paid less than men for work rated as equivalent then it is impossible to say that the difference in pay was genuinely due to a material factor other than the difference of sex.

ENFORCEMENT

10. Individual enforcement of the Act

A woman (or man) may enforce an equality clause by presenting a complaint to an industrial tribunal. Such a complaint may be referred to a tribunal by an individual, an employer or, in certain circumstances, by the Secretary of State for Employment. If the tribunal finds that an individual is entitled to equal pay, it may make a declaration to that effect and award up to two years' back pay. Claims must be brought within 6 months of the end of the contract, where the applicant has left employment: *see Fletcher* v. *Midland Bank plc* (1996). This rule also appears to apply to claims brought under Article 119. The burden of proving that s. 1(2) is satisfied lies upon the complainant. It the employer wishes to rely on the genuine material factor defence, he must establish it. It should be remembered that the tribunal must follow a special procedure where a claim is based on work of equal value.

10

DISCRIMINATION IN EMPLOYMENT

INTRODUCTION

1. Scope of the chapter

In this chapter a number of Acts of Parliament are considered, together with associated regulations. The enactments which will be considered are the Sex Discrimination Act 1975 (as amended by the Sex Discrimination Act 1986), the Race Relations Act 1976 and the Disability Discrimination Act 1995. It should be noted that although these Acts are concerned with eliminating discrimination on certain grounds in a number of areas, this chapter is concerned with their impact in the context of employment. In addition, the Asylum and Immigration Act 1996, which makes it an offence for an employer to employ someone who does not have permission to work in the United Kingdom, is considered.

It will be remembered from Chapter 9 that, in broad terms, the Equal Pay Act 1970 is concerned with less favourable treatment of a person of one sex as compared to another in respect of matters (pay and terms and conditions) governed by the contract under which a person is employed, while the Sex Discrimination Act deals with matters not covered by the contract. The two Acts are designed to be complementary.

SEX DISCRIMINATION ACT 1975

2. Scope of the 1975 Act

In relation to employment, the Sex Discrimination Act is intended to render discrimination on grounds of sex and/or the fact that a person is married (irrespective of age) unlawful as regards those areas of employment not dealt with by the terms of the contract (which are the province of the Equal Pay Act: *see* Chapter 9). The Act applies to the Crown: s. 85.

The Act renders discrimination on the above grounds unlawful except in the following cases.

(a) Discrimination by way of 'special treatment afforded to women in connection with pregnancy or childbirth': s. 2(2).

(b) Where in the previous year there were no or few members of one sex doing a particular job, certain discrimination in favour of members of that sex is allowed: s. 48.

(c) Discrimination in the selection, promotion or training of a person is permissible where being a man or a woman is a 'genuine occupational qualification'.

(d) There are special rules relating to the police, prison officers and ministers of religion: ss. 17–19.

(e) There are special rules relating to death or retirement: s. 6(4)(a)–(c). Detailed consideration of these complex provisions, which were inserted in the Act with effect from the beginning of 1993 by virtue of the Social Security Act 1989, is beyond the scope of this book, but the recent amendments are intended to provide for the equal treatment of men and women in occupational pension schemes. The position here has been much influenced by European Community law, which in turn led to the amendment of the 1975 Act by the Sex Discrimination Act 1986. The original position under Community law was that discriminatory retirement ages for men and women were viewed as lawful: *see Burton* v. *British Railways Board* (1982). However, the matter is no longer so clear cut following the decision of the European Court of Justice in *Barber* v. *Guardian Royal Exchange Assurance Group* (1990), the legal issues in which were extremely complex. Among a number of other matters, the ECJ held that a pension paid under a contracted-out private occupational pension scheme falls within the scope of Article 119 and that entitlement to a deferred pension (for men, as against women who were entitled to an earlier retirement age under the scheme) was contrary to Article 119. This was the case even though the deferred pension arrangements in the contracted-out scheme reflect those in the state pension legislation.

The position with regard to discrimination which *flows from* differential retirement ages has also been problematic. In *Garland* v. *British Rail Engineering* (1982), all employees enjoyed concessionary rail travel during their employment and this concession extended to their immediate families. After retirement, however, the families of retired women (but not of retired men) lost these concessions. Following a reference by the House of Lords the European Court of Justice ruled that the different concessionary arrangements were discriminatory under Article 119 on the basis that 'pay' included indirect benefits. In the light of the European Court of Justice ruling the House of Lords held that the provision of different travel facilities for retired male and female employees was unlawful discrimination; this involved interpreting the exception to the general principle contained in s. 6(4) of the Act as originally drafted narrowly.

The difficulty with such an approach is that it would not always be possible to construe the statute in such a way: *Duke* v. *Reliance Systems Ltd* (1988).

Additionally, in *Marshall* v. *Southampton and South West Hampshire Area Health Authority (Teaching)* (1986), the European Court of Justice held that the exclusion of the right of a woman to bring an unfair dismissal claim after she reached the age of 60 (whereas the age is 65 for men) was contrary to the Equal Treatment Directive.

Subsequently, and also in the light of the decision of the European Court in *Commission of the European Communities* v. *UK* (1984), the 1986 Act was passed in order to bring the 1975 Act into line with Treaty obligations.

The present position is that under s. 6(4) provisions in relation to death or retirement are excluded from the operation of the Act, and except insofar as they apply to provisions relating to retirement, it remains unlawful to discriminate in relation to promotion, transfer, training, demotion or dismissal. What this means in practice is that if there is a fixed retirement age for men with a particular employer, a woman cannot be compelled to retire at a lower age. However, it should be noted that although the Act applies, in this context, *to retirement*, it does not directly affect matters relating to differential *pension* ages. Accordingly, as has been indicated at the beginning of this section, there are still some problematic issues to be resolved in this area.

3. Positive discrimination

The general position under the Act is that positive discrimination in favour of either sex is rendered unlawful by the Act. Mention has already been made of s. 48 which expressly permits positive discrimination in relation to training, or encouraging members of one sex to take advantage of opportunities for doing particular kinds of work or holding certain posts in an organisation, where in the preceding twelve months there were no, or very few, persons, proportionally, of that sex undertaking those posts or doing work in the organisation. This is in line with the Equal Treatment Directive, which, while prohibiting all direct or indirect discrimination on grounds of sex, does provide in Article 2(4) that this is 'without prejudice to measures to promote equal opportunity for men and women, in particular by removing existing inequalities which affect women's opportunities. . . .' In *Kalanke* v. *Freie Hansestadt Bremen* (1995) the issue before the ECJ was whether a national law which provided that women should have priority for posts if they did not represent 50 per cent of the workforce and were equally qualified with male candidates was contrary to the Equal Treatment Directive. The court held that Article 2(4) had to be construed strictly and held that the national law fell outside its scope.

4. Areas of employment covered

Section 6 provides that the following areas of employment are within the scope of the Act.

(a) (Section 6(1)(a)). Arrangements for selecting employees and the making of offers of employment, e.g. discriminatory arrangements for holding interviews, refusing to employ members of one sex for certain kinds of jobs etc. *See Saunders*

v. *Richmond-upon-Thames Borough Council* (1977) for a case dealing with allegedly discriminatory interviewing of candidates.

(b) (Section 6(1)(b)). The terms upon which employment is offered but not the terms themselves when employment has been obtained, this latter matter being within the scope of the Equal Pay Act (*see* above). *See Greig* v. *Community Industry and Ahern* (1979).

Following the decision of the EAT in *Clymo* v. *Wandsworth London Borough Council* (1989), it is clear that the provisions of s. 6(1) deal only with situations which arise before a contract of employment is entered into. Alleged discriminatory acts which occur once the employment has commenced fall under s. 6(2).

(c) (Section 6(2)(a)). Access to promotion, training, transfer or any other benefit, facilities or services. *See Peake* v. *Automotive Products* (1977) for a case which examined the general objectives of the Act.

(d) (Section 6(2)(b)). Dismissal or the subjecting of a person to any other detriment, e.g. suspension from work.

There are a number of examples in the cases of situations where a 'detriment' has been said to apply to an employee, but a particularly significant and important issue in this context is that of sexual harassment. In *Strathclyde Regional Council* v. *Porcelli* (1986), the applicant, one of three laboratory technicians in a school, alleged that she had been subjected to a campaign of harassment by the two male technicians, which included sexual harassment. She alleged that this was designed to make her leave her place of employment. The Court of Session held that since the treatment meted out to her was only meted out to her because she was a woman, she had been subjected to a detriment under s. 6(2)(b). It was irrelevant that there was no sexual motive behind the harassment: *see also Wadman* v. *Carpenter Farrer Partnership* (1993) and the European Commission Code of Practice on Measures to Combat Sexual Harassment.

In *Burton and Rhule* v. *De Vere Hotels* (1996) the EAT ruled that an employer had subjected employees to a 'detriment' by causing or permitting harassment serious enough to amount to a detriment to occur. Thus, where employees were subjected to verbal harassment by an after-dinner speaker at a function at the hotel where the employees worked it was held that the employer was liable to the employees. The EAT said that it would have been good employment practice for the manager to have been vigilant and to have withdrawn the employees from the area where the verbal harassment happened once matters became unpleasant.

5. Advertisements

It is unlawful to publish or cause to be published an advertisement which indicates, or might reasonably be taken to indicate, an intention to do an act which is contrary to the Act: s. 38(1). Use of terms such as 'salesgirl' or 'waiter' in job advertisements are thus precluded: s. 38(3). The term 'advertisement' is defined as including 'every form of advertisement whether to the public or not': s. 82. The publisher, as opposed to the person causing it to be published, has a defence if he can prove that he acted reasonably in reliance upon a statement by the person causing the advertisement to be published to the effect that the publication would not be unlawful: s. 38(4).

The provisions relating to advertisements are enforceable only by the Equal Opportunities Commission (*see* 1:**28**) seeking a declaration and/or a county court injunction to restrain publication. *See Equal Opportunities Commission* v. *Robertson* (1980).

6. The meaning of discrimination

The Act embodies three kinds of discrimination.

(a) *Direct discrimination*: s. 1(1)(a) and s. 3(1)(a) – this is 'less favourable' treatment on grounds of sex/being married, e.g. operating a rule that female employees' contracts of employment automatically terminate on marriage: *North East Midlands Co-operative Society* v. *Allen* (1977); *see also Hurley* v. *Mustoe* (1981).

Statistical evidence relating to the employer's business may be used as rebuttable evidence of discrimination, e.g. the fact that no woman is employed by an employer may suggest that there is a policy of discrimination and vice versa, but this is not automatically so: *see Johnson* v. *Timber Tailors (Midlands) Ltd* (1978).

Note that there can only be direct discrimination if there can be a direct comparison between men and women. Thus in *Schmidt* v. *Austicks Bookshops Ltd* (1977) it was held that it was not direct discrimination for an employer to impose rules relating to the way his employees dressed even though the precise content of those rules differed as between the sexes.

This case was distinguished in *Smith* v. *Safeway plc* (1995). The applicant had been dismissed because the length of his hair breached the employer's rules for male staff. By a majority the EAT found that he had been discriminated against on the grounds of his sex in that the employer's rules were capable of being applied to both men and women and also in that, unlike other requirements as to appearance (which is what the *Schmidt* case was concerned with), a restriction on hair length did not have effect just during working hours but all the time. This was regarded as detrimental and clearly unfair to men and was inconsistent with the objectives of the Sex Discrimination Act.

An interesting and topical illustration of the way in which these provisions can operate is afforded by *Webb* v. *Emo Air Cargo (UK) Ltd.* (1994), where an employee who had been recruited to replace a member of staff who was due to take maternity leave herself informed her new employer that she was pregnant. She was dismissed by the employer, who argued that she had been treated no less favourably than a new male recruit would have been if he had announced that he would be absent from work for a comparable period. The Court of Appeal held that the dismissal of a pregnant woman for a reason arising out of, or related to, her pregnancy can in law be, but is not necessarily, direct discrimination under s. 1(1)(a), and accordingly the applicant's claim was dismissed. The House of Lords referred the following question arising from the appeal from the Court of Appeal to the European Court of Justice for a preliminary ruling:

"Is it discrimination on grounds of sex . . . for an employer to dismiss a female employee

(a) whom he engaged for the specific purpose of replacing (after training) another female employee during the latter's forthcoming maternity leave;

(b) when, very shortly after appointment, the employer discovers that the appellant herself will be absent on maternity leave during the maternity leave of the other employee, and the employer dismisses her because he needs the job-holder to be at work during that period;

(c) had the employer known of the pregnancy of the appellant at the date of appointment, she would not have been appointed; and

(d) the employer would similarly have dismissed a male employee engaged for this purpose who required leave of absence at the relevant time for medical or other reasons?"

The ECJ held that it is contrary to the Equal Treatment Directive to dismiss a woman who is employed for an unlimited period who, shortly after being engaged by the employer, is found to be pregnant, notwithstanding that she was appointed to replace another employee who is on maternity leave. Such a dismissal is direct discrimination on grounds of sex; this kind of situation cannot be compared with the dismissal of a male employee in similar circumstances on grounds of ill health. *See also Dekker* v. *Stichting Vormingscentrum voor Jong Volwassenen Plus* (1991). When the case came back to the House of Lords (1995) it was formally held that the employers had breached the Sex Discrimination Act and the case was remitted back to the industrial tribunal to assess compensation.

(b) *Indirect discrimination*: s. 1(1)(b) and s. 3(1)(b) – this is where the complainant must show that:

(*i*) the employer applies a 'requirement or condition' which he applies or would apply to members of the other sex / single persons; and

(*ii*) the proportion of the complainant's sex / married persons who 'can comply with it is considerably smaller than the proportion of' the other sex / single persons who can comply with it;

(*iii*) the employer cannot show the requirement or condition is justifiable irrespective of the sex of the person to whom it is applied

(*iv*) that it is to the complainant's detriment because he / she cannot comply with it.

It should be noted that if it is proved that, despite indirect discrimination, the respondent did not *intend* to treat the complainant less favourably, no compensation can be awarded: s. 66(3).

An example of the operation of this provision would be where an employer requires all his employees to be over six feet tall. Point (*i*) would be satisfied; point (*ii*) could be established by reference to established statistics; point (*iii*) would require the employer to establish that the nature of the job demanded employees of that height and point (*iv*) would mean that a complaint could only be presented if the complainant was less than six feet tall.

Price v. *Civil Service Commission* (1978). Held: a Civil Service condition that candidates for certain posts should be no more than 28 years of age was indirect discrimination because women in their late twenties were frequently occupied in having and bringing up children. The word 'can' in s. 1(1)(b) should not be so strictly construed as to mean that any woman could comply because women were not bound to have children. It is necessary to consider not merely the 'theoretically possible' but also whether a person can do something 'in practice': *see also Jones* v. *University of Manchester* (1993).

Clarke v. *Eley (IMI) Kynoch Ltd* (1982). Held: that the redundancy procedure of the employers which provided that part-time workers would be selected before full-time workers applied a requirement or condition within the meaning of s. 1(1)(b) in that in order to qualify for selection on the basis of 'last in first out' (the second stage of the employer's procedure) an employee had to be employed full-time. The proportion of women who can satisfy the requirement of working full-time is considerably smaller than the proportion of men. Accordingly such a procedure was found to be indirectly discriminatory.

Turner v. *The Labour Party and the Labour Party Superannuation Society* (1987). Held: that an alleged discriminatory condition, whereby the applicant argued that an occupational pension provision discriminated against her as a single parent (who are mostly women) in the arrangements for the pension entitlements of her dependants on her death, was not to her detriment. The reason for the decision was that the conditions for benefit from a pension fund have to be satisfied in the future, and not at the date when a contribution was made. Accordingly, the alleged discriminatory condition could not be held to be to her 'detriment' because she 'cannot comply with it' (s. 1(1)(b)(iii)). It cannot be said of a single woman that she 'cannot' marry.

Two recent cases which illustrate the care which employers need to exercise in their consideration of the contractual arrangements under which employees work are *London Underground Ltd* v. *Edwards* (1995) and *Meade-Hill* v. *British Council* (1995).

In the London Underground case the applicant was a train operator who worked under a shift system which she was able to organise in such a way as to meet her responsibilities as a single mother. The employer introduced a new rostering system which meant that she could no longer continue to balance her different responsibilities and she left her employment voluntarily. She claimed that she had been indirectly discriminated against under the Act on the basis that the employer had applied to her a condition with which a considerably smaller proportion of train operators who were female single parents could comply than those who were male single parents. The EAT found that the correct pool for comparison was not the pool of single parent train operators. The case was remitted back to the industrial tribunal, which went on to hold that London Underground had failed to justify the indirect discrimination. In *London Underground Ltd* v. *Edwards (No. 2)* (1997) the EAT rejected the employer's appeal. It said that there was evidence to justify the conclusion that the employer could, and should, have accommodated the requirements of the employee, who had been working for London Underground for nearly 10 years and whose family demands were of a temporary nature. The EAT went on to say, in an *obiter dictum*, that employers should recognise the need to take a reasonably flexible attitude to accommodating the particular needs of their employees – it said that the 'more clear it is that the employers unreasonably failed to show flexibility in their employment practices, the more willing the tribunal should be to make a finding of unlawful discrimination.'

In *Meade-Hill* v. *British Council* the issue concerned a mobility clause in a contract. The applicant had been promoted to a higher grade, but she was required to work anywhere in the United Kingdom if so directed by her employer. She would have found this difficult to do, because her husband earned more in his job than she did in her job. She sought a declaration that the mobility clause was unlawful, given that a higher proportion of women than men in employment are secondary earners. The Court of Appeal accepted this argument subject to the possible defence of justifiability by the employer (see below). The case was remitted to the county court to consider whether the term was justifiable.

7. Justifiability

Direct discrimination is unlawful *per se*. Indirect discrimination is not unlawful if it can be shown to be justifiable under s. 1(b)(ii). In *Clarke* v. *Eley (IMI) Kynock Ltd (supra)* the EAT considered whether the discriminatory requirement was 'justifiable'. In the years immediately following the passing of the SDA the test for justifiability was stringent: an employer had virtually to establish that the requirement or condition imposed was 'necessary' rather than merely 'convenient': *see Steel* v. *Union of Post Office Workers* (1978). However, this test has been eroded and the matter is now much more open to the application of the discretion of an industrial tribunal applying the open-ended test adopted in the *Clarke* case of 'was it right and proper in the circumstances to adopt the requirement?' Nevertheless, in applying this test the EAT found that the industrial tribunal had not misdirected itself in finding that the requirement was not justifiable.

On the question of justifiability, *see also Cobb* v. *Secretary of State for Employment and Manpower Services Commission* (1989); *Greater Manchester Police Authority* v. *Lea* (1990); and *London Underground Ltd* v. *Edwards (No. 2)* (1997).

8. Discrimination by victimisation: s. 4

This is discrimination against a person who has brought proceedings, given evidence or information, alleged a contravention etc. under the Sex Discrimination Act or Equal Pay Act. Such a person must not be treated 'less favourably' by the alleged discriminator than another person in those circumstances is or would be treated.

For the limits of the availability of the remedy *see Waters* v. *Metropolitan Police* (1995).

9. Genuine occupational qualifications

In relation to discrimination on grounds of sex (as opposed to discrimination against married persons), s. 7 provides that certain kinds of employment are excluded from the operation of the Act, namely where being a member of one sex is a 'genuine occupational qualification' for the job. Two general points should be noted:

(*i*) These provisions do not apply to the terms upon which employment is offered, dismissal or subjecting a person to any other detriment.

(*ii*) With the exception of **(g)** below, these provisions do not apply to the filling of a vacancy where the employer already has male (or female) employees capable of filling it and whom it would be reasonable to employ on those duties and whose numbers are sufficient to meet the employer's likely requirements without undue inconvenience.

Being a man (or woman) is a genuine occupational qualification for a job where:

(a) The essential nature of the job calls for a man for reasons of physiology or authenticity, e.g. actors, models (s. 7(2)(a)).

(b) (*i*) For reasons specified by s. 7, the job needs to be held by a man to preserve decency or privacy: *see Wylie* v. *Dee and Co.* (1978) and *Timex Corporation* v. *Hodgson* (1981) (s. 7(2)(b)).

(*ii*) The job is likely to involve the holder of the job doing his work, or living, in a private home and needs to be held by a man (or woman) because objection might be taken to allowing a woman (or man) the degree of physical or social contact with a person living in the home (s. 7(2)(b)).

(c) The nature or location of the establishment effectively requires the employee to 'live in' and, in the absence of separate sleeping accommodation and sanitary facilities, it is not reasonable to expect the employer to provide such things (it should be noted, however, that the absence of sanitary facilities is not generally a lawful reason for refusing to employ members of one sex) (s. 7(2)(c)).

(d) The nature of the establishment where the work is done, i.e. a hospital, prison or special care establishment virtually exclusively for men, requires that the job be held by a man (s. 7(2)(d)).

(e) The holder of the job provides personal services relating to welfare, education or similar and those services can most effectively be provided by a man (s. 7(2)(e)).

(f) The job needs to be held by a man because it is likely to involve the performance of duties outside the United Kingdom in a country whose laws or customs are such that the duties could not, or could not effectively, be performed by a woman.

(g) The job is one of two held by a married couple.

10. Sexual orientation

Section 1(1)(a) of the Act establishes that there is discrimination where a woman (or man) is treated less favourably by an employer than he would have treated a man (or woman). The European Court of Justice has recently had to consider the position of transsexuals in *P* v. *S* (1996). In this case the applicant, P, was a manager at an educational establishment. S was its chief executive. P had been born a male, but she had announced her intention to undergo a sex change. When she was dismissed she argued that it was because she had announced her intention; S argued that she had been dismissed because of redundancy. The industrial tribunal found that the true reason for the dismissal was her intention to undergo a sex change, but that there was no remedy under the 1975 Act because the Act dealt only with people who belong to one sex or another – it did not recognise a transsexual condition. However, the tribunal stayed the proceedings pending a determination by the ECJ as to whether the Equal Treatment Directive had been breached. The ECJ found that the scope of the Directive was not confined to discrimination based on the fact that a person was of one or other sex, but also extended to discrimination which arose from the gender reassignment of a person. It held that where a person is dismissed on the ground that he or she intends to undergo, or has undergone, gender reassignment, he or she is treated unfavourably by comparison with persons of the sex to which he or she was deemed to belong before undergoing gender reassignment. Accordingly, dismissal of such a person, unless justified under Article 2(2) (which it was not, in this case), is contrary to the Equal Treatment Directive.

The approach taken by the ECJ in the above case should be contrasted with that of the Court of Appeal in *R.* v. *Ministry of Defence ex p Smith* (1996) which concerned the question of the employment of homosexuals in the armed forces. The Ministry of Defence had, in 1994, reaffirmed its policy that homosexuality was incompatible with service in the armed forces and that persons known to be homosexual would be discharged. The applicant in this case, who had been discharged, argued that the decision to discharge him breached Article 2 of the Equal Treatment Directive. The Court of Appeal dismissed the appeal on the basis that the policy pursued by the Ministry of Defence could not be stigmatised as irrational and also on the ground that the Directive was not directed to discrimination on grounds of sexual orientation; *see also Smith* v. *Gardner Merchant Ltd* (1996) where the EAT held that discrimination on the grounds of homosexuality in either sex was discrimination on grounds of sexual orientation and not discrimination on grounds of sex – since neither the 1975 Act nor the Equal Treatment Directive mentioned sexual orientation or preference, they provided no protection.

11. Enforcement of the Act

It should be remembered that the Equal Opportunities Commission has important functions in connection with the enforcement of the Sex Discrimination Act.

As regards individual enforcement of the Act, an individual may complain to an industrial tribunal: s. 63. A complaint must normally be presented within three months of the alleged discrimination (s. 76) although it would seem that the tribunals have a wide discretion to hear cases out of time: *see Hutchison* v. *Westward Television Ltd* (1977) and, for a particularly interesting example of the width of this discretion, the decision of the EAT in *Foster* v. *South Glamorgan Health Authority* (1988).

The burden of proof is on the complainant but normally the tribunal would hear what the respondent has to say: *see Moberly* v. *Commonwealth Hall (University of London)* (1977) and *Humphreys* v. *Board of Managers of St. George's Church of England (Aided) Primary School* (1978). There is a special pre-tribunal procedure facilitating the obtaining of information and effective presentation of a complaint: s. 74 and Sex Discrimination (Questions and Replies) Order 1975 *but see Science Research Council* v. *Nasse* (1979) as to the issue of whether a complainant is entitled to see confidential reports, references, etc.

If the tribunal finds the complaint well-founded it can make a declaration and recommend that the respondent take a certain course of action (but note *Irvine* v. *Prestcold* (1981): a tribunal cannot recommend the increase in pay of the complainant under s. 65(1)(c) and/or award compensation: s. 65(1)(b)).

12. Compensation

Until November 1993 there was a ceiling on awards of compensation under the Sex Discrimination Act 1975, but following the landmark decision of the ECJ in *Marshall* v. *Southampton and South-West Area Health Authority (No. 2)* (1993) the Sex Discrimination and Equal Pay (Remedies) Regulations 1993 were implemented. The regulations removed the maximum amount of compensation for sex discrimination, which had previously been tied to the compensatory award for unfair dismissal. They also allow an award of interest on awards of compensation under the Equal Pay Act and the Sex Discrimination Act to run from the date of the act of discrimination complained of, and not just from the date of the decision of the tribunal as had been the case hitherto.

It should be noted that compensation awards under s. 65 can include a sum for injury to feelings: *see Coleman* v. *Skyrail Oceanic Ltd* (1981) and *Orlando* v. *Didcot Power Station Sports and Social Club* (1996).

13. Miscellaneous provisions

The following points should be noted:

(a) By virtue of s. 39, it is unlawful for any person (e.g. an employer) who has authority over another person (e.g. an employee) to instruct him to discriminate. Enforcement of this provision is by the Equal Opportunities Commission: s. 72.

(b) Section 40 provides that pressure (by providing a benefit or subjecting to a detriment) to discriminate is unlawful. Enforcement of this provision is by the Equal Opportunities Commission: s. 72.

(c) Section 41 provides that where an employee does an act of discrimination in the course of his employment, it is deemed to have been done by his employer:

see, for example, *Strathclyde Regional Council* v. *Porcelli* (1986) and *Enterprise Glass Co. Ltd* v. *Miles* (1990). It is a defence for the employer to show 'that he took such steps as were reasonably practicable to prevent the employee from doing . . . in the course of his employment acts of that description'. Thus, in *Balgobin & Francis* v. *London Borough of Tower Hamlets* (1987), an employer which did not know of the unlawful discrimination but had taken adequate steps to supervise staff and publicise its equal opportunities policy was able to rely on this defence.

(d) Section 42 provides that any person who knowingly aids another person to discriminate is treated as though he had discriminated himself. It is a defence to show that he acted reasonably in reliance upon a statement made to him by the other person that the act would not be unlawful.

RACE RELATIONS ACT 1976

References in this section are to the Race Relations Act 1976.

14. Scope of the Act

The 1976 Act is concerned with discrimination on grounds of 'colour, race, nationality or ethnic or national origin': s. 3(1). Some difficulty has been experienced over the question of the meaning of 'ethnic . . . origin' and in particular its relationship with 'race'. However in *Mandla* v. *Lee* (1983) the House of Lords resolved the matter. The question was whether Sikhs are a group of persons defined by ethnic origin so as to fall within the protection of s. 3(1). It was held that Sikhs did constitute an ethnic group; 'ethnic' was used in the Act in a sense much wider than that of 'race', and an ethnic group can be identified by some or all of such essential factors as a long history, cultural tradition, common geographical origin, common language and a common religion (different from neighbouring groups); *see also Commission for Racial Equality* v. *Dutton* (1989).

In *Dawkins* v. *Department of the Environment* (1993) the Court of Appeal held that although Rastafarians are a separate group with identifiable characteristics, they have not established a separate identity by reference to their ethnic origins. Applying the decision in *Mandla* v. *Lee (supra)* it was held that the word 'ethnic' has a racial flavour and, in comparing Rastafarians with the rest of the Afro-Caribbean community, there was nothing to set them aside as a separate ethnic group.

It should be noted that a racial group cannot be defined by the factor of language alone: accordingly, a requirement that applicants for a post as an assistant in a local authority residential home be Welsh speakers did not constitute a breach of the Act: *Gwynedd County Council* v. *Jones* (1986). The EAT in that case held that even if the language requirement had been discriminatory under the Act, it was nevertheless justifiable.

The 1976 Act is concerned not only with employment but covers also such things as the provision of services, housing etc. Otherwise, *mutatis mutandis*, the 1976 Act is based on similar principles to the Sex Discrimination Act 1975 and, as such, it is not intended to discuss in detail the areas of employment covered, advertisements, the meaning of discrimination and the enforcement of the Act.

15. Exceptions

As with the Sex Discrimination Act 1975, there are a number of exceptions to the 1976 Act including where being of a certain race etc. is deemed to be a 'genuine occupational qualification'. These are somewhat narrower than those in the 1975 Act but include, in addition, employment involving 'working in a place where food and drink is . . . provided to and consumed by members of the public or a section of the public in a special ambience for which, in that job, a person of that racial group is required for reasons of authenticity': s. 5(2), e.g. a Chinese waiter for a Chinese restaurant.

Under s. 5(2)(d) it is provided that being of a certain race, etc. is a genuine occupational qualification where the holder of the job provides persons of that racial group with personal services promoting their welfare and those services can most effectively be provided by a person of that racial group. A broad construction was given to this exception in *Tottenham Green Under Five's Centre* v. *Marshall* (1991), where the Employment Appeal Tribunal held that a childrens playgroup which catered for a wide variety of ethnic groups was entitled to advertise for someone of Afro-Caribbean origin; this was because the personal services which were provided included the maintenance of the cultural links of the children and the requirement to be able to talk and read in West Indian patois; but see also *Lambeth London Borough* v. *Commission for Racial Equality* (1990).

16. Enforcement of the Act

The Act may be enforced by individuals, but the Commission for Racial Equality also has wide powers of investigation.

An individual may complain to an industrial tribunal within three months of the act of discrimination. If the tribunal finds that the complaint is justified it may make a declaration of the rights of the individual (and the respondent), it may order compensation, and it may recommend action to be taken by the respondent to obviate or reduce the effect of the discrimination on the complainant.

By virtue of the Race Relations (Remedies) Act 1994, previous limits on compensation for discrimination on grounds of race were removed. Compensation may include compensation for injury to feelings. Useful guidance on the assessment of compensation was provided by the Court of Appeal in *Alexander* v. *Home Office* (1988):

(a) The object of an award for unlawful racial discrimination is restitution.

(b) Where the discrimination has caused actual pecuniary loss (e.g. the refusal of a job) then damages can be calculated relatively easily.

(c) The calculation of loss occasioned by injury to feelings 'depends on the experience and good sense of the judge and his assessors' (*per* May LJ). Awards should not be minimal, because that would trivialise the policy of the Act, but they should be restrained. Excessive awards also damage the policy of the Act.

(d) The measure of damages may be affected by the conduct of the applicant as well as by the conduct of the respondent.

The Commission for Racial Equality may conduct formal investigations (by virtue of s. 48) and may serve a non-discrimination notice on an employer where it discovers unlawful discriminatory acts in the course of an investigation. This notice may require the employer not to commit such discriminatory acts and to inform the Commission of steps taken to remedy the situation. Where the non-discrimination notice is not being complied with at any time within five years of the issue of the notice, the Commission can seek an injunction in the county court restraining the employer from continuing to commit discriminatory acts.

17. Codes of practice

The Commission for Racial Equality is empowered to issue codes of practice on certain matters: s. 47(1). A Code of Practice for the elimination of racial discrimination and the promotion of equality in employment came into force in April 1984 and it provides practical guidance to employers (and trade unions) on how to achieve the broad aims of the 1976 Act. Employers are recommended to adopt an equal opportunity policy to ensure that no unlawful discrimination occurs and that equal opportunity is genuinely available. Such a policy should be regularly monitored. It should be noted that the Code is not legally binding and that a failure to comply with the Code does not necessarily amount to discrimination. However, it is likely that a failure to comply with the Code will have a persuasive influence before a tribunal: *see Carrington* v. *Helix Lighting Ltd.* (1990).

DISABILITY DISCRIMINATION ACT 1995

References in this section are to the Disability Discrimination Act 1995 and to the Code of Practice for the Elimination of Discrimination in the Field of Employment Against Disabled Persons or Persons who have had a Disability.

18. Scope of the Act

The Disability Discrimination Act 1995 is the first comprehensive legislative attempt to address the issues of discrimination which affect people who are disabled. Its provisions cover the field of employment, the provision of goods, facilities and services and the disposal or management of premises. The Act also establishes the National Disability Council which has wide powers and duties in relation to a range of matters connected with disability.

The employment provisions came into force in December 1996, alongside the

Disability Discrimination (Employment) Regulations 1996. The Disability Discrimination (Meaning of Disability) Regulations 1996 are also in force.

Section 1 of the Act gives wide definitions to 'disability' and 'disabled persons': it provides that, subject to Schedule 1 of the Act, a person has a disability for the purposes of the Act if he has a physical or mental impairment which has a substantial and long-term effect on his ability to carry out normal day-to-day activities. Schedule 1 provides further definitions of what is meant by 'impairment', 'long-term effects' and 'normal day-to-day' activities. The Disability Discrimination (Meaning of Disability) Regulations 1996 were issued under Schedule 1, and provide further elucidation of the meaning of disability.

Section 4 is a key section, and it prohibits discrimination by employers against applicants for jobs and existing employees in relation to the following matters:

(a) in the arrangements which he makes for the purpose of determining to whom he should offer employment

(b) in the terms on which he offers that person employment; or

(c) by refusing to offer, or deliberately not offering, him employment

(d) in the terms of employment which he affords him

(e) in the opportunities which he affords him for promotion, a transfer, training or receiving any other benefit

(f) by refusing to afford him, or deliberately not affording him, any such opportunity

(g) by dismissing him, or subjecting him to any other detriment.

'Discrimination' is defined differently from the comparable term in both the Sex Discrimination Act 1975 and the Race Relations Act 1976. Under the 1995 Act there are two broad elements to the meaning of discrimination. An employer is regarded as discriminating against a disabled person if:

(a) for a reason which relates to the disabled person's disability he treats him less favourably than he treats others, and he cannot show that treatment to be justified (s. 5(1)(a),(b))

(b) he fails to comply with the duty required of him by s. 6 of the Act, and he cannot show that failure to be justified (s. 5(2)(a),(b)).

Section 6 requires an employer to make adjustments to working practices, and the workplace itself, to the extent that is reasonable in all circumstances of the case so as to ensure that the disabled person concerned is not at a substantial disadvantage in comparison with persons who are not disabled. Section 6(3) sets out some examples of steps which an employer may have to take in order to comply with the section. These steps include such matters as:

- making adjustments to premises
- allocating some of the disabled person's duties to another person
- altering his working hours

- allowing him to be absent during working hours for rehabilitation, assessment or treatment
- acquiring or modifying equipment
- providing a reader or interpreter.

Some guidance is given in s. 6(4) on the meaning of reasonableness in this context, and the subsection provides that regard will be had to such matters as the extent to which it is practicable for the employer to take the step, the financial and other costs which would be incurred by the employer and the extent of the employer's financial and other resources.

An exemption is provided, by virtue of s. 7, for employers with fewer than 20 employees.

19. Enforcement

In common with the 1975 and 1976 Acts, the remedy for an aggrieved person is by way of complaint to an industrial tribunal, within three months of the act complained of; it should be noted that the tribunal has a discretion to consider a complaint out of time if it considers it just and equitable to do so.

If the tribunal finds the complaint well-founded, the following remedies are available to it under s. 8(2):

(a) A declaration of the rights of the complainant and respondent

(b) An order of compensation

(c) Recommending that the respondent take, within a specified period, action appearing to the tribunal to be reasonable in all the circumstances of the case for the purpose of obviating or reducing the adverse effect on the complainant of any matter to which the complaint relates.

It should be noted that the National Disabilities Council does not play any comparable role to the Equal Opportunities Commission or the Council for Racial Equality in relation to enforcement – its main duties relate to the provision of advice to the Secretary of State.

20. Code of Practice

The Code of Practice for the Elimination of Discrimination in the Field of Employment against Disabled Persons or Persons who have had a Disability came into force at the same time as the employment provisions of the Act in 1996. Like other codes of practice, it does not itself impose legal obligations and is not an authoritative statement of the law; however, it is admissible in evidence in any proceedings under the Act and must be taken into account in determining any relevant issue under the Act. The Code of Practice is a lengthy and detailed document. It provides general guidance to help avoid discrimination, deals in detail with the main employment provisions of the Act and in particular deals with the s. 6 duty to make reasonable adjustments.

21. The Asylum and Immigration Act 1996

The main objectives of this Act are to strengthen the UK's asylum procedures so that false claims and appeals can be dealt with more quickly and to reduce the economic incentives which attract people to the United Kingdom in breach of its immigration laws. Under s. 8 of the Act it is provided that if an employer employs someone who has not been granted leave to enter or remain in the UK, or where the leave of the individual is subject to a condition precluding the taking up of employment, then the employer is guilty of an offence. The employer has a defence if he can prove that, before the employment began, 'there was produced to the employer a document which appeared to him to relate to the employee and to be of a description specified in an order made by the Secretary of State.' It appears that even where a document is forged, an employer may still have a defence.

By virtue of s. 8(8) a contract of employment is defined in terms of a contract of service; accordingly, a person is not guilty of an offence under the Act if he engages a self-employed sub-contractor.

11

TERMINATION OF EMPLOYMENT (1): METHODS

There are a number of ways in which a contract of employment may come to an end and these are examined in this chapter. The consequences of a termination of employment vary with the circumstances and are considered in the following three chapters. Unless otherwise indicated, statutory references in this chapter are to the Employment Rights Act 1996.

DISMISSAL WITH NOTICE

1. Effect of notice

At common law, a contract of employment could be validly terminated by an employer giving notice to an employee in accordance with the terms of the contract (express or implied) or, in the absence of such a term, by giving reasonable notice. If sufficient notice was given, the employee had no further rights and this meant that dismissal could be entirely arbitrary. However, if an employee has been unfairly dismissed (see Chapters 13 and 14), he may be entitled to compensation for loss of his job despite the fact that he was given notice. It should be noted that, once notice has been given, it can only be effectively withdrawn with the consent of the other party: *see Brennan* v. *Lindley and Co.* (1974).

2. Amount of notice: employer to employee

The length of notice which must be given by an employer to an employee is determined by reference to the following criteria to be applied in the following order. It should be noted, however, that these periods of notice apply only where notice is necessary lawfully to terminate the contract. They do not apply, for example, where the employer is entitled to dismiss an employee summarily on account of his gross misconduct.

(a) *Express terms of the contract.* If the contract of employment expressly provides for a period of notice, this must be observed unless that period is less than the statutory minimum to which that particular employee is entitled under (d) below.

It should be noted that the written statement supplied to employees under s. 1 of the Employment Rights Act 1996 ought to state the length of notice to be given by both parties to the contract (these periods may differ).

(b) *Implied term of the contract.* In the absence of an express term it may be possible to imply a term into the contract, e.g. from custom. Again, such a period may not be less than the statutory minimum. In *Davson* v. *France* (1959) a musician was given one week's notice to terminate his engagement. He claimed that this was wrongful dismissal in so far as it was an implied term of his contract (by virtue of a custom of the music trade) that he should receive at least fourteen days' notice. Held: such a term would be implied and the dismissal was therefore wrongful.

(c) *Reasonable period.* If there is no express or implied term of the contract, the courts may rely on a 'reasonable' period. What is 'reasonable' depends upon such factors as the status of the employee, salary, length of employment with that employer, age, etc. The 'reasonable' period cannot be less than the statutory minimum.

Thomas v. *Gatti* (1906): chorus-girl – two weeks.

Adams v. *Union Cinemas* (1939): manager of 120 cinemas – six months.

Mulholland v. *Bexwell Estates Co. Ltd* (1950): manager of estate agencies – three months.

Phillips v. *Alkem* (1969): a senior female clerk who had been employed for eighteen years – four weeks. (Note that this was merely her statutory minimum at that time.)

Hill v. *C.A. Parsons and Co. Ltd* (1972): a senior professional engineer who had been employed for thirty-five years – at least six months.

(d) *Statutory minima.* In the absence of any of the above criteria, or where they produce a period less than the following, the statutory minima in s. 86 of ERA 1996 must be applied in respect of those employees covered by that section. Section 86 provides that for an employee continuously employed for between one month and two years, the notice period is one week; for an employee employed for more than two years, he is entitled to one week for each year of continuous employment subject to a maximum of twelve weeks' notice after twelve years of employment. Thereafter an employee is entitled to at least twelve weeks notice.

It should be noted that these rights of minimum notice do not apply to a contract for the performance of a specific task which is not expected to last for more than three months, unless the employee has been continuously employed for a period of more than three months.

3. Date of termination of the contract

For the purposes of the legislation on unfair dismissal and redundancy the date of termination of the contract is referred to as the 'effective date of termination' (s. 97(1) of the 1996 Act) and the 'relevant date' (s. 153 of the 1996 Act) respectively. It is often important to identify these dates precisely, e.g. for the purposes of determining whether an employee has sufficient qualifying service to pursue an unfair dismissal or redundancy claim, or for calculating his period of continuous service. The basic rules for determining these dates are:

(a) Where notice is given, the date on which it expires.

(b) Where a contract is terminated without notice, in a situation where the employer may lawfully summarily dismiss the employee without notice, the date when the termination takes effect.

(c) Where a fixed term contract expires without being renewed, the date of expiry.

One problem which has exercised the courts and tribunals is that of identifying the date of termination where, as is common, the employee is dismissed with salary in lieu of notice. Although the matter is not without difficulty, it is submitted that the date of termination is the date of dismissal, not the expiry of the period in respect of which salary in lieu is paid: *see Dedman* v. *British Building and Engineering Appliances* (1974); *Robert Cort* v. *Charman* (1981). Sometimes, however, the facts of the case may mean that the tribunals will hold that the true construction of the dismissal is simply that the employee is not being required to work the notice period, in which case the effective date of termination is the date of the expiry of the notice: *see Leech* v. *Preston Borough Council* (1985).

In certain situations the effective date of termination will be deemed to be the date when the statutory minimum notice would have expired. In *Lanton Leisure Ltd* v. *White* (1987) the EAT ruled that employers cannot deprive an employee of the benefit of this provision by simply labelling the reason for dismissal as 'gross misconduct' and invoking their right to dismiss without notice for good cause. The existence of an internal appeal does not rebut the general principle that a person is dismissed when the notice is given. In *Batchelor* v. *British Railways Board* (1987) the Court of Appeal held that a notice containing words 'you are dismissed with immediate effect' terminated the employee's employment immediately, despite the existence of an internal appeal.

In cases of constructive dismissal, the effective date of termination will generally be the date on which the employee departs his employment: *Western Excavating (ECC) Ltd* v. *Sharp* (1978), although where the employee resigns with effect from a stated date, that will be regarded as the effective date of termination: *see Crank* v. *HMSO* (1985).

It should be noted that, under s. 97(2), if the statutory period of notice would have expired later than the effective date of termination, then for certain purposes the later date is deemed to be the effective date of termination. These purposes are:

(a) Ascertaining the qualifying period for the right to a written statement of reasons for dismissal (*see* 12:**11**).

(b) Ascertaining the qualifying period for the right not to be unfairly dismissed (*see* 13:**4**).

(c) Calculation of the basic award for unfair dismissal (*see* 13:**31**).

(d) Ascertaining the period of continuous employment for the purposes of redundancy payments (*see* 14:**15**).

4. Rights during notice

An employee's rights during the period of notice are the same as during the continuance of the contract and are protected by sections 87–91 of the Act.

SUMMARY DISMISSAL

5. Meaning of summary dismissal

Summary dismissal is where an employer dismisses an employee without giving the employee the amount of notice (*see* **2** above) to which that employee may be entitled by virtue of the contract of employment. If there is no justification for the summary dismissal, such dismissal is wrongful. An action for wrongful dismissal may be brought by an employee who has been summarily dismissed without the period of notice to which he is entitled.

The remedy for wrongful dismissal is damages representing the loss of wages during the period of notice that ought to have been given (*see* 12: **1**). However, wrongful dismissal may also be 'unfair dismissal' within the meaning of the 1996 Act (*see* 13:**10**), although both actions could not be taken by the aggrieved employee. Nevertheless, in certain circumstances a dismissal which is wrongful will not be deemed to be unfair (e.g. where a person is dismissed for misconduct without notice which makes it not 'unfair' but the misconduct is not such as to justify dismissal without notice); and conversely, a dismissal may be unfair but not wrongful, i.e. because the correct notice has been given.

It may sometimes be difficult to decide whether there has actually been a 'dismissal' or whether the employer has been merely angry or abusive towards the employee, e.g. where the employer tells the employee in no uncertain terms, to go away. It would seem that the test is: 'How would a reasonable employee in all the circumstances have understood what the employer intended by what he said and did?': *Tanner* v. *Kean Ltd* (1978) and *Chesham Shipping Ltd* v. *Rowe* (1977).

6. Circumstances which justify summary dismissal

The question of what justifies summary dismissal is not one that can be answered with a simple rule since each case must be decided according to the particular circumstances. However, a general principle has emerged that summary dismissal is justified if the conduct of the employee is such that it prevents 'further satisfactory continuance of the relationship': *Sinclair* v. *Neighbour* (1967). The attitude of the courts towards the issue of conduct justifying summary dismissal has tended to alter with changing social attitudes: compare *Turner* v. *Mason* (1845) with *Laws* v. *London Chronicle Ltd* (1959) below.

The status of the employee in question is a relevant consideration as is the fact that the employee has a history of misconduct as opposed to an isolated incident.

In *Turner* v. *Mason* (1845) a domestic servant sought permission from her employer to visit her mother whom she said was dying. The employer refused permission but the servant disobeyed the prohibition and was summarily dismissed. Held: the dismissal was not wrongful.

In *Laws* v. *London Chronicle Ltd* (1959) the plaintiff had been employed for only three weeks as secretary to an advertising manager. The manager 'walked out of' an editorial conference following an argument and the plaintiff followed him despite an order from the managing director for her to remain. The plaintiff was summarily dismissed. Held: the dismissal was wrongful.

In *Jupiter General Insurance Co. Ltd* v. *Shroff* (1937) an insurance company had refused a proposal for insurance but shortly afterwards an employee of the company, who knew of the previous refusal, granted a policy on the same proposal. He was summarily dismissed. Held: the dismissal was not wrongful.

> 'It must be remembered that the test to be applied must vary with the nature of the business and the position held by the employee . . . and . . . it can be in exceptional circumstances only that an employer is acting properly in dismissing an employee on his committing a single act of negligence' (Lord Maugham).

In *Sinclair* v. *Neighbour* (1967) the manager of a betting shop borrowed money from the till, without attempting to hide the fact and with every intention of returning it, although he was aware that this practice was forbidden. He was summarily dismissed. Held: the dismissal was justified.

In *Pepper* v. *Webb* (1969) a gardener who had been 'acting in a very unsatisfactory way' for some time, refused an order which was within the scope of his contract of employment and was abusive in this refusal. He was summarily dismissed. Held: the dismissal was justified and the fact that there was a history of misconduct was a relevant consideration.

In *Denco Ltd* v. *Joinson* (1991) an employee who gained unauthorised access to a part of the employer's computer database was summarily dismissed. The EAT observed, in remitting the case to an industrial tribunal for a rehearing on the issue of unfair dismissal, that the unauthorised use of, or tampering with, computers is an extremely serious industrial offence and that if an employee uses an unauthorised password to enter a computer containing information to which he is not entitled, that of itself is gross misconduct which prima facie will attract summary dismissal. The EAT drew a strong analogy between the conduct in this case and dishonesty.

At common law there was no need for an employer to state the reason for summary dismissal provided that one existed which was sufficient to justify his action: *see Boston Deep-Sea Fishing and Ice Co.* v. *Ansell* (1888). However, under s. 92 of the 1996 Act, an employee with two years continuous service is entitled to be provided by his employer, on request, with a written statement of the reasons for dismissal (*see* 12:**11**).

7. Dismissals procedures

The following two principles apply to dismissals procedures which form part of the contract of employment of an employee who is dismissed with or without notice.

(a) If the contract states that dismissal is to be according to an established pattern (e.g. that there will be two warnings before dismissal occurs), it is a breach of contract if the procedure is not observed: *Tomlinson* v. *LMS Railway* (1944)

It should be noted that, even if there has been a failure to follow a contractual procedure, that does not entitle an industrial tribunal to reach a finding that the dismissal was unfair and award compensation based on the statutory principles, if the employee is not otherwise entitled to claim a remedy for unfair dismissal. In *Focsa Services (UK) Ltd* v. *Birkett* (1996) an employee was dismissed after four months service with the employer. The employer did not follow the contractually agreed disciplinary procedure. The industrial tribunal implied a term in the contract of employment to the effect that the employee had a right not to be unfairly dismissed under his contract, and awarded compensation to the same extent as would have been awarded for a statutory unfair dismissal. The EAT allowed the employer's appeal; it was not open, where none of the recognised tests for implying such a term were made out, for the tribunal to imply a term into the contract in the way that it had. Accordingly, the tribunal had erred in disregarding the ordinary common law rule that loss in wrongful dismissal cases is limited to those sums which would have been payable to the employee if the contract had been terminated lawfully.

(b) If the contract states that the dismissal may only occur for certain specified reasons, a dismissal is wrongful (and probably unfair also) if the reason for the dismissal is other than specified in the contract.

8. Waiver of rights

If an employer wishes to allege that an employee's conduct justified a summary dismissal, the right must have been exercised within a reasonable time of the conduct which allegedly justified the action since delay may amount to a waiver of the breach of contract.

EMPLOYEE LEAVING

9. With notice

An employee is entitled to terminate employment at any time by giving the amount of notice required by the contract. In determining the amount of notice to be given, the criteria are the same as in 2 above except that the statutory minimum for employee to employer is simply that where the employee has been continuously employed for at least one month, he must give at least one week's notice: s. 86(2). If the employee is deemed to have been entitled to terminate employment by reason of the employer's conduct, that may constitute a 'constructive dismissal' and the fact that he gave notice makes no difference (*see* 13:7).

10. Without notice

An employee is entitled to terminate his employment without notice if the conduct of the employer justifies it. Such a circumstance may well constitute a 'constructive dismissal' and the employee may act accordingly (*see* 13:7).

TERMINATION BY AGREEMENT

11. General principle

The parties to a contract of employment, as with any other contract, may terminate their relationship by agreement at any time upon such terms as they may agree, e.g. payment of money as a 'golden handshake'. It should be noted that a termination by agreement is not a 'dismissal' for the purposes of the redundancy and unfair dismissals provisions of the 1996 Act: *see Birch and Humber* v. *University of Liverpool* (1985). *See also* Chapters 13 and 14. However, the tribunals are concerned to ensure that any alleged agreement to terminate a contract of employment is real and not merely the result of pressure imposed on an employee who is unaware of the significance of agreeing to terminate the contract and who faces dismissal as an alternative to so agreeing: *see Lees* v. *Arthur Greaves (Lees) Ltd* (1973).

It should be noted that s. 203 of the 1996 Act places restrictions on the rights of parties to contract out of the provisions of the Act. This provision is plainly designed to protect employees, and the tribunals will endeavour to give effect to this policy: *see Tracey* v. *Zest Equipment* (1982). Nevertheless, in the situation where there is an agreement to end a contract of employment, made without undue pressure and following proper advice, the tribunals will not activate s. 203: *see Logan Salton* v. *Durham County Council* (1989).

12. Agreement as to length of contract

Where the parties to a contract of employment decide at the outset what the length of the contract shall be, then the contract will end automatically at the end of that period. The nature of such an agreement is not affected by the fact that the contract contains provisions which allow for earlier termination in certain circumstances: *see Wiltshire County Council* v. *NATFHE* (1980).

13. Variation of the contract

Any variation of the contract of employment must be mutually agreed since a unilateral variation of the contract is a breach of its terms, unless the other party to the contract has agreed to the variation. Unilateral variations may be agreed through the vehicle of a collective agreement. Thus in *Airlie* v. *City of Edinburgh District Council* (1996), where the employer had introduced a new bonus scheme which had the effect of reducing the earnings of the employees, it was held by the EAT that an individual contract of employment can be varied without consent where the contract itself provides for unilateral variation. In this case the employers had relied on a collective agreement which was incorporated into the individual contracts of employment and which allowed the employer to vary the bonus scheme in such a way as to meet managerial needs.

Where an employer has made a unilateral change to the contract, and the employee has continued to work under the contract, this does not necessarily mean that the employee can be regarded as having accepted the variation. In *Aparu* v. *Iceland Frozen Foods plc* (1996), the EAT said that even where an employee has worked for more than 12 months without objecting to the new terms, that did not mean that the employee could be regarded as having accepted them. In cases where a unilateral alteration by the employer does not have an immediate effect on the employee, a tribunal must proceed very cautiously before reaching a conclusion that the employee has consented to the variation.

TERMINATION BY FRUSTRATION

14. Meaning of the term

'Frustration occurs whenever the law recognises that without default of either party a contractual obligation has become incapable of being performed because the circumstance in which performance is called for would render it a thing different from that which was undertaken by the contract': Lord Radcliffe in *Davis Contractors* v. *Fareham UDC* (1956).

In the context of a contract of employment, the term 'frustration' means that circumstances have arisen, without the fault of either party, that make it impossible for the contract to be performed in the way that may be reasonably expected and the contract thereby automatically terminates without the need for notice to be given. Frustration of the contract is not deemed to be a 'dismissal' for legislative purposes.

15. Circumstances which may frustrate

The question of whether a contract of employment is frustrated depends on the circumstances of each case but the following may be frustrating circumstances.

(a) *Sickness*. It is suggested that the question of whether a contract of employment is frustrated by the employee's sickness may be determined by reference to Phillips J's judgment in *Egg Stores (Stamford Hill) Ltd* v. *Leibovici* (1977):

'There will have been frustration of the contract, even though at the time of the event the outcome was uncertain, if the time arrives when looking back one can say that at some point (even if it is not possible to say precisely when) matters had gone on so long, and the prospects for the future were so poor, that it was no longer practical to regard the contract as still subsisting. Among the matters to be taken into account in such a case in reaching a decision are these:

(1) the length of the previous employment
(2) how long it had been expected that the employment would continue
(3) the nature of the job
(4) the nature, length and effect of the illness or disabling event
(5) the need of the employer for the work to be done, and the need for a replacement to do it
(6) the risk to the employer of acquiring obligations in respect of redundancy payments or compensation for unfair dismissal to the replacement employee
(7) whether wages have continued to be paid
(8) the acts and statements of the employer in relation to the employment including the dismissal of, or failure to dismiss, the employee
(9) whether in all the circumstances a reasonable employer could be expected to wait any longer'.

In *Williams* v. *Watsons Coaches Ltd* (1990) the EAT added a further two factors:

(10) the terms of the contract as to the provisions for sick pay
(11) a consideration of the prospects of recovery.

The courts, as a general rule, have been reluctant to hold that a contract has been frustrated because of sickness (and indeed generally), because a wide acceptance of the doctrine would undermine the aims of the employment protection legislation: *see Harman* v. *Flexible Lamps Ltd* (1980). Nevertheless, where the circumstances of the case point unequivocally to frustration, the courts will not flinch from finding that the contract has been frustrated.

In *Notcutt* v. *Universal Equipment Co.* (1986), a worker, with 27 years service, who was two years from retirement suffered a permanently incapacitating heart attack. The court decided that this rendered performance of the contract impossible and therefore the contract was frustrated as he was unable to perform his obligation to work. The employee was therefore not entitled to sick pay during his statutory period of notice.

(b) *Imprisonment.* The question as to whether imprisonment frustrates a contract of employment has also caused problems. The same guidelines as for sickness have been used in the cases: *see Hare* v. *Murphy Brothers Ltd* (1974). Again the courts and tribunals have been reluctant to apply the doctrine in cases relating to imprisonment because of the loss of employment rights: *Norris* v. *Southampton City Council* (1982).

However, the Court of Appeal has allowed a four-year apprenticeship contract to be frustrated by a six-month borstal sentence: *FC Shepherd & Co. Ltd* v. *Jerrom* (1986). In this case the court held that such a period of imprisonment made the performance of the contract impossible.

12

TERMINATIONOF EMPLOYMENT (2): CONSEQUENCES

The consequences of a termination of employment inevitably vary with the circumstances but the two most significant are undoubtedly a complaint of unfair dismissal (*see* Chapter 13) and a claim for a redundancy payment (*see* Chapter 14). There are, however, a number of other possible actions which are examined in this chapter.

ACTION FOR WRONGFUL DISMISSAL

1. General principle

An employee who has been wrongfully dismissed (i.e. unjustifiably with no notice or with insufficient notice) may bring an action for damages against his former employer representing the amount of wages owed to him in respect of work already done and in respect of wages that the employee would have earned had he been given the amount of notice to which he was entitled (*see* 11:2). The amount of wages that may be recovered is assessed in accordance with the ordinary principles of the law of contract, i.e. the loss which arises from the breach of contract in the 'ordinary course of things' and any loss of which the employer ought to have been aware. Hence, the wages lost includes money which was normally earned and any additional benefits, such as 'tips', which are lost as a result of the breach.

In *Manubens* v. *Leon* (1919) a hairdresser was wrongfully dismissed and claimed damages. Held: he was entitled to damages representing lost wages and also a sum representing 'tips' since the employer must be taken to be aware that such a loss would be sustained.

Damages for wrongful dismissal cannot normally include compensation for injured feelings or pride or the fact that future earnings are affected: *Addis* v. *Gramophone Co.* (1909), but see *Cox* v. *Phillips Industries Ltd* (1976) and *Bliss* v. *SE Thames RHA* (1985). Similarly, an employee who has been wrongfully dismissed cannot seek compensation for the loss of some right which has lapsed on the termination of employment. In *Micklefield* v. *SAC Technology Ltd* (1990) the High Court held that where one of the consequences of a wrongful dismissal is that the employee loses an option to purchase shares, in circumstances where the contract with the employee provided that in the event of termination of the contract for any reason the option lapsed, then the employee is not entitled to recover damages for the loss he has suffered as a consequence of the lapse of the option. In certain circumstances damages for wrongful dismissal may include compensation for loss of opportunity to enhance reputation (*see* 6:3).

It should be noted that where an employee is dismissed without receiving the period of notice to which he is contractually entitled, this may have the effect of preventing his acquiring the necessary qualifying period to bring an unfair dismissal claim. In such a case, the loss of his statutory right may be a quantifiable head of loss for the purpose of damages for wrongful dismissal: *Stapp* v. *Shaftesbury Society* (1982).

You should also note that an industrial tribunal is not entitled, in a wrongful dismissal case, simply to treat the dismissal as one which is unfair and award compensation based on statutory principles: *see Focsa Services (UK) Ltd* v. *Birkett* (1996) (supra 11:7).

2. Deductions from damages

The object of damages is to compensate the innocent party for what he actually lost, not to punish the party in breach of contract, and therefore the courts have developed principles to ensure that the employee who has been wrongfully dismissed receives compensation only for his actual loss. Consequently, a number of deductions are made from the sum which represents the loss of wages during the period of notice that ought to have been given.

(a) *Other earnings.* Earnings from other employment which the employee obtains during the time representing the notice period that he ought to have received must be deducted, or a sum representing the amount that the court considers he would have earned had he made reasonable efforts to find employment. This is part of the duty of the innocent party to mitigate his loss. However, the employee is only obliged to take reasonable steps and is therefore entitled to expect to find similar employment: *Yetton* v. *Eastwoods Froy* (1967).

It has been argued that such a deduction ought not to be made, since, if the employer had paid wages in lieu of notice, the employee would be under no obligation to return any part of the wages already paid by the former employer. This argument seems to have considerable merit: *Norton Tool Co. Ltd* v. *Tewson* (1972).

(b) *Tax.* Awards of damages for wrongful dismissal are not taxed to the extent of the first £30,000 of the payment. Accordingly, where damages are awarded they must be reduced by the amount of tax that *would* have been payable on the damages if they had been paid as wages: *see British Transport Commission* v. *Gourley* (1956). By virtue of ss. 148 and 188 of the Income and Corporation Taxes Act 1988, damages for wrongful dismissal *are* chargeable to tax to the extent that they exceed £30,000. A good example of the application of the above principles was provided in *Shove* v. *Downs Surgical plc* (1984).

(c) *National Insurance contributions.* While an employee is unemployed, his National Insurance contributions are normally credited by the State on his behalf. Since these contributions would have been paid by the employer, a sum representing those contributions during the notice period is deducted: *Cooper* v. *Firth Brown Ltd* (1963).

(d) *Unemployment benefit.* Any sum received under the state unemployment benefit scheme is normally deducted in accordance with the general rule of compensation rather than punishment. It has been argued that this ought not to be deducted since it is simply in the nature of an insurance scheme to which the employee has contributed: *Parry* v. *Cleaver* (1970).

Money received under private insurance schemes or by way of income support is not deducted.

(e) It should also be noted that the total damages award may be reduced in order to take account of the fact that it may represent an accelerated payment to the plaintiff: *see Shove* v. *Downs Surgical plc* (*supra*).

DAMAGES AGAINST EMPLOYEE

3. General principle

Where an employee fails to give sufficient notice to his employer, the employer may sue the employee for damages representing the loss which follows from the breach of contract.

4. Quantification of loss

In practice, such actions are infrequent because the loss is often minimal; but it may be possible to quantify the loss, e.g. the difference (if any) in rates of payment between the employee in breach and the replacement and the cost of advertising, or, in the case of an employee involved in a manufacturing process, the loss of production (if any) resulting from the failure to give correct notice.

SPECIFIC PERFORMANCE

5. Meaning of the term

Specific performance is an order from the court directing that the parties to a contract perform their contractual obligations.

6. Non-availability

It is a fundamental principle of labour law that specific performance is never granted to compel performance of a contract of employment and this principle is embodied in s. 236 of the Trade Union and Labour Relations (Consolidation) Act 1992. However, it should be noted that industrial tribunals have the power to order the reinstatement or re-engagement of an employee who has been unfairly dismissed (*see* 13:**28**) and may reinforce such an order by awarding additional compensation if it is not complied with.

INJUNCTION

7. Meaning

An injunction is an order from a court forbidding certain conduct, e.g. the breaking of a term of the contract of employment. Hence it may be used to prevent a breach of a covenant restraining an employee from taking employment with a rival of his former employer (*see* 5:**21**).

8. Effect

In certain circumstances, the granting of an injunction may be tantamount to ordering specific performance of the contract. In general, the courts have been aware of this and have refused to grant an injunction if the effect would be to compel performance: cf. *Warner Bros. Pictures Inc.* v. *Nelson* (1937) and *Page One Records* v. *Britton* (1967). By virtue of s. 236 of the 1992 Act, no court may issue an injunction if the effect of such an order would be to compel an employee to do any work or to attend at any place for work.

However, where the injunction compelling performance is to the benefit of the employee, the court may be prepared to grant such an order.

In *Hill* v. *C.A. Parsons and Co. Ltd* (1972) the defendant employers wished to enter into an agreement with an organisation of workers whereby it was agreed that all employees in certain sections, including the plaintiff, would be obliged to join that organisation. This arrangement was legal at the time but under the Industrial Relations Act 1971 (which was not then in force although it had been passed) it would have been invalid. The plaintiff did not wish to join the organisation and he was dismissed with four weeks' notice. He claimed that this was wrongful dismissal. Held by the Court of Appeal: the plaintiff had been wrongfully dismissed since he was entitled to at least six months' notice, and furthermore an injunction was awarded which prevented the employee from being dismissed until that time elapsed by which time he would have a remedy under the 1971 Act.

The decision in *Hill* (*above*) is arguably a case limited to its own particular facts as it was the trade union applying the pressure and therefore trust and confidence remained between the employer and employee. It should also be noted from the case that damages were seen as an inadequate remedy and therefore the injunction was granted.

Recent decisions, which although not many in number are significant enough to mention, have increasingly allowed the employee to elect which remedy to take, i.e. damages or injunction. In *Powell* v. *London Borough of Brent* (1987) the Court of Appeal granted an interlocutory injunction requiring employers who had selected an employee at an interview to retain her for that job, despite their wish to re-advertise the post. The crucial factor in the decision was that the court found that the employers had sufficient confidence in her ability and therefore trust and confidence remained. Similar reasoning was adopted in *Hughes* v. *London Borough of Southwark* (1988). The case did not concern dismissal but an injunction was granted restraining an employer from requiring its employees to perform services beyond the scope of their contractual duties. The point to note is that the injunction was granted because mutual trust and confidence existed between the employer and employee; indeed the very reason why the extra work was demanded by the employer was because of the competence of the employees.

The essence of the cases where injunctions have been granted has been the existence of sufficient mutual trust and confidence between the parties so as to enable the employment to continue. *Robb* v. *London Borough of Hammersmith and Fulham* (1991) shows that where the purpose of the injunction which has been sought is simply to preserve the existence of the employment relationship between the parties, for example so that the contractually agreed disciplinary procedure can run its course, then injunctive relief may be granted. In such circumstances as this, where the employee is not continuing with the duties of his employment – e.g. he is being treated as suspended – the fact that the mutual trust and confidence of the parties has broken down is irrelevant.

DECLARATION

9. General principle

A declaration is an order from a court which simply determines the rights of the parties in the case. It has no binding force in itself and is not available to all employees, being restricted to those persons whose employment is derived from statute: *Vine* v. *National Dock Labour Board* (1957).

In *McClelland* v. *NIGHSB* (1957) it was held by the House of Lords that a declaration could be granted to determine the rights of an employee of the Board (the defendants) who had been dismissed in contravention of the terms of her appointment: *see also Gunton* v. *Richmond-upon-Thames London Borough Council* (1980).

10. Order of industrial tribunal

In exercising the various jurisdictions which they have, the industrial tribunals have the power to declare the rights of the parties (*see* 1:**4**).

WRITTEN STATEMENT OF REASONS FOR DISMISSAL

11. Claim by employee

Under s. 92 of the ERA 1996 an employee who has been continuously employed for at least two years and who has been dismissed is entitled to receive, upon request, a written statement of the reasons for his dismissal. This statement, which must be provided within fourteen days of the request being made, is admissible in any proceedings, e.g. before an industrial tribunal hearing a complaint of unfair dismissal.

12. Remedy for infringement

A claim may be presented to an industrial tribunal by an employee that his employer has 'unreasonably failed' to provide a written statement of the reasons for dismissal or that it is 'inadequate or untrue': s. 93(1). *See Lang and Sons Ltd* v. *Aubrey* (1977); *Horsley Smith and Sherry Ltd* v. *Dutton* (1977), and *Daynecourt Insurance Brokers Ltd* v. *Iles* (1978). The right to a written statement only arises where the employee has been dismissed or been given notice of dismissal by his employer; occasionally the situation arises where the employee maintains that he has been dismissed but the employer maintains that he has resigned. In *Broomsgrove* v. *Eagle Alexander Ltd* (1981) the EAT held that the test to be applied in this situation is an objective one: 'Where the employer reasonably believes that there was no dismissal, it may well be difficult to say that he unreasonably refused to give the reasons for a dismissal which he genuinely believed never occurred'. It should be noted that where an employee is given written reasons for dismissal without having requested them, the employee cannot subsequently use s. 92 as a vehicle to complain that the reasons were untrue. Following *Catherine Haigh Harlequin Hair Design* v. *Seed* (1990), it is clear that a request for reasons is necessary before the provisions of s. 92 come into effect.

If the tribunal finds the complaint well-founded, it may make a declaration as to what the reasons for the dismissal were and make an award of two weeks' pay to the complainant.

SUSPENSION

13. On full pay

In accordance with the general principle that an employer fulfils his contractual obligation by paying wages in accordance with the contract of employment, he may suspend an employee on full pay without being in breach of contract (*see* 6:2).

14. Without pay

An employer may only suspend an employee without pay if the contract expressly or impliedly provides for this: *Marshall* v. *English Electric Co. Ltd* (1945). If the contract does not so provide, it is a breach of contract for an employer to suspend an employee without notice: *Hanley* v. *Pease* (1915). Therefore, an employee who is suspended without contractual authority may treat himself as dismissed and claim accordingly.

13

UNFAIR DISMISSAL

INTRODUCTION

References in this chapter are to the Employment Rights Act 1996.

1. Significance

The significance of the concept of unfair dismissal is that it represents a most important element of the property right which an employee has in his job. It is no longer possible, as was the case under the common law, for an employer to end a contract by simply giving notice and thereby totally discharging his responsibilities.

2. Basic principle

Section 94 of the 1996 Act provides that, subject to certain specified exceptions, every employee has the right not to be unfairly dismissed. It should be noted that a complaint of unfair dismissal does not depend upon the employer having acted in breach of contract but simply that the employer has terminated the contract in circumstances which are unfair.

3. Qualifying period of employment

By virtue of changes made under the Unfair Dismissal (Variation of Qualifying Period) Order 1985 employees who, at the effective date of termination of the contract, have been continuously employed for less than two years do not, in general terms, enjoy protection against unfair dismissal. However, this issue has been the subject of recent litigation which is as yet not concluded. In *R. v. Secretary of State for Employment ex p Seymour-Smith* (1997) the applicant complained that she had been unfairly dismissed, but because she did not have two years service at the date of dismissal she was unable to register her application to an industrial tribunal to obtain compensation for unfair dismissal. She applied for judicial review of the 1985 Order as the instrument which established the qualifying period as two years. She argued that it was contrary to the Equal Treatment Directive (76/207/EEC) on the basis that the proportion of women who can comply with that period is smaller than the proportion of men who can comply; accordingly, she argued that the two-year qualification period indirectly discriminated against women. In the Court of Appeal the court examined statistical data relating to the employment of men and women over the period 1985–91 and reached the conclusion that in that period there were considerable and persistent differences between the numbers and percentages of men and women in the groups which did comply and in the groups which did not comply with the two-year qualification period. On this basis the Court of Appeal found that the qualification period was indirectly discriminatory. The Secretary of State sought to argue that this was justifiable in the context of seeking to maximise employment opportunities. However, the court was unconvinced by both the factual and the opinion evidence on this matter and found that the Secretary of State had not established an objective justification for the discriminatory impact of the two-year qualification period. The Court of Appeal granted a declaration to the applicant to the effect that the qualification period was indirectly discriminatory.

The Secretary of State appealed to the House of Lords. In following the decision in *Marshall* v. *Southampton and South-West Area Health Authority* (1986) it found it clear that a Directive, in this case the Equal Treatment Directive, has no effect upon the private rights of employees and employers where the employer is not the State or an emanation of the State. The real difficulty that the House of Lords had with the decision of the Court of Appeal was not the finding that the United Kingdom legislation *is* incompatible with European law, but that it *was* incompatible in 1991 – the end of the period in respect of which statistical evidence had been adduced. Other evidence showed that by 1993 the gap between the ratios of men and women who qualified had narrowed. Accordingly, the declaration made by the Court of Appeal neither enabled the employee to sue for unfair dismissal nor told the Government that United Kingdom legislation needed to be changed because it was incompatible with European law.

The House of Lords discharged the declaration made by the Court of Appeal and adjourned further consideration of the matter until after consideration by the European Court of Justice of a number of questions referred to it by the House of Lords. *Inter alia*, these questions include the following:

'What is the legal test for establishing whether a measure adopted by a Member State has such a degree of disparate effect as between men and women as to amount to indirect discrimination for the purposes of Article 119 of the EC Treaty unless shown to be based on objectively justified factors other than sex?'

'When must this legal test be applied to a measure adopted by a Member State? In particular, at which of the following points in time, or at what point in time, must it be applied to the measure:

(a) when the measure is adopted
(b) when the measure is brought into force
(c) when the employee is dismissed?

'What are the legal conditions for establishing the objective justification, for the purposes of indirect discrimination, under Article 119, of a measure adopted by a

Member State in pursuance of its social policy? In particular, what material need the Member State adduce in support of its grounds for justification?'

It should be noted that in *Nolte* v. *Landesversicherungsanstalt Hannover* (1996) the ECJ held that social policy is a matter for Member States. Accordingly, Member States have a broad margin of discretion in exercising their competence to choose the measures capable of achieving the aims of their social and employment policy. Thus, a legislative measure which is chosen to reflect a legitimate social policy is likely to be one based on objective factors unrelated to discrimination on grounds of sex – this may be sufficient to provide a defence of justification to a claim of indirect discrimination; *see also Megner and Scheffel* v. *Innungskrankenkasse Vorderpfalz* (1996). This will be the kind of argument which is likely to be used by the Secretary of State in order to justify the increase of the qualification period from one to two years.

The House of Lords judgment was published in the early part of 1997, but it is likely to be a further two years before the ECJ rules on the questions which have been referred to it. The future implications of the litigation in this case remain unclear, but the quandary facing any draftsman of legislative provisions in employment law where time periods are considered necessary for employment protection purposes is an acute one. It remains arguable that where the *same* qualification period is applied to men and women, it may be *indirectly* discriminatory in effect; if a draftsman includes *different* qualification periods, the effect will be *directly* discriminatory.

One fear which many employers may have is that the effect of the ECJ decision, when it is known, may be to release a flood of backdated claims for unfair dismissal from women who have been dismissed before the expiry of the two-year qualification period. However, in *Biggs* v. *Somerset County Council* (1996) the Court of Appeal ruled, in a parallel context (relating to the old qualifying thresholds for part-time employees under the Employment Protection (Consolidation) Act 1978), that where there is a three-month time limit to make an application to an Industrial Tribunal and the applicant has not pursued the application because of a mistake of law, it would be contrary to the principle of legal certainty to allow past transactions to be reopened and for limitation periods to be circumvented, because the law had been misunderstood.

> *Note*: Employees are not excluded from the right to present a complaint of unfair dismissal where the reason for the dismissal is one which is regarded in the legislation as automatically unfair. These reasons include dismissal for trade union membership or activities, dismissal for assertion of a statutory right, dismissal on grounds of sex or race, and dismissal for a reason connected with the transfer of an undertaking except where there are organisational, technical or economic reasons to justify the dismissal. In all of these cases there is no minimum qualifying period of employment.

4. Excluded categories of employees

Certain categories of employees are excluded from the right to present a complaint of unfair dismissal:

(a) Persons over retiring age.

(b) Persons employed in the police service.

(c) Share fishermen.

(d) Employees who ordinarily work outside Great Britain.

(e) Employees employed on certain fixed-term contracts.

(f) Persons covered by a designated dismissals procedure agreement.

(g) Under earlier unfair dismissal legislation, persons who were employed on a part-time basis (which for these purposes was less than 16 hours per week, except in the case of an employee who has worked for more than 8 hours per week for more than 5 years) were excluded from the right to claim a remedy for unfair dismissal. However, in a decision of considerable importance in *R. v. Secretary of State for Employment ex p Equal Opportunities Commission* (1994) the House of Lords ruled that such a qualifying threshold, in the context of redundancy pay, was incompatible with Article 119 of the Treaty of Rome, the 'Equal Pay' Directive (No. 75/117/EEC) and the 'Equal Treatment' Directive (No. 76/207/EEC).

Accordingly, these threshold requirements were removed by the Employment Protection (Part-Time Employees) Regulations 1995 and it is now the case that *all* employees have the right to a redundancy payment and bring a claim for unfair dismissal after two years of service, irrespective of their hours of work.

DISMISSAL

5. Burden of proof

If an action for unfair dismissal is to succeed, the employee must first establish that he was 'dismissed' within the meaning of s. 95. In most cases the fact of dismissal is conceded but in cases of alleged 'constructive dismissal' (*see* 7 below), the employee must establish it.

6. Definition

Section 95(1) provides that:

'... an employee is dismissed by his employer if ...

(a) the contract under which he is employed is terminated by the employer (whether with or without notice)

(b) he is employed under a contract for a fixed term and that term expires without being renewed under the same contract, or

(c) the employee terminates the contract under which he is employed (with or without notice) in circumstances in which he is entitled to terminate it without notice by reason of the employer's conduct.'

As regards (a) *see* 11:**1** and **6**; as regards (b) *see* 3:**16**.

7. Constructive dismissal

Section 95(1)(c) refers to the concept of so-called 'constructive dismissal'. If an employee leaves employment entirely voluntarily, there is no 'dismissal' but if the employee is deemed to be 'entitled to terminate it without notice by reason of the employer's conduct', it is a 'dismissal' irrespective of whether the employee gave notice or not.

The courts and tribunals have been concerned to define the circumstances in which an employee is entitled to regard himself as constructively dismissed. Before *Western Excavating (ECC) Ltd* v. *Sharp* (1978), the tribunals found that sufficiently 'unreasonable' behaviour on the part of an employer entitled an employee to leave his job and claim constructive dismissal. However, in *Western Excavating*, the Court of Appeal rejected the 'unreasonableness' test and established that the correct test is one based on strict contractual principles. Accordingly an employee is only able successfully to argue constructive dismissal where the employer has breached the contract in such a way as to justify the employee in treating himself as discharged from further performance. The action of an employer may involve breach of an express or implied term.

(a) *Express term.* In *Hill Ltd* v. *Mooney* (1981) the EAT held: 'The obligation of an employer to pay remuneration is one of the fundamental terms of a contract. In our view, if an employer seeks to alter that contractual obligation in a fundamental way . . . such attempt is a breach going to the very root of the contract and is necessarily a repudiation.' *See also Industrial Rubber Products* v. *Gillon* (1977); *Gillies* v. *Richard Daniels & Co. Ltd* (1979).

In *Coleman* v. *S. & W. Baldwin* (1977) it was held that by taking away an important part of an employee's responsibilities and leaving him with residual duties of a humdrum nature, the employer had repudiated the contract of employment. *See also Woods* v. *W.M. Car Services (Peterborough) Ltd* (1982); *Wadham Stringer Commercials (London) Ltd* v. *Brown* (1983).

In *Derby City Council* v. *Marshall* (1979) it was held that by instructing an employee (who worked as a warden of an old people's home) that she was to be on call during the whole of a five-day duty period, the employer had expressed an intention not to be bound by the contract so that the employee was entitled to treat it as at an end. But note, where the employer has the contractual right to alter working hours, changing the hours without the consent of the employee is not a breach of contract: *Dal* v. *Orr* (1980).

(b) *Implied term.* Following *Western Excavating (ECC) Ltd* v. *Sharp* (1978) some uneasiness was felt in the tribunals and EAT about the relative narrowness of the strict contract test compared with the earlier, and wider, 'unreasonableness' test. The crux of the problem is that, before 1978, a series of minor intrusions by the employer upon the contractual relationship might well have amounted to unreasonable behaviour on his part, justifying the employee in resigning, even though no single incident amounted to a repudiation of the contract. Following *Western Excavating* the problem has been that a strict application of the contract test would allow the employer more latitude than hitherto. Since 1978 the matter has been resolved; tribunals and courts have been prepared to imply and interpret the terms of the contract in such a way as to bring the present position close to the position before *Western Excavating*. In particular, the development of doctrine surrounding the implied duty of trust and confidence owed by employers has been important: *see* 6:7. Thus in *Woods* v. *W.M. Car Services* (1981), the EAT said:

> 'Experience in this Appeal Tribunal has shown that one of the consequences of the decision in the *Western Excavating* case has been that employers who wish to get rid of an employee or alter the terms of his employment without becoming liable either to pay compensation for unfair dismissal or a redundancy payment have had to resort to methods of 'squeezing out' an employee. Stopping short of any major breach of the contract, such an employer attempts to make the employee's life so uncomfortable that he resigns or accepts the revised terms. Such an employer, having behaved in a totally unreasonable manner, then claims that he has not repudiated the contract and therefore that the employee has no statutory right to claim either a redundancy payment or compensation for unfair dismissal. It is for this reason that we regard the implied term we have referred to as being of such importance. In our view, an employer who persistently attempts to vary an employee's conditions of service (whether contractual or not) with a view to getting rid of an employee or varying the employee's terms of service, does act in a manner calculated or likely to destroy the relationship of confidence and trust between employer and employee. Such an employer has therefore breached an implied term.'

It is not possible to determine with absolute precision just when the tribunals will, and when they will not, be prepared to imply particular terms into a contract of employment. There are many illustrations, however, of when such terms have been implied in particular contracts of employment. Thus, when an employee resigned because of the failure of the employer to treat her complaint of persistent sexual harassment seriously, this was held to be a constructive dismissal justified by breach of an implied term: *see Bracebridge Engineering Ltd.* v. *Darby* (1990). Similarly in *Hilton International Hotels (UK) Ltd.* v. *Protopapa* (1990) it was held that an unmerited reprimand which had been given in a humiliating and degrading manner amounted to a repudiatory breach of an implied term. On the other hand, in *Dryden* v. *Greater Glasgow Health Board* (1992) it was held that the introduction of a no-smoking policy is not likely to constitute a repudiation of the contract, because the right of an individual to smoke at work is unlikely to be secured in the contract of employment.

> *Note*: If the employer commits a repudiatory breach of the contract of employment, the employee can if he chooses continue to work, or he can accept the repudiation, in which case the contract is at an end and he has been constructively dismissed. The employee does not have to elect to affirm the contract or accept the repudiation within any reasonable or other time, and mere delay does not constitute affirmation of the contract. However, prolonged delay on the part of the employee may constitute implied affirmation: *W.E. Cox Toner* v. *Crook* (1981).

In *Goold (Pearmak) Ltd* v. *McConnell* (1995) the Employment Appeal Tribunal upheld the finding of an industrial tribunal that the failure of an employer to provide and implement a grievance procedure amounted to the breach of an implied term in a contract of employment to the effect that an employer should promptly afford a reasonable opportunity to its employees to obtain redress of any grievance they may have.

The implication of terms into a contract of employment is not necessarily always in favour of the employee as the decision of the Court of Appeal in *Courtaulds Northern Spinning Ltd* v. *Gibson* (1988) shows. Here an employee, a heavy goods vehicle driver, claimed constructive dismissal when he was moved from one depot to a depot one mile away. The contract of employment made no express reference as to mobility. A term was implied to the effect that the employee could be transferred anywhere within reasonable commuting distance of his home. The transfer, in this case, did not breach the contract and the complaint of unfair dismissal therefore failed.

8. Early termination by employee

Section 95(2) provides that where an employee has been given notice by his employer, he may give counter-notice to terminate the contract before it was due to expire and he is nevertheless to be regarded as 'dismissed' for the reason for which the employer gave notice originally.

9. Repudiation by the employee

From time to time it has been suggested that an employee who, by his conduct, repudiated the contract, thereby terminated his contract so that in law there was no dismissal. However, the better view today is that termination of the contract does not occur until the repudiation of the contract is accepted by the employer. Accordingly in law a dismissal takes place: *London Transport Executive* v. *Clarke* (1981).

WHEN IS DISMISSAL UNFAIR?

10. General considerations

Establishing the fact of dismissal is only one part of a complete unfair dismissal action. Once a dismissal has been proved (and in most cases this will, of course, be admitted) it will be up to the employer to show what the reason for the dismissal was, and that it was one of the categories of reason regarded as acceptable in the statute, and for the tribunal to be satisfied as to the reasonableness of the employer's action in dismissing for that reason. Those matters are considered in detail below, but the relevant statutory provision is as follows:

– 's. 98(1) In determining . . . whether the dismissal of an employee was fair or unfair, it is for the employer to show:
(a) the reason (or, if more than one, the principal reason) for the dismissal, and
(b) that it is either a reason falling within subsection (2) or some other

substantial reason of a kind such as to justify the dismissal of an employee holding the position which that employee held.

(2) A reason falls within this subsection if it

(a) relates to the capability or qualifications of the employee for performing work of the kind which he was employed by the employer to do

(b) related to the conduct of the employee

(c) is that the employee is redundant, or

(d) is that the employee could not continue to work in the position which he held without contravention (either on his part or on that of his employer) of a duty or restriction imposed by or under an enactment.'

Section 98(4) goes on to provide:

'Where the employer has fulfilled the requirements of subsection (1), the determination of the question whether the dismissal is fair or unfair (having regard to the reason shown by the employer)-

(a) depends on whether in the circumstances (including the size and administrative resources of the employer's undertaking) the employer acted reasonably or unreasonably in treating it as a sufficient reason for dismissing the employee, and

(b) shall be determined in accordance with equity and the substantial merits of the case.'

In the light of the above statutory provisions, the following general observations can be made:

(a) 'The expression "unfair dismissal" is in no sense a common-sense expression capable of being understood by the man in the street, which at first sight one would think it is': Phillips J in *Devis and Sons Ltd* v. *Atkins* (1977).

(b) Whether a dismissal is unfair is affected, but not conclusively determined, by whether one or both parties has broken the terms of the contract of employment.

(c) The employer cannot, in seeking to show that a dismissal was not unfair, rely on alleged misconduct not known to him at the time of the dismissal: *Devis and Sons Ltd* v. *Atkins* (1977). This may, however, affect the amount of compensation awarded (*see* **30–33** below).

(d) An otherwise fair dismissal is not automatically rendered unfair by a failure to give proper notice: *Treganowan* v. *Robert Knee and Co. Ltd* (1975).

11. Reasonableness

As s. 98(1) makes clear, it is for the employer to establish the reason for the dismissal. In addition, the tribunal must then satisfy itself as to whether 'in the circumstances (including the size and administrative resources of the employer's undertaking) the employer acted reasonably or unreasonably in treating it as a sufficient reason for dismissing the employee': s. 98(4)(a). This provision is of considerable significance and means that the tribunal must be satisfied that, in dismissing the employee, the employer acted reasonably both in terms of the substantive decision to dismiss for the reason alleged and in the procedure which led up to the dismissal.

In judging whether the employer has acted reasonably in taking the decision to dismiss it is clear that the tribunal must not substitute its own view of whether the decision was reasonable for that of the employer. The EAT laid down the following general principles in *Iceland Frozen Foods Ltd* v. *Jones* (1982):

(a) In applying s. 98(4), a tribunal must consider the reasonableness of the employer's conduct and not simply whether they (the members of the tribunal) consider the dismissal fair.

(b) In judging the reasonableness of the employer's conduct a tribunal must not substitute its own decision as to what was the right course to adopt for that of the employer.

(c) In many cases there is a band of reasonable responses to the employee's conduct within which one employer might take one view and another quite reasonably take another.

(d) The function of a tribunal is to determine whether in the particular circumstances of the case the decision to dismiss fell within the band of reasonable responses which a reasonable employer might have adopted. If the dismissal falls within the band it is fair; if it falls outside the band it is unfair. *See also British Leyland (UK) Ltd* v. *Swift* (1981).

Under s. 98(4) there is no formal burden of proof on the employer to prove that he has acted reasonably, and indeed where an industrial tribunal falls into error and refers to such a burden being placed on an employer then this could lead to a successful appeal to the Employment Appeal Tribunal: *see Post Office Counters Ltd.* v. *Heavey* (1989) and *Boys and Girls Welfare Society* v. *McDonald* (1996). In practice, of course, employers will wish to demonstrate their reasonableness in using the reason they have established in reaching a decision to dismiss and the practical position does seem to have been acknowledged at the highest level by the House of Lords in *Smith* v. *City of Glasgow District Council* (1987).

12. Code of Practice

In deciding whether an employer acted reasonably, the industrial tribunal is required to have regard to the provisions of the ACAS Code of Practice 'Disciplinary Practice and Procedures in Employment' (*see* 1:**14**). In broad terms this provides that the disciplinary rules (and the likely consequences of breach thereof) and procedures ought to be made known to each employee and that a disciplinary procedure ought to contain certain essential features, e.g. provide for an individual to be given an opportunity to state his case before disciplinary decisions are reached and to be allowed to be accompanied by a trade union representative or similar. In addition, the Code suggests that no employee should be dismissed for a first breach of discipline except in the cases of serious misconduct and that there ought to be a right of appeal against disciplinary decisions. In operating the procedure, a system of warnings ought to be used so that employees are given an opportunity to improve their conduct. Records of such warnings etc. should be kept but disregarded after a specified period of satisfactory conduct.

The provisions of the Code of Practice are not to be regarded as a rigid set of rules which, if not observed, will inevitably result in a finding of unfair dismissal, but rather as an important set of guidelines which, if not observed, will make it difficult though not impossible for the employer to establish that he acted reasonably and hence that the dismissal was fair: *Retarded Children's Aid Society* v. *Day* (1978); *Wood* v. *Kettering Co-operative Chemists Ltd* (1978).

ACAS have subsequently produced a Handbook: *Discipline at Work* (1987). Although this does not have the status of a code of practice, it does provide a compendium of useful practical advice.

The importance of the above procedural requirements received a severe set-back by the formulation of the so-called 'no difference' principle. The principle was formulated by the EAT in *British Labour Pump Co. Ltd* v. *Byrne* (1979). The effect of the principle was that procedural unfairness may be allowed if the employer could show, on the balance of probabilities, that even if a proper procedure had been followed the employer would still have dismissed the employee and that he would have been acting reasonably in so acting. In other words, the unreasonableness of the procedure made 'no difference' to the decision. The Court of Appeal approved the principle in *W. & J. Wass Ltd* v. *Binns* (1982).

The 'no difference' principle was overruled by the House of Lords in *Polkey* v. *A.E. Dayton Services Ltd.* (1987). The effect of the decision was to restore the importance of procedural requirements in determining the reasonableness of the dismissal. It should be noted that the effect of *Polkey* is to prevent an employer introducing retrospective claims that the procedure would have made 'no difference'. However, if at the time of the dismissal the employer felt that any consultation or warning 'would be utterly useless he might well have acted reasonably even if he did not observe the provisions of the code', *per* Lord Mackay in *Polkey*, although it should be noted that the major significance of the decision is to emphasise the importance of procedural fairness in reaching dismissal decisions: *see Stoker* v. *Lancashire County Council* (1992).

REASONS FOR DISMISSAL

13. Introduction

As shown above in **10**, the effect of s. 98(1) and s. 98(2) is that there are five categories of reasons which, if one is established by the employer, may make the dismissal fair provided that the tribunal is satisfied that the employer acted reasonably. These may be summarised under the following heads:

(a) Capability or qualifications.

(b) Conduct.

(c) Redundancy.

(d) Illegality of continued employment.

(e) Some other substantial reason.

These are dealt with in the next five paragraphs.

14. Capability or qualifications

The employer may show a reason which 'related to the capability or qualifications of the employee for performing work of the kind which he was employed by the employer to do': s. 98(2)(a):

(a) 'Capability' is defined as 'assessed by reference to skill, aptitude, health or any other physical or mental quality': s. 98(3)(a).

Thus an employer may seek to show that the employee was incompetent, but it must be remembered that the employer must also show that he acted reasonably in dismissing for that reason. Consequently the tribunal may wish to be satisfied that, for example, there had been a proper appraisal of the employee's performance, that he had been given adequate training and supervision, and opportunity, to improve his performance and the necessary facilities to enable him to be competent: *see Winterhalter Gastronom Ltd* v. *Webb* (1973); *Littlewoods Organisation Ltd* v. *Egenti* (1976); *Cook* v. *Linnell and Sons Ltd* (1977). The need for appraisal, supervision and guidance is particularly important in the case of probationary employees: *Post Office* v. *Mughal* (1977); *ILEA* v. *Lloyd* (1981). (*See* 3:**14**.) In exceptional circumstances, one serious error of judgment might justify dismissal on grounds of capability: *Taylor* v. *Alidair Ltd* (1978). Similarly, where it is alleged that an employee's ill health justified his dismissal, the tribunal will wish to be satisfied that the employer only dismissed the employee after having gathered sufficient information upon which to base such a decision: *East Lindsey District Council* v. *Daubney* (1977); *Spencer* v. *Paragon Wallpapers* (1977). The employer may also be required to consider offering the employee suitable alternative employment in such circumstances, but there is no obligation on him to create a special job for an employee in poor health: *Merseyside and North Wales Electricity Board* v. *Taylor* (1975).

(b) 'Qualifications' means 'any degree, diploma or other academic, technical or professional qualification relevant to the position which the employee held': s. 98(3)(b). Qualifications can also relate to aptitude or ability: *Blue Star Ship Management Ltd* v. *Williams* (1979). In *Blackman* v. *Post Office* (1974) a telegraph officer was required to pass an aptitude test. He failed it three times which was the maximum number of attempts permitted. Held: dismissal was fair.

15. Conduct

This term is not defined in the 1996 Act but the cases establish that a wide range of different kinds of misconduct may be used to justify a dismissal. However, probably the most important consideration in deciding whether a dismissal for misconduct is reasonable (and hence fair) is whether the provisions of the Code of Practice (*see* **12** above) have been complied with in respect of the dismissal, having regard to such matters as only 'serious misconduct' being sufficient to justify a dismissal for first breach of discipline and an employee being provided with an opportunity to state his case prior to a decision to dismiss being taken. Thus in *Budgen and Co.* v. *Thomas* (1976) a dismissal was held to be unfair as the employee had not been given an opportunity to explain herself despite the fact that on the face of it she had been dishonest. On the other hand, provided a proper investigation is carried out, a dismissal for alleged misconduct may be fair even though it subsequently transpires that the employee had not committed the 'offence': *Ferodo Ltd* v. *Barnes* (1976). It is impossible to list all the kinds of misconduct which may justify dismissal but the following categories are perhaps the most commonly used:

(a) Refusal to obey reasonable instructions from the employer: *Farnborough* v. *Governors of Edinburgh College of Art* (1974); *Boychuk* v. *H.J. Symons Holdings Ltd* (1977).

(b) Dishonesty towards the employer: *British Home Stores Ltd* v. *Burchell* (1978); *British Leyland UK Ltd* v. *Swift* (1981); *Sillifant* v. *Powell Duffryn Timber Ltd* (1983); *United Distillers* v. *Conlin* (1992).

(c) Criminal conduct outside employment but affecting it: *Singh* v. *London Country Bus Services Ltd* (1976); *Moore* v. *C. & A. Modes* (1981).

(d) Sexual misconduct: *Nottinghamshire County Council* v. *Bowly* (1978); *Wiseman* v. *Salford City Council* (1981).

(e) Drunkenness: *Connely* v. *Liverpool Corporation* (1974).

(f) Fighting: *Parsons* v. *McLoughlin* (1978).

(g) Absenteeism: *Williams* v. *Lloyds Retailers Ltd* (1973); *Hutchinson* v. *Enfield Rolling Mills Ltd* (1981).

(h) Interference with 'clocking-in' machine: *Dalton* v. *Burton's Gold Medal Biscuit Co.* (1974); *Elliot Bros. (London) Ltd* v. *Colverd* (1979).

(i) Misuse of employer's computer: *Denco Ltd.* v. *Joinson* (1991).

(j) Breach of implied contractual duty of fidelity: *Adamson* v. *B & L Cleaning Services Ltd* (1995).

One of the difficulties with the concept of conduct relates to the question of group misconduct where, despite all reasonable investigations, the employer is unable to identify the culprit. Previously, it has been decided that it was fair to dismiss two people in such a situation (*Monie* v. *Coral Racing Ltd* (1981)). The law has now considered the situation where there are three employees under suspicion in *Whitbread & Co.* v. *Thomas and others* (1988). In this case, despite repeated attempts by the employer, it was not possible to identify which one employee out of the three concerned was responsible for numerous stock losses over a period of years. The EAT laid down three criteria to be adopted when making a decision in such a case: **(a)** the act complained of would have justified dismissal if the culprits could have been identified, **(b)** that act had clearly been committed by a member or members of the group in question, and **(c)** all reasonable steps had been taken, including a full investigation, to ascertain the real culprits. On the facts the EAT held that as all three criteria were satisfied the decision to dismiss the three employees was fair.

16. Redundancy

The employer may show that the dismissal was because the employee was redundant: s. 98(2)(c). In such a case, the employer must establish that the employee was redundant and is unable to rely on the presumption of redundancy which arises by virtue of s. 163(2) of the 1996 Act: *Midland Foot Comfort Centre Ltd* v. *Moppett* (1973).

However, s. 105 provides:

(1) An employee who is dismissed shall be regarded for the purposes of this Part as unfairly dismissed if –

(a) the reason (or, if more than one, the principal reason) for the dismissal is that the employee was redundant,
(b) it is shown that the circumstances constituting the redundancy applied equally to one or more other employees in the same undertaking who held positions similar to that held by the employee and who have not been dismissed by the employer, and
(c) it is shown that any of subsections (2) to (7) applies.'

Subsections (2) to (7) list a series of categories of employee to whom the s. 105 right applies. These include:

- employees who are pregnant
- employees who are health and safety representatives
- employees who are trustees of an occupational pension scheme
- employees who have brought proceedings against an employer to assert a statutory right.

Such employees already have protection against unfair dismissal, but the effect of s. 105 is to increase the force of those statutory rights by making it clear that an employer cannot fall back onto a dismissal based on redundancy to justify as fair the dismissals of employees in the above categories.

In addition to s. 105, the cases establish that s. 98(4) also applies to dismissals for redundancy (i.e. the employer must show that he acted reasonably in dismissing for that reason) although it is clear that an industrial tribunal must not make a finding of unfair dismissal simply as a means of 'topping up' what it regards as an inadequate redundancy payment or out of sympathy for a redundant employee: *Lifeguard Assurance Ltd* v. *Zadrozny* (1977).

Tribunals have been cautious not to come to the conclusion too readily that a dismissal on the grounds of redundancy is unfair, but in *Williams* v. *Compair Maxam Ltd* (1982) the EAT set out the following standards of behaviour by which tribunals should be guided:

(a) As much warning as possible of impending redundancy should be given to employees (and trade unions: *see* 14:**21**).

(b) Trade unions should be consulted so as to decide the best means by which the desired management objectives can be achieved fairly and with as little hardship as possible. Employers and unions should seek to agree the criteria for selection for redundancy.

(c) Criteria for selection should not depend solely upon the opinion of the person making the selection; criteria should be capable of objective certification, e.g. attendance record, efficiency at the job, experience, length of service.

(d) The employer should ensure that the selection is made fairly in accordance with these criteria.

(e) The employer should investigate whether it is possible to offer an employee alternative employment rather than dismiss him.

The EAT emphasised that the above guidelines are not principles of law, failure to comply with which will result in a dismissal for redundancy being unfair. You should note that these guidelines are expanded in considerable detail at ss. 188–198 of the Trade Union and Labour Relations (Consolidation) Act 1992 in relation to the obligation to consult with trade unions in the case of collective redundancies. These provisions are covered in more detail in the next chapter.

17. Illegality of continued employment

The employer may show 'that the employee could not continue to work in the position which he held without contravention (either on his part or that of his employer) of a duty or restriction imposed by or under an enactment': s. 98(2)(d). This provision might therefore include an employee whose contract requires him to hold a driving licence losing that licence: *see Fearn* v. *Tayford Motor Co.* (1975). Nevertheless, the employer must still act reasonably and should therefore consider giving the employee an opportunity, if he so wishes, of making satisfactory alternative arrangements to cover the period of his disqualification: *Mathieson* v. *Noble and Sons Ltd* (1972).

It should be noted that, for an employer to rely on s. 98(2)(d) as a ground for dismissal, the continued employment of the employee must in fact breach a statutory enactment; it is not enough if the employer merely genuinely though mistakenly believes that an enactment is being breached: *Bouchaala* v. *Trust House Forte Hotels Ltd* (1980).

18. Some other substantial reason

The employer may show 'some other substantial reason of a kind such as to justify the dismissal of an employee holding the position which the employee held': s. 98(1)(b). Thus reasons other than those discussed above may be used to justify a dismissal.

It is impossible to compile an exhaustive list but the following are among those which have been used under this category in the particular circumstances of the case.

(a) Unreasonable refusal to agree to the inclusion in the employee's contract of a restrictive covenant relating to soliciting business from the employer's clients: *R.S. Components* v. *Irwin* (1973).

(b) Irreconcilable conflict of personalities principally caused by the dismissed employee: *Treganowan* v. *Robert Knee and Co.* (1975). Where such a conflict exists every step short of dismissal should be taken to try and improve the situation: *Turner* v. *Vestric Ltd* (1981).

(c) Unreasonable refusal to agree to an alteration in working hours and arrangements: *Ellis* v. *Brighton Co-operative Society Ltd* (1976); *Hollister* v. *National Farmers' Union* (1978); but *see also Evans* v. *Elmeta Holdings Ltd* (1982) and *St. John of God (Care Services) Ltd* v. *Brooks* (1992).

(d) An ultimatum from a key customer requiring a particular employee's dismissal: *Scott Packing and Warehousing Co.* v. *Patterson* (1978); but *see also Dobie* v. *Burns International Security Services (UK) Ltd* (1984).

In all the above cases, the employer must nevertheless establish that he acted reasonably. Thus in (c), for example, it would be unreasonable if the employer did not give the employee adequate opportunity to comply with the request to change his working hours.

19. Dismissal on grounds of pregnancy

It is automatically unfair to dismiss an employee because she is pregnant or for any other reason connected with her pregnancy. This is the effect of s. 99 of the Employment Rights Act 1996. The previous statutory provisions provided a defence where the employer could prove that the woman had, or would, become unable to do adequately the work she was employed to do, but this defence has now been removed and the right not to be unfairly dismissed is an absolute one. It should be noted that, by virtue of s. 108 of the 1996 Act, there is no minimum qualifying period of employment before the employee is protected against dismissal on pregnancy-related grounds.

DISMISSAL FOR TRADE UNION REASONS

References in this section are to the Trade Union and Labour Relations (Consolidation) Act 1992.

20. Trade union membership or activities

Under s. 152 of the Act a dismissal is automatically unfair if the employee can establish that the principal reason for it was:

(a) that the employee was, or proposed to become, a member of an independent trade union (*see* 14:**6**); or

(b) that the employee had taken or proposed to take part in the activities of an independent trade union at any appropriate time; or

(c) that the employee was not a member of any or a particular trade union, or had refused or proposed to refuse to become or remain a member.

It is conceivable that situations may arise where trade unions may seek to put industrial pressure on an employer, for example to secure the dismissal of an employee who is not a member of the trade union. An industrial tribunal, when it considers what was the reason, or the principal reason, for the dismissal, is obliged by virtue of s. 107(2) of the Employment Rights Act 1996 not to take account of any such pressure. However, under s. 160(1) of the 1992 Act the employer may ask that the tribunal directs that the trade union be joined as a party to the unfair dismissal proceedings. Under s. 160(3) the tribunal may then order that compensation for the unfair dismissal shall be paid by the trade union rather than by the employer, or apportioned between them on a just and equitable basis.

'Appropriate time' means a time which is either outside working hours or a time within working hours at which, by virtue of an express or implied agreement with the employer or assent given by the employer, it was permissible to take part in such activities: s. 152(2); and *see Marley Tile Co.* v. *Shaw* (1980) and *Zucker* v. *Astrid Jewels Ltd* (1978). A distinction must be drawn between trade union activities, e.g. an employee seeking assistance from a trade union to assist him in discussions with his employer, and an employee who does something which might be associated with a trade union, but which is essentially an individual and not a trade union activity, e.g. presenting a petition to an employer as spokesman for fellow employees: *see Chant* v. *Aquaboats Ltd* (1978). It should be noted that the protection of s. 152(2) does not extend to the situation where employees are dismissed following the activities of their trade union, rather than their own activities as trade unionists: *Therm A Stor Ltd* v. *Atkins* (1983). In *Bass Taverns Ltd* v. *Burgess* (1995) the Court of Appeal had to consider the meaning of s. 152 in the context of a member of a trade union who had been given approval to recruit new members to the union at an induction meeting for new staff. At the meeting he was critical of the employer. He was subsequently demoted, upon which he resigned and claimed he had been constructively dismissed. The Court of Appeal upheld his claim for unfair dismissal. It found that the employer's consent to the meeting was not subject to any implied condition that nothing critical of the employer would be said; accordingly it held that the only conclusion which could be drawn from the circumstances was that the employee had been dismissed for taking part in trade union activities at an appropriate time. Consequently, he was entitled to compensation.

There is no continuous employment qualification period for the right not to be dismissed for trade union reasons.

> *Note* that participation in industrial action is not to be regarded as participating in trade union activities.
>
> *Note* also that if, for similar reasons, action short of dismissal is taken against an employee, a complaint may be presented to an industrial tribunal (*see* generally Chapter 8).

21. Dismissal in health and safety cases

Under s. 100 of the Employment Rights Act 1996 the dismissal of an employee shall be regarded as having been unfair if the reason, or the principal reason, for the dismissal, was that the employee, having been designated by the employer to carry out activities in connection with preventing or reducing risks to health and safety at work, carried out or proposed to carry out such activities, or because he was carrying out the functions of a safety representative or a member of a safety committee.

The compensation rules which apply to such a dismissal are dealt with at **24** below.

OTHER REASONS FOR DISMISSAL

22. Industrial action

Under s. 237(1) of the 1992 Act an employee has no right to complain of unfair dismissal if at the time of the dismissal he was taking part in an unofficial strike or other unofficial industrial action. Under s. 238, an industrial tribunal cannot determine the fairness or otherwise of a dismissal if it is shown that at the date of dismissal the employer was conducting or instituting a lock-out or the complainant was taking part in an official strike or other official industrial action, unless it is shown:

(a)   that one or more relevant employees of the same employer have not been dismissed, or

(b)   that any such employee has, before the expiry of the period of three months beginning with that employee's date of dismissal, been offered re-engagement and that the complainant has not been offered re-engagement: s. 238(2).

It is often difficult to determine whether an employee participated in a strike. In *Coates and Venables* v. *Modern Methods and Materials Ltd* (1982) the issue was whether an employee who had not crossed a picket line during a strike was participating, even though the motive for not doing so was fear of the consequences rather than sympathy with the aims of the strike. The Court of Appeal held by a majority that the motives or reasons of the employee in not crossing the picket line were not relevant. As Stephenson L J said:

'. . . participation in a strike must be judged by what the employee does and not by what he thinks or why he does it. If he stops work when his workmates come out on strike and does not say or do anything to make plain his disagreement, or which could amount to a refusal to join them, he takes part in their strike . . . In the field of industrial action those who are not openly against it are presumably for it'.

In *Manifold Industries Ltd.* v. *Sims* (1991) the Employment Appeal Tribunal held that the question of whether an employee is on strike is an objective factual question, not involving the knowledge or lack of knowledge on the part of the employer; it should also be noted that a person away from work through illness or on holiday may still be regarded as taking part in a strike or other industrial action if his actions disclose that that is his intent: *see Bolton Roadways Ltd.* v. *Edwards* (1987).

It should be noted that 'relevant employees' in relation to a strike are defined as 'those employees at the establishment of the employer at or from which the complainant works who at the date of his dismissal were taking part in the action': s. 238(3)(b). The practical effect of this is that where an employer dismisses employees who are participating in a strike, the fact that other employees who were previously participating in the strike have drifted back to work before the date of dismissal, and have not been dismissed, does not enable those dismissed to complain of unfair dismissal.

'Re-engagement' in relation to dismissed strikers means re-engagement in the job which the employee held immediately before the dismissal or in a different job which would be reasonably suitable in his case: s. 238(4) and *see Williams* v. *National Theatre Board Ltd* (1982).

In **15** above, the question of group dismissals has been discussed. It is important to remember that where an individual is being dismissed, for alleged misconduct arising out of a strike, the basic principles of unfair dismissal still apply. In *McLaren* v. *National Coal Board* (1988), M was dismissed for allegedly assaulting a working miner during the 1984–85 miners' dispute. The colliery manager, who was under a duty to investigate such matters, decided that in the prevailing circumstances he would allow the police to investigate the matter. If charges were brought by the police then the manager indicated that he would dismiss M. The police decided to charge M and he was dismissed. The Court of Appeal decided that 'standards of fairness are immutable' and further 'no amount of heat in industrial warfare can justify failing to give an employee the opportunity of offering an explanation'. The case was remitted to a differently constituted industrial tribunal for the matter to be reconsidered.

23. National security

If an employee is shown to have been dismissed on grounds of national security, as conclusively evidenced by a certificate signed by or on behalf of a Minister of the Crown, the tribunal must dismiss the complaint. The concept of 'national security' was at issue in the decision of the House of Lords in *Council of Civil Service Unions* v. *Minister for the Civil Service* (1985) (the 'GCHQ' case). The court held that the requirements of national security outweighed those of fairness when the Minister decided to ban trade unions at GCHQ, without prior consultation with the trade unions. Further it was for the executive (in this case the Minister) and not for the courts to decide upon the appropriate national security implications of the case. Workers who refused to give up their trade union membership were subsequently fairly dismissed. It has recently been announced by the Minister that trade union membership at GCHQ is no longer incompatible with the interests of national security; accordingly GCHQ employees will, once more, be allowed to join a trade union.

PROCEDURE

24. Application

An employee who considers that he has been dismissed unfairly may present a complaint to the Central Office of Industrial Tribunals (this is usually done on the prescribed form IT1) within three months of the effective date of termination (*see* 11:3) or 'within such further period as the tribunal considers reasonable in a case where it is satisfied that it was not reasonably practicable for the complaint to be presented before the end of that period of three months': s. 111(2) ERA 1996. The question of whether it was not reasonably practicable for the time limit to be met is essentially a question of fact for the industrial tribunal. The onus of proof is on the complainant: *see Wall's Meat Co. Ltd v. Khan* (1979); *see also Marley (UK) Ltd v. Anderson* (1996).

A copy of the application is sent to the employer as respondent. If the employer wishes to contest any aspect of the complaint, he must enter a 'notice of appearance' (usually on the prescribed form IT3) within fourteen days, although tribunals have a wide discretion to grant an extension of time. Once this has happened, a date is set down for the hearing of the case by an industrial tribunal.

25. Conciliation

A copy of the application is also sent to a conciliation officer (*see* 1:13). He is under a statutory duty, either at the request of the parties or on his own initiative, to endeavour to promote a voluntary settlement of the issue, either by way of an agreement to reinstate or re-engage the complainant or an agreement as to the payment of compensation in respect of the dismissal: s. 18 Industrial Tribunals Act 1996 and *see Moore v. Duport Furniture Products Ltd* (1982).

There is no legal duty upon the parties to co-operate with the conciliation officer and anything communicated to him is not subsequently admissible in evidence in the tribunal. If no settlement is reached and the complaint is not withdrawn, the tribunal will hear the case.

26. Pre-hearing reviews

Under Schedule 1 of the Industrial Tribunals (Constitution and Rules of Procedure) Regulations 1993 provision is made for a pre-hearing review to be undertaken by the tribunal at any time before the hearing of the originating
application. Such a review can be sought by either party to the proceedings, or
can be instituted by the tribunal itself. If upon the pre-hearing review the tribunal
considers that the contentions put forward by either party have no reasonable
prospect of success, the tribunal may make an order against that party requiring
him to pay a deposit, not exceeding £150, as a condition of being permitted to
continue to take part in the proceedings. Where such an order is made a
summary record of the order will be sent to each of the parties, accompanied by
a note which explains that if the party against whom the order is made persists
in participating in the proceedings, he may have an award of costs made against
him *and* he could lose his deposit. The purpose of such a review is to filter out
cases where there is 'no reasonable prospect of success' (Rule 7(4)) and to put a
party on notice that he runs the risk of having to pay costs and lose the deposit
if he persists with the case and loses.

27. Tribunal hearing

At the tribunal (*see* 1:**3**), it is for the complainant to establish that he was
dismissed (unless dismissal is conceded). It is then for the tribunal to satisfy itself
as to whether the dismissal was fair or unfair in accordance with the principles
stated above. If the dismissal is found to be unfair, the tribunal will consider the
remedies which may be awarded. An appeal, on a point of law only, lies from
an industrial tribunal to the Employment Appeal Tribunal (*see* 1:**9**).

REMEDIES

The references in this section are to ss. 113–132 of ERA 1996.

28. Reinstatement and re-engagement orders

If the tribunal finds the dismissal unfair, it must explain to the complainant the
remedies which are available and ask if he wishes to be reinstated or re-engaged.
Reinstatement means that the employer must treat the employee in all respects
as if he had not been dismissed—in other words, there must be no loss of
seniority etc. and arrears of pay etc. since the dismissal must be paid. Re-engagement means that the employer (or his successor) or an associated employer must
take the employee into employment comparable to that from which he was
dismissed or into other suitable employment on such terms as the tribunal may
specify, e.g. no loss of pension rights.

If the complainant indicates that he would like to be reinstated or re-engaged,
the tribunal must first consider whether to make an order for reinstatement. In
so deciding, the tribunal must consider, by virtue of s. 116, the complainant's

wishes, whether it is 'practicable' for the employer to comply with such an order and whether, if the complainant caused or contributed to any extent to his dismissal, it would be 'just' to order his reinstatement. In deciding whether it is 'practicable' for the employer to comply with the order, the tribunal must normally disregard the fact that the employer has already engaged a replacement for the dismissed employee.

If the tribunal decides not to make an order for reinstatement, it must next consider making a re-engagement order. In so doing, the tribunal must again take into account the complainant's wishes, whether it is 'practicable' for the employer to comply with the order and whether, if the complainant caused or contributed to his dismissal, it would be 'just' to make such an order.

If the tribunal decides not to make either order, it must make an award of compensation (*see* **30** below).

29. Failure to reinstate/re-engage

If the employer complies, but not fully, with a reinstatement or re-engagement order, the tribunal may make an award of compensation of such amount as it thinks fit having regard to the complainant's loss subject to a maximum of £11,300 (at the time of writing) in consequence of the failure to comply fully with the terms of the order.

If the employer completely fails to comply with an order for reinstatement or re-engagement then, unless the tribunal is satisfied that it was not practicable to comply with the order, an additional award of compensation must be made (additional, that is, to the normal award of compensation which will be made in respect of the unfair dismissal). In other words, the additional award is designed to 'punish' the employer for his failure to comply with the order. The additional award is between thirteen and twenty-six weeks' pay (maximum £210 a week at the time of writing), other than in the cases where the dismissal was on the grounds of sex or race discrimination. In these cases a higher additional award of between twenty-six and fifty-two weeks' pay is payable.

Thus it is clear that, while an employer cannot ultimately be compelled to take an employee back, he may be 'persuaded' to do so by the imposition of an additional award.

> *Note:* Special rules apply in relation to dismissals for trade union reasons and dismissals connected with health and safety; see **34** below.

30. Compensation

In addition to the principles set out above, or where a reinstatement order or re-engagement order is not made, the tribunal must make an award of compensation on the basis of the principles stated in the next two paragraphs.

31. Basic award

The basic award is assessed in the same way as a redundancy payment (*see* **14:5**). The maximum basic award is therefore £6,300 (at the time of writing).

The basic award is reduced by the amount of any redundancy payment paid (which would normally be the same amount). In addition, the amount of the basic award may be reduced to such extent as the tribunal considers just and equitable if: **(a)** the employee has unreasonably refused an offer of reinstatement; or **(b)** the employee's conduct prior to the dismissal justifies it (this could include misconduct by the employee not known by the employer at the time of the dismissal but discovered subsequently (*see* **10(c)** above)).

32. Compensatory award

The compensatory award is 'such amount as the tribunal considers just and equitable in all the circumstances having regard to the loss sustained by the complainant in consequence of the dismissal in so far as the loss is attributable to action taken by the employer' subject to a maximum of £11,300 (at the time of writing).

The tribunal will specify the amount of compensation which it awards under the following heads (*see Norton Tool Co.* v. *Tewson* (1972)):

(a) *Expenses incurred as a result of dismissal.* This could include expenses incurred in seeking new employment and loss of fringe benefits such as a company car or accommodation which went with the job. It does not include the cost of presenting the complaint of unfair dismissal to an industrial tribunal.

(b) *Wages lost up to the date of hearing.* This can include: (*i*) net (of tax) wages payable during a period of notice which should have been, but was not, given; and (*ii*) net (of tax and social security contributions) wages which would have been earned from the end of the notice period to the date of the hearing.

(c) *Estimated future loss of earnings.* If the employee has already obtained other employment, it will be possible to assess his loss under this head (if any) precisely. If, however, the complainant has not obtained employment, the tribunal, taking account of local employment conditions and personal factors affecting the complainant, will award a sum representing his loss of earnings; *see Fougere* v. *Phoenix Motor Co. (Surrey) Ltd* (1976). The tribunal will usually allow a maximum of two years' earnings but, in exceptional cases, it could be longer. Total figures are, of course, subject to the statutory maximum.

(d) *Manner of dismissal.* If there is 'cogent evidence' that the manner of the dismissal made a complainant less acceptable to potential employers, compensation can be awarded under this head, although it rarely is.

(e) *Loss of protection against future dismissal.* In so far as, in any new employment, the complainant will have to acquire a period of continuous employment before being 'protected' in respect of unfair dismissal, compensation is awarded in respect of this. The amount awarded, however, is usually restricted to a small sum, although in some situations the amount may be not insignificant: *see Daley* v. *A E Dorsett Ltd* (1981).

(f) *Loss of pension rights.* Where the complainant can establish that, because of the dismissal, he has lost pension rights, compensation will be awarded to cover this. Calculation of this sum has always been notoriously difficult, but the Government Actuary's Department has produced a document 'Industrial Tribunals – compensation for Loss of Pension Rights' providing a suggested method for assessing loss of pension rights under an occupational pension scheme following an unfair dismissal. The methods of calculation set out in the document have been used as a basis for consideration by tribunals: *see Tradewinds Airways Ltd* v. *Fletcher* (1981), although it should be noted that there is no statutory requirement that tribunals must make use of this document in assessing compensation under this heading: *see Bingham* v. *Hobourn Engineering Ltd* (1992). For the general principles to be applied, *see Copson* v. *Eversure Accessories Ltd* (1974); *Powrmatic Ltd* v. *Bull* (1977).

Certain deductions may be made from the compensatory award:

(*i*) The complainant must mitigate his loss in so far as possible (e.g. by taking reasonable steps to find other employment) and if he fails to do so, the award may be reduced: *see Gardiner-Hill* v. *Roland Berger Technics Ltd* (1982).

(*ii*) As with the basic award, the tribunal may reduce the award to such extent as it considers 'just and equitable' if it considers that the employee caused or contributed to his dismissal. It seems that the amount of the reduction on this ground should not normally exceed 80 per cent: *Kemp* v. *Shipton Automation Ltd* (1976); but *see also W Devis & Sons Ltd* v. *Atkins* (1977). However, if the tribunal considers that it would be 'just and equitable' not to make any compensatory award at all (e.g. because, although subsequently discovered misconduct cannot be used to justify the dismissal, it might be 'just and equitable' not to make a compensatory award) it may do so: *Moncrieff (Farmers)* v. *MacDonald* (1978).

(*iii*) The amount by which any redundancy payment exceeds the basic award may be taken from the compensatory award.

33. Interim relief

There are special procedures which allow for interim relief pending a full hearing in the case of dismissals in health and safety cases (s. 128 ERA 1996) and where the reason for the dismissal is alleged to be for trade union membership or non-membership or for trade union activities (TULR(C)A, s. 161). In such cases the application for interim relief must be presented to the tribunal within seven days of the effective date of termination and it will be determined by the tribunal as soon as practicable. The tribunal has the power to order a continuation of the employee's contract pending the final hearing of the application, should the employer be unwilling to reinstate or re-engage pending that hearing.

34. Special compensation rules for dismissals in health and safety and trade union cases

Where the dismissal is for one of the reasons prohibited by s. 100 of ERA 1996 (health and safety cases) or s. 152 of the 1992 Act (trade union cases), the tribunal will make a 'special award' of compensation. The detailed provisions relating to the totality of the compensation possibilities which apply in such a case are beyond the scope of this book, but the special award which is available constitutes a high and punitive award against the employer. The special award is one week's pay multiplied by 104, and is subject to a minimum payment of £13,775 and a maximum of £27,500. Where a reinstatement or re-engagement order has been made by the tribunal and this has not been complied with by the employer, the special award will be a week's pay multiplied by 156 and is subject to a minimum of £20,600, with no statutory maximum.

14

THE LAW OF REDUNDANCY

References in this chapter (up to and including **16**) are to the Employment Rights Act 1996.

INTRODUCTION

1. Purpose of the legislation

Prior to the passing of the now-repealed Redundancy Act 1965, the only circumstances in which a redundancy or severance payment had to be paid was where it had been contractually agreed. The significance of the 1965 Act was that it gave certain employees the right to claim a payment from the employer if redundancy occurred. The original object of the 1965 Act was as stated in *Wynes* v. *Southrepps Hall Broiler Farm Ltd* (1968) by the President of the industrial tribunals:

> 'The stated purpose of the redundancy payments scheme is two-fold: it is to compensate for loss of security, and to encourage workers to accept redundancy without damaging industrial relations. A redundancy payment is compensation for loss of a right which a long-term employee had in his job . . . redundancy pay is to compensate a worker for loss of a job, irrespective of whether that loss leads to unemployment. It is to compensate him for loss of security, possible loss of earnings and fringe benefits . . . and the anxiety of change of job.'

However, the redundancy payment scheme as originally envisaged in 1965, and now as continued in the 1996 Act, is seen as something rather different than in the 1960s. At that time the scheme was seen as one designed to encourage the mobility of labour and as a contribution to providing a more efficient and appropriately skilled workforce. Today employers are encouraged *not* to make employees redundant where redundancy can be avoided. Many employers will seek to redeploy staff within the organisation, through retraining or job sharing, in order to avoid making members of the workforce redundant. The changing legislative framework has contributed to this in that, unlike at the time of the inception of the scheme, employers are no longer able to look to a central Redundancy Fund for a rebate of any redundancy payments which may have to be made. Ironically, where the issue of redundancy is being considered by an industrial tribunal it will usually be an employer, rather than an employee, who will argue that the employee is redundant, given that since 1971 redundancy has been one of the grounds on which an employer will seek to argue that a dismissal is fair.

2. Persons covered

The redundancy provisions of the 1996 Act (Part XI of the Act) apply to all persons who work under a contract of employment with the following exceptions:

(a) Persons who have been employed by that employer for less than two years: s. 155. It should be noted, however, that issues relating to time periods for qualification now need to be considered with special caution in the light of the decision of the House of Lords in *R.* v. *Secretary of State for Employment ex p. Seymour-Smith* (1997) *(see* 13:**3**).

(b) Persons over the age of 65.

(c) Persons employed under a fixed-term contract for two years or more who agree in writing, before the contract expires, to forgo their rights to claim a redundancy payment: s. 197. In *Pfaffinger* v. *City of Liverpool Community College* (1996) the Employment Appeal Tribunal held that an employee employed under a series of fixed-term contracts was constructively dismissed by reason of redundancy, when the employee resigned following the decision of the employer to reduce the hourly rate of pay for reasons of efficiency.

(d) Crown employees.

(e) Under s. 157 of the 1996 Act, where a joint application is made by a trade union and an employer who have made an agreement providing for payments on the termination of contracts of employment, the Secretary of State for Employment may by order grant an exemption from the requirement on an employer to make redundancy payments under the Act. It should be noted that the Secretary of State will not make an order unless provision is made in the agreement for disputes to be referred to an industrial tribunal for decision.

(f) A period of continuous service for the purposes of claiming a redundancy payment cannot begin until the employee is 18.

DISMISSAL

3. Prerequisite for claim

An employee to whom Part XI of the 1996 Act applies may claim a redundancy payment if he can establish that he has been 'dismissed' and the employer cannot rebut the presumption of redundancy which arises. An employee is treated as having been 'dismissed' by his employer if, but only if:

(a) the contract of employment is terminated by the employer whether with or without notice; or

(b) it is a fixed-term contract which has expired without being renewed; or

(c) the employee terminates the contract with or without notice in circumstances such that he is entitled to terminate it without notice by reason of the employer's conduct (*see* 13:7): s. 136(1).

In addition, where the contract is deemed to come to an end because of some act on the part of the employer or some event affecting him (e.g. the employer's death), it is deemed to be a 'dismissal': s. 136(5).

4. Variation of contract

If the parties to a contract mutually agree to vary the terms of their contract, no dismissal occurs if the employee later leaves because he regrets the variation. If, however, there is a unilateral variation of the contract by the employer to which the employee does not assent, this may be regarded as a breach of the contract by the employer and the employee may treat himself as 'dismissed'.

In *Marriott* v. *Oxford and District Co-operative Society Ltd* (1970) the claimant was employed as a foreman and was sent a letter by his employer stating that in future he had to be employed at a lower status with less wages. Held: this was a termination of a contract by the employer which the claimant could treat as 'dismissal'.

The problem is not unlike that of constructive dismissal (*see* 13:7 above) in that a breach of contract has to be shown. The problem then is to identify a breach and the relationship with reorganisation must be examined. An employer has a discretion, often referred to as managerial prerogative, to reorganise his business. The question to be asked in this context is whether or not the reorganisation amounts to a breach of contract, and hence a dismissal, and then whether a redundancy situation arises.

A good example of the difficulties is provided by the question of a change in the shift working patterns of an employee and whether or not this amounts to a breach of contract. The courts and tribunals have avoided the issue by saying it is a question of fact depending on the circumstances of each case. In *Lesney Products Co. Ltd* v. *Nolan* (1977) and *Johnson* v. *Nottinghamshire Combined Police Authority* (1974) it was held that a change in shift patterns was merely a reorganisation as 'an employer is entitled to reorganise his business so as to improve its efficiency'. However in *Macfisheries Ltd* v. *Findlay* (1985) a change from night shift to day shift was held to be a breach of contract as the employee had a contractual right not to be required to transfer to the day shift. Further problems of this kind arise in relation to an employer instructing an employee to move from one place of work to another. In *O'Brien* v. *Associated Fire Alarms Ltd* (1968) the requirement to move 120 miles to new work (in the absence of an express term of the contract requiring mobility) was held to be a breach of contract, but in *Courtaulds Northern Spinning Ltd* v. *Gibson* (1988) (*see* 13:7 above) the requirement to move within a reasonable commuting distance was held not to be a breach of contract. Clearly it is a question of fact in the circumstances of each case.

REDUNDANCY

5. Presumption of redundancy

When dismissal has been established, a presumption arises by virtue of s. 163(2) that the reason for the dismissal was redundancy and it is for the employer to show that the dismissal was for some reason other than redundancy. It should be noted that an employer cannot rely on the presumption of redundancy to show that a dismissal was not unfair (*see* 13:**16**).

6. Dismissal for misconduct

If the employee is dismissed for misconduct he is not entitled to a redundancy payment. However, if the dismissal for misconduct occurs during the period of notice which has already been given for redundancy, the tribunal may award the claimant the whole or part of the payment as it considers 'just and equitable'. See *Simmons* v. *Hoover Ltd* (1977).

7. Definition of redundancy

Redundancy is defined by s. 139(1) as where:

'. . . dismissal is wholly or mainly attributable to—(a) the fact that his employer has ceased or intends to cease (i) to carry on the business for the purposes of which the employee was employed by him, or (ii) to carry on that business in the place where the employee was so employed, or (b) the fact that the requirements of that business (i) for employees to carry out work of a particular kind, or (ii) for employees to carry out work of a particular kind in the place where the employee was so employed by the employer, have ceased or diminished or are expected to cease or diminish.'

Part (a) of s. 139(1) has given rise to few problems, but (b) has been subject to considerable interpretation, particularly in connection with changing duties required of an employee.

In *North Riding Garages* v. *Butterwick* (1967) the claimant had been employed for thirty years at a garage and had become workshop manager. The appellants acquired ownership of the garage and some time later the claimant was dismissed because of alleged inefficiency in so far as he was unable to adapt to new methods of work which required that he perform certain administrative functions. The claimant alleged that the changed nature of the work showed that the requirements of the business for employees to carry out that particular kind of work must be diminishing and therefore he had been dismissed for redundancy. Held: the claimant was not entitled to a redundancy payment because the reason for the dismissal was his inability to assimilate new techniques rather than redundancy. Widgery J:

'For the purpose of the Act, an employee who remains in the same kind of work is expected to adapt himself to new methods and techniques, and cannot complain if his employer insists on higher standards of efficiency than those previously required; but if new methods alter the nature of the work required to be done, it may follow that no requirement remains for employees to do work of the particular kind which is being superseded, and that they are truly redundant.'

In *Vaux and Associated Breweries Ltd* v. *Ward* (1969) the claimant had been employed as a barmaid. The owners of the public house wished to cater for a different kind of customer and therefore dismissed the claimant in order to replace her with a younger woman. Held: the claimant was not redundant because there was no less need for this kind of work to be done. In *Hindle* v. *Percival Boats Ltd* (1969) it was held that the dismissal of an employee because he was too good and too slow did not amount to redundancy. Merely shedding surplus labour is not redundancy.

In *Chapman* v. *Goonvean and Rostowrack China Clay Co.* (1973) it was held that where a free transport service to and from work was withdrawn because it was uneconomical, the employees who found it more difficult to get to work were not redundant. In *Gimber and Sons* v. *Spurrett* (1967) it was held that a person is to be regarded as redundant if he is dismissed to make way for a fellow employee who is redundant, since s. 139(1)(b) does not refer specially to the claimant's own job.

It should be remembered, when dealing with the situation where an employer has sought to invoke a geographical mobility clause in the contract, that the employee will not be regarded as being redundant if the employer seeks to require the employee to work in another location. In *Rank Xerox Ltd* v. *Churchill* (1988) the employee worked at the London headquarters of the employer. A term in the contract of the employee provided that 'The company may require you to transfer to another location.' The employee refused to move when the company transferred its headquarters to another location and claimed that she had been made redundant. The Employment Appeal Tribunal found for the employer and said that the words 'the place where the employee was so employed' in s. 139(1)(a) are not to be construed as the place where the employee actually works, but as the place where by the contract the employee can be required to work. Accordingly the company had not ceased to carry on its business in the place where the employee was employed, and she was therefore not redundant.

In *Johnson* v. *Peabody Trust* (1996) the applicant was employed as a roofer, but his contract required him to work flexibly and carry out multi-trade operations where necessary. At the time he was selected for redundancy he was carrying out more multi-trade work than roofing work. He argued that his dismissal was unfair because the employer had sought to justify his redundancy in terms of a diminution in requirements for roofing work. However, the EAT held that where an employee is employed to carry out a particular well-recognised and well-defined category of skilled trade, it is that basic contractual obligation which should be considered. In the view of the EAT the fact that the applicant could be required to assist in multi-trade operations on the occasions when roofing work was not available to be done did not alter the essential fact that he was contracted as a roofer. It followed that the reason for his dismissal was redundancy.

VOLUNTARY REDUNDANCIES

8. Volunteers

A method of reducing hardship in a redundancy situation is to ask for volunteers. Employers, in order to attract volunteers, will offer either enhanced redundancy payments or an early pension. Both these payments are matters arising out of the contract of employment. What is clear is that there will be no right to a statutory redundancy payment as well in such a situation. The principle is illustrated by the decision in *Littlewoods Organisation plc* v. *Pickersgill* (1987). P applied for voluntary redundancy and entered the lengthy process of obtaining civil service employment. The voluntary redundancy scheme depended on the employee obtaining a comparable job elsewhere. Before P finalised the new job and left, the employers withdrew the scheme. The EAT decided there had been no dismissal and therefore any claim P might have was contractual.

It should be remembered that where the termination of the contract is consensual, that will preclude a finding that the employee was dismissed for reasons of redundancy. In *Birch and Humber* v. *University of Liverpool* (1985) where employees took early retirement under the employer's Premature Retirement Compensation Scheme, it was held by the Court of Appeal that the employees had not been dismissed for redundancy, but that their contracts had been terminated by mutual agreement when their applications for retirement under the scheme had been accepted, despite the fact that the retirements were expressed to be 'in the managerial interest.' In the course of this judgment in the case Lord Justice Ackner observed that where an employer envisages that at some time in the future he will have to slim down his workforce and makes an offer to those who are prepared to resign rather than to wait to volunteer for redundancy, and supports that offer with a financial inducement which is far in excess of what is likely to be obtained under the redundancy legislation, then if that offer is accepted there can be no question of there having been a dismissal.

9. Lay-off and short time

Sections 147 and 148 of the Act make provision in relation to employees who are laid off or on short time (i.e. receive less than half the normal weekly earnings) other than as a result of an industrial dispute. If an employee's contract of employment does not contain any provision that the employee may be laid off or placed on short time, such action by the employer inevitably constitutes dismissal for redundancy: *Hanson* v. *Wood* (1967). However, if the contract does permit it, the following provisions apply:

(a) If the employee is laid off or on short time for four consecutive weeks or six out of the previous thirteen, he may give written notice to the employer stating his intention to claim a redundancy payment. The employee may then claim the payment if he gives notice as required by the contract.

(b) The employer, however, can either make the payment or, within seven days of the employee's notice of intent to claim, issue a written counter-notice contesting the claim and stating that there is a reasonable chance that, within four weeks of the date of the counter-notice, the employee will commence a period of thirteen weeks' consecutive full employment. If the claim and the counter-claim are not withdrawn, the matter must be resolved by the tribunal on the basis of whether it considers that there was a reasonable prospect of full employment for thirteen consecutive weeks.

(c) If the employer withdraws the counter-notice or fails to give thirteen weeks' full employment, the employee is entitled to a payment.

ALTERNATIVE OFFERS

10. General principle

An employee who has been dismissed by reason of redundancy will lose his right to a payment if he unreasonably refuses an offer from his employer to renew the contract on the same terms or if he unreasonably refuses an offer from his employer to re-engage him on different terms if that offer is deemed to be of 'suitable employment'. Such an offer whether in writing or not, must be made before the termination of the original contract so as to commence not later than four weeks following such termination: s. 141(1).

To be regarded as an offer of 'suitable employment', regard must be had to the employee's status, the nature of the work to be done, the remuneration and the other terms and conditions.

In *Taylor* v. *Kent County Council* (1969) the claimant was a headmaster of a school. He was made redundant but offered a place in a 'pool' of teachers to act as a supply to schools which were temporarily without a teacher. There was to be no loss of salary or other rights. He refused the offer. Held: the offer was not suitable because of the loss of status in so far as he would no longer be headmaster of his own school. Parker LCJ: '. . . "suitable" in relation to that employee means conditions of employment which are reasonably equivalent to those under the previous employment . . . it does not seem to me that by "suitable employment" is meant employment of an entirely different nature . . .'

In *Bowman* v. *NCB* (1970) an offer was made to a colliery worker which involved a loss of 20 per cent of wages, downgrading and the possibility that the new work might only last three years. Held: the offer was not suitable.

If the offer is to renew the contract or, in the case of an offer to re-engage on different terms, is 'suitable', the employee loses his right to a payment unless he has reasonable grounds for refusing it. In deciding whether the employee has such grounds, the tribunal may have regard to personal factors affecting the employee, e.g. travel difficulties, housing or domestic problems.

In *White* v. *Bolding and Sons Ltd* (1966) it was held that a refusal was reasonable where the claimant and her husband were purchasing a house in the place where she was employed.

In *Rawe* v. *Power Gas Corporation* (1966) it was held that a move from the South East of England to Teesside was reasonably refused because of the possibility of marital difficulties.

In Souter v. Henry Balfour and Co. Ltd (1966) it was held that where the claimant, who was skilled in a particular trade, wished to remain in the same kind of work as he was formerly doing, his refusal of a suitable offer was reasonable.

In *Wragg & Sons* v. *Wood* (1976) it was held that in deciding whether a refusal is reasonable, the tribunal is entitled to consider the employee's fear of future redundancy and the fact that he has already obtained other employment.

In *Tocher* v. *General Motors Scotland Ltd* (1981) it was held that even though the alternative work may have been suitable, in the sense that it was within the capacity of the employee, refusal was justified where it involved a loss of status and loss of salary.

An interesting example of the potential width of grounds which may be regarded as reasonable occurred in *Spencer and Griffin* v. *Gloucestershire County Council* (1985). The employees were school cleaners employed by the County Council. Following a proposal to reduce the number of cleaners at the school where the employees worked, the employees were offered new conditions of employment with reduced hours of work. It was accepted by the employer that a consequence of this would be that the standard of cleaning at the school would inevitably be lower, and on this basis the employees had refused the new terms and claimed a redundancy payment. The Court of Appeal held that whilst it is for the employer to decide what is the appropriate standard of work, the question of whether it is reasonable for a particular employee to refuse to work to that standard is a separate consideration and will depend on the facts of the case. Accordingly it was found that on the facts of this case the employees had not acted unreasonably in refusing an offer of suitable alternative employment.

11. Effect of accepting alternative offer

Where an employee accepts an alternative offer, his employment is deemed to continue for the purposes of determining the period of 'continuous employment' (*see* 2:**15**).

12. Transfer of a business

In the situation where an employer transfers his undertaking to a new employer the effect of the change of ownership on individual contracts of employment is governed to a large extent by the Transfer of Undertakings (Protection of Employment) Regulations 1981 (SI 1981/1794). This topic is covered in detail in the next chapter.

13. Trial period

If the employment of the employee is renewed on the basis of different terms (either by that employer or a new employer), the employee is entitled to have a trial period of four weeks (or such longer period as the parties may agree in advance).

If during the trial period, the employee terminates the contract, the employee is treated as having been dismissed on the date on which the previous contract terminated for the reason then applying: *see McKindley* v. *William Hill (Scotland) Ltd* (1985). It must then be determined whether the offer of alternative employment was suitable and whether the employee had reasonable grounds for not continuing the employment: s. 138.

It should be noted that the right of an employee to a trial period is a statutory one; thus in *Elliot* v. *Richard Stump Ltd* (1987), where the employer offered alternative employment to an employee, but denied him a trial period, leading to a rejection by the employee of the alternative employment offer, it was held by the EAT that the dismissal was unfair.

CLAIMING A PAYMENT

14. Procedure

An employee who considers that he has been dismissed for redundancy must make a claim to his employer in writing; if the employer refuses to make such a payment, the matter must be referred to an industrial tribunal. This must normally be done within six months of the termination of the contract: *see* s. 164. The payment is made by the employer.

15. Amount of payment

If the right to a payment is established, it is paid to the employee free of tax. The actual sum is calculated by reference to three factors (s. 162 of the 1996 Act):

(1) age of claimant

(2) length of continuous employment of claimant

(3) the weekly pay of the claimant.

Table 1: Amount of payment

Age (inclusive)	Amount (weeks' pay for each year of employment)
18–21	½
22–40	1
41–65 (men and women)	1½

(a) For each month a claimant is over sixty-four the amount is reduced by one-twelfth for each complete month worked.

(b) Any earnings over £210 per week are disregarded and only the last twenty years' employment may be counted. Hence the maximum payment at the time of writing is £6,300, i.e. 20 years × 1½ × £210.

(c) If an employee's employment has straddled an age barrier, the different age rates are applied. For example, if an employee has been employed from the age of thirty-five to forty-five, he has 6 years at 1 week's pay and 4 years at 1½ weeks' pay.

16. A week's pay

The computation of a week's pay varies with each individual case but the principles are laid down in ss. 220–227. If the employee is on a fixed weekly rate, the contractual rate is adopted. If an employee's remuneration for employment in normal working hours does not vary with the amount of work done, a week's pay is the amount payable under the contract. If the amount of remuneration does vary, a week's pay is determined by taking an average over the last twelve weeks of employment. If there are no normal working hours, a week's pay is determined by taking an average over the last twelve weeks of employment. Overtime hours are not included as 'normal working hours' for determining a week's pay unless it was obligatory on both the employer and the employee: *Tarmac Roadstone Holdings* v. *Peacock* (1973); *Lotus Cars Ltd* v. *Sutcliffe and Stratton* (1982); *British Coal Corporation* v. *Cheesbrough* (1990).

PROCEDURES FOR HANDLING REDUNDANCIES

References in this section are to ss. 188–198 of the Trade Union and Labour Relations (Consolidation) Act 1992 (as amended by the Trade Union Reform and Employment Rights Act 1993).

17. Consultation

Where an employer is proposing to dismiss as redundant 20 or more employees at one establishment within a period of 90 days or less, the employer is obliged to consult about the dismissals with the persons who are the appropriate representatives of any of the employees who may be dismissed. The obligation on the employer is to begin the consultation in good time, and in any event if he is proposing to dismiss 100 or more employees there must be at least 90 days consultation before the first dismissals take effect and in the case of more than 20 dismissals there must be at least 20 days consultation: s. 188(1)(1A).

Until the relevant provisions relating to redundancy consultation were amended in 1995, there was an obligation on the employer to consult with a recognised trade union even in the case of a single redundancy. When the Collective Redundancies and Transfer of Undertakings (Protection of Employment) (Amendment) Regulations 1995 came into force a number of trade unions sought to challenge them by way of judicial review so as to prevent changes to the principal statute. Such attempts were rejected in *R.* v. *Secretary of State for Trade and Industry ex p. UNISON* (1996).

The employer, in the consultation, shall consult on such matters as ways of avoiding the dismissals, how to reduce the numbers of employees to be dismissed and how to mitigate the consequences of the dismissals. Under s. 1882(2) this 'shall be undertaken by the employer with a view to reaching agreement with the appropriate representatives.' Section 188(1B) defines appropriate representatives of the employee as

'(a) employee representatives elected by them, or
(b) if the employees are of a description in respect of which an independent trade union is recognised by the employer, representatives of the trade union, or . . . either employee representatives elected by them, or representatives of the trade union, as the employer chooses.'

Under s. 196 persons are employee representatives if

(a) they have been elected by employees for the specific purpose of being consulted by their employer about dismissals proposed by him, or

(b) have been elected by employees, other than for that specific purpose, and it is appropriate to consult them about dismissals proposed by the employer.

The consequence is that, unlike before the Collective Redundancies and Transfer of Undertakings (Protection of Employment) (Amendment) Regulations 1995 which amended the consultation provisions dramatically, the requirement to consult applies to any employer intending to make 20 or more people redundant and not just to those who recognise a trade union. Even where the employer recognises a trade union he has the choice as to which representatives to consult if s. 188(1B) applies. Note that the obligation to consult applies whether the particular employees are entitled to a redundancy payment or not: *see Association of University Teachers* v. *University of Newcastle-upon-Tyne* (1987), where although the employee in question was not entitled to a redundancy payment (he was employed on a three-year fixed-term contract and had agreed in writing to waive his redundancy rights in the case of non-renewal of the contract) it was held that the employer had to consult with the union where the contract was not renewed because of redundancy. In any case consultation must begin 'in good time'.

It should be remembered that the amended s. 188 provdes that consultation shall 'be undertaken by the employer with a view to reaching agreement with the appropriate representatives'.

In consulting the trade union representatives, the employer must disclose certain information. Under s. 188(4) the employer must provide the following initial information, in writing:

The reasons for the proposed redundancies.
The numbers and descriptions of employees whom it is proposed to dismiss as redundant.
The total number of employees of any such description employed by the employer at the establishment in question.
The proposed method of selecting the employees who may be dismissed.

The proposed method of carrying out the dismissals, with due regard to any agreed procedure, including the period over which the dismissals are to take effect.

The proposed method of calculating any redundancy payments to be made.

If the employer can show that there were 'special circumstances', e.g. the fact that the employer was genuinely hoping to find a buyer for the business: *APAAC* v. *Kirvin Ltd* (1978), which made it not 'reasonably practicable' for the employer to comply with the obligation to consult, he need only take such steps as are reasonably practicable in the circumstances: *see Bakers' Union* v. *Clarks of Hove Ltd* (1978) and *USDAW* v. *Leancut Bacon Ltd* (1981).

18. Failure to consult

If the employer fails to consult as required, the employee representatives or trade union, as the case may be, may present a complaint to an industrial tribunal to that effect. If the tribunal finds the complaint well-founded it must make a declaration to that effect; it may also make a 'protective award' i.e. an award directing that those employees concerned be paid for a specified period (the 'protected period') not exceeding ninety days or thirty days depending on whether the proposed redundancies relate to more than 100 or more than 20 employees. If the employer fails to pay remuneration under a protective award, an individual employee may present a complaint to an industrial tribunal which, if it finds the complaint well-founded, will order the employer to comply. For a consideration of the basis on which a protective award is made, *see Talke Fashions Ltd* v. *ASTWKT* (1977). It should reflect the loss suffered by the employees and not be used to penalise the employer for his failure to consult. *See also Spillers-French (Holdings) Ltd* v. *USDAW* (1980) and *GKN Sankey Ltd* v. *NSMM* (1980).

19. Notification of redundancies

If an employer is proposing to dismiss as redundant more than a hundred employees at one establishment within ninety days, or more than twenty employees within thirty days, he must notify the Secretary of State for Employment of this ninety or thirty days before the first of such dismissals takes effect, unless there are 'special circumstances' preventing compliance with this (in which case all such steps as are reasonably practicable must be taken).

If an employer fails to comply with this requirement then, by virtue of s. 194, the employer commits an offence and is liable to a fine on summary conviction.

TIME OFF WORK TO LOOK FOR NEW EMPLOYMENT

20. General principle

An employee who has been dismissed by reason of redundancy is entitled to have 'reasonable' time off work with pay during the period of notice to look for new employment or to make arrangements for training for future employment: s. 52 of the 1996 Act. To be eligible for this right, an employee must have been continuously employed (*see* 2:**15**) for two years at the date on which the notice is due to expire. The employee does not have to provide the employer with evidence of interviews or appointments before being entitled to exercise the right to time off work for this purpose: *Dutton* v. *Hawker Siddeley Aviation Ltd* (1978).

21. Complaint to industrial tribunal

If an employer refuses to allow an employee time off or fails to pay him for it, a complaint may be presented to an industrial tribunal, normally within three months. The tribunal, if it finds the complaint well-founded, may award compensation of up to two-fifths of a week's pay.

15

TRANSFER OF UNDERTAKINGS

INTRODUCTION

References in this chapter are to the Transfer of Undertakings (Protection of Employment) Regulations 1981 as amended by the Trade Union Reform and Employment Rights Act 1993 and the Collective Redundancies and Transfer of Undertakings (Protection of Employment) (Amendment) Regulations 1995.

1. Background

This chapter is concerned with the legal consequences for the employees of a business when the business is sold. The old common law rule was set out by the House of Lords in *Nokes* v. *Doncaster Amalgamated Collieries Ltd* (1940) and was to the effect that, under the then prevailing notions of freedom of contract, nothing was transferable by a company that was not transferable by an individual: and in particular '... no one (has) suggested that contracts of service could be transferred' (per Lord Atkin). Such a position can, of course, work considerable hardship on an employee because at common law the person to whom the business was transferred was under no obligation to offer employment to any of the original employees. In such circumstances the only remedy available to an employee, at least after the enactment of the Redundancy Payments Act 1965, would be to claim a redundancy payment from the employer.

The Council of Ministers of the European Community adopted the Social Action Programme in 1974 and this in turn led to the adoption of the Acquired Rights Directive (77/187/EEC) in 1977. The main purpose of this Directive was to protect the rights of employees in the case of the change of ownership of a business. This Directive led, in turn, to the implementation of the Transfer of Undertakings (Protection of Employment) Regulations 1981. Interpretation of the Regulations has not been without difficulty, and a number of amendments were made by the 1993 Act. These brought the Regulations more closely into line with the requirements of the Directive, although there are still some important differences between them. The Regulations are complex and, although their practical consequences may not be as significant as was feared by some at the time of their original implementation, they have given rise to some important and far-reaching litigation.

2. Scheme of the Regulations

The main purpose of the Regulations is to ensure that on a relevant transfer the contracts of employment of individual employees are not terminated. The way they achieve this is as follows:

(a) The Regulations apply to a transfer of an undertaking from one person to another, whether the transfer is effected by sale of the undertaking or otherwise: Reg. 3.

(b) A relevant transfer shall not operate so as to terminate the contract of employment of any person employed by the transferor or in the undertaking and all the transferor's rights, powers, duties and liabilities shall be transferred to the transferee: Reg. 5(1),(2). However, if the employee informs the transferor or the transferee that he objects to becoming employed by the transferee, then the transfer of the undertaking operates so as to terminate his contract of employment with the transferor – but this is not treated as a dismissal: Reg. 5(4A), (4B).

(c) Where at the time of a relevant transfer there exists a collective agreement made between the transferor and a trade union recognised by the transferor in respect of employees whose contract of employment is preserved in the transfer, the provisions of that collective agreement survive the transfer in respect of those employees: Reg. 6.

(d) Where, either before or after a relevant transfer, any employee of the transferor or transferee is dismissed, that employee shall be treated as unfairly dismissed if the transfer, or a reason connected with it, is the reason or the principal reason for the dismissal: Reg. 8(1). However, where there is an economic, technical or organisational reason which entails changes to the workforce of the transferor or transferee and results in the dismissal of the employee, the reason shall be regarded as being for a substantial reason of a kind such as to justify dismissal: Reg. 8(2).

(e) There is a duty to consult with appropriate representatives of affected employees about the fact that a transfer is to take place, when it is to happen, the reasons for it and the legal, economic and social implications for the affected employees: Reg. 10.

3. Meaning of 'undertaking'

The Regulations apply to the transfers of 'undertakings'. These are further defined in Regulations 2(1) and 2(2) as including 'any trade or business' and to 'part of an undertaking'. Following amendments made by the 1993 Act it is clear that 'trade or business' can refer to non-commercial undertakings. This now renders obsolete a number of cases decided prior to 1993 on the question of whether a particular activity was commercial or not. The only significant issue with which a court may be faced today on the question of what constitutes an undertaking is whether or not there is some economic entity which has been transferred: *see Sophie Redmond Stichting* v. *Bartol* (1992). In the situation where part of an

171

undertaking is transferred, the essential issue is whether that part is being 'transferred as a business'. In *Secretary of State for Employment* v. *Spence* (1986) the Court of Appeal held that it is not vital to the existence of an undertaking that it has a workforce – accordingly, where the workforce has been dismissed in the morning but the business has been transferred in the afternoon, there was nevertheless the transfer of an undertaking. However, in interpreting the provisions of the Acquired Rights Directive, the ECJ has held that in order to constitute a transfer of an undertaking the transfer must relate to a stable economic entity whose activity is not limited to the carrying out of a single fixed-term contract: *see Rygaard* v. *Strø Mølle Akustik A/S* (1986). This decision was considered by the EAT in *BSG Property Services* v. *Tuck* (1996). In this case the applicant was employed by the Direct Services Organisation of Mid-Bedfordshire District Council. The DSO decided to terminate the contract for housing maintenance and gave notice to terminate the contract of employment of the applicant on 15 May on the basis of there no longer being any work for him to do. On 14 May the District Council had reached agreement with BSG for housing maintenance. Both the Council and BSG believed there was no transfer of an undertaking and the applicant was not engaged by BSG. The EAT held that the activities of the DSO constituted an undertaking capable of being transferred for the purposes of the Regulations; the requirement of a 'stable economic entity' referred to in the *Rygaard* case covers short-term, one-off contracts rather than the continuing and recurrent maintenance activities with which the present case was concerned. Accordingly the EAT went on to hold that the dismissal was unfair.

RELEVANT TRANSFERS

4. Relevant transfer

The Regulations apply whether the transfer is effected by sale or by some other disposition, and an undertaking can be transferred by a series of transactions. It should be noted that by defining a 'transfer' in terms of a transfer of an undertaking from one person to another the Regulations do not deal with the situation where ownership of a company may change by share transfer. Because the company has a separate legal identity its identity as an employer does not change in such circumstances.

There have been a number of important ECJ decisions, dealing with the Directive, which have provided important indications as to what is meant by the transfer of a business:

(a) 'It is necessary to determine whether what has been sold is an economic entity which is still in existence . . .' (*Spijkers* v. *Gebroeders Benedik Abattoir CV* (1986)).

(b) '. . . (The) decisive criterion for establishing whether there is a transfer within the meaning of the Directive is whether the business retains its identity, as would be indicated, in particular, by the fact that its operation was either continued or resumed. . . .' (*Rask and Christensen* v. *ISS Kantineservice A/S* (1993); *see also Securicor Guarding Ltd* v. *Fraser Security Services Ltd* (1996)).

(c) However, the reorganisation of administrative functions as between one public authority and another does not constitute the transfer of an undertaking within the terms of the Directive: *see Henke* v. *Gemeinde Schierke and Verwaltungsgemeinschaft 'Brocken'* (1996).

There have been a large number of decisions in the UK in recent years which have addressed the question of what is meant by a relevant transfer within the meaning of the Regulations. The criteria used by the tribunals have been along the following lines:

> '. . . it is necessary to take into account all the surrounding circumstances . . . and to see whether there is a recognisable economic entity, a going concern (this can include the provision of services) which is run or operated or carried on by the alleged transferor and which is being continued by the alleged transferee . . . One must look at the substance of what has occurred and not the form; it is a transfer or transmission or translation of the economic entity, the going concern' (EAT in *Wren* v. *Eastbourne Borough Council and UK Waste Control Ltd* (1993).

However, in *Dines* v. *Initial Health Care Services* (1995) the question was whether there had been a transfer in the situation where the contracts of employees were terminated on the grounds of redundancy where, following a competitive tendering process, a cleaning contract had been awarded to another company. The employees argued that there had been a relevant transfer, but the industrial tribunal had found that, although the provision of cleaning services constituted an undertaking within the meaning of Regulation 2(1), the termination of the cleaning contract following competitive tendering meant that the business of the employers ceased and a new business commenced when the new company was awarded the contract. Thus it found that there was no transfer of an undertaking. This was overturned by the Court of Appeal which said that where one company took over the provision of services from another company as a result of competitive tendering, the business or undertaking of the first company did not necessarily come to an end. The Court of Appeal said that the facts of the case indicated a transfer of an undertaking and that this had happened in two phases – the return by the employers of the cleaning services to the authority and, then, the grant of the services by the authority to the new company the following day. This approach was followed by the EAT in *Isles of Scilly Council* v. *Brintel Helicopters Ltd* (1995) where the following test was set out:

> 'The decisive criterion for establishing whether there has been a transfer is whether the business in question retains its identity following the event alleged to constitute the transfer (the relevant events). Retention of identity is indicated, *inter alia*, by examining whether the activities which were carried out before the relevant events are being carried out afterwards in the same or similar manner. In other words, one should examine the similarity between the work done before and after relevant events and the identity of those carrying out the work . . .'

The formulation in the above case indicates the very flexible approach which is taken by the tribunals in determining whether or not there has been a transfer. It does not matter that there has been no goodwill transferred because one business has come to an end and another one has started up. An important issue, as indicated in the *Brintel Helicopters* case, is whether the work which was done before the relevant events continues afterwards; the fact that the business is 'labour only' does not prevent it from being transferred. The EAT stressed that in considering these issues it should be borne in mind that it is necessary to take a purposive approach towards the interpretation of the Regulations, so as to ensure, as far as possible, that the rights of the employees are safeguarded in the event of a change of employer by allowing them to remain in employment with the new employer on the terms and conditions which have been agreed with the transferor.

5. A series of two or more transactions

Under Regulation 3(4) it is declared that a transfer of an undertaking may be effected by a series of two or more transactions. The meaning of this was considered by the EAT in *Longden* v. *Ferrari Ltd and Kennedy International Ltd* (1994). Administrative receivers were appointed to F Ltd; K Ltd was interested in purchasing some or all of F Ltd's undertaking, but K Ltd was unable to conclude a binding agreement as swiftly as the receivers wished because of lack of information. The receivers threatened to close down the whole undertaking, dismissing all the staff, so K Ltd agreed to pay them £4,000 to keep F Ltd operational for a further week. L was dismissed by the receivers; negotiations continued with K Ltd and two weeks later the undertaking was transferred to K Ltd. L's claim for unfair dismissal failed before an industrial tribunal, on the grounds that the transfer had been effected at the end of the two-week period, rather than by a series of two or more transactions beginning prior to the dismissal. Accordingly the industrial tribunal held that L was not employed by F Ltd immediately before the transfer and thus could not claim for unfair dismissal against K Ltd. The EAT confirmed the decision of the industrial tribunal. It found that there had been a succession of events which could be loosely described as causally linked to one another and to the ultimate agreement of sale, but that is not sufficient for the language of the Regulations. They require that the transfer is 'effected' by the series of transactions – in this case the transfer was not effected by a series of transactions; it was effected by the single agreement.

EFFECT ON CONTRACTS OF EMPLOYMENT

6. Effect of relevant transfer on contracts of employment

Other than where an employee objects, a relevant transfer does not operate so as to terminate contracts of employment; what happens is that any contract which would otherwise have been terminated by the transfer now has effect as if originally made between the employee and the transferee. Regulation 5(2)(a) specifically provides that 'all the transferor's rights, powers, duties and liabilities under or in connection with . . . (the contract of employment) . . . shall be transferred . . . to the transferee.' The force of this Regulation was demonstrated by the EAT in *Wilson* v. *St Helens Borough Council* (1996) in a controversial decision. There had been a transfer of an undertaking between Lancashire County Council and St Helens Borough Council and at the time of the transfer changes to the terms and conditions of employment of the employees affected by the transfer were made by the transferee. The EAT held that if the operative reason for the variation in the contracts of employment is the transfer of the undertaking then the variation would be ineffective. There was no evidence in the case that the reason for the variation was anything other than the transfer itself – there was no subsequent separate agreement varying the terms of the employment after the transfer. The employer's argument, that the subsequent conduct of the employees was consistent with their affirmation of the variation, was rejected on the basis that, if there can be no agreement to vary terms and conditions by reason of the transfer, there cannot be any subsequent effective affirmation of that variation. It remained prohibited by the Regulations; *see also Foreningen af Arbejdsledere i Danmark* v. *Daddy's Dance Hall A/S* (1988); *Meade* v. *British Nuclear Fuels Ltd* (1996).

7. Persons employed immediately before the transfer

Under Regulation 5(3) the protection afforded to employees by the Regulation is afforded to a person employed 'immediately before the transfer'. The courts and tribunals have had some difficulty in interpreting these words. In *Secretary of State for Employment* v. *Spence* (1986) the Court of Appeal had to deal with the situation where employees were dismissed in the morning and the business was sold to a purchaser in the afternoon. Some of the employees claimed redundancy payments against the Secretary of State, as the original employer was insolvent. The Secretary of State argued that the liability to make the payments had passed to the purchaser of the business. The Court of Appeal held that the employees were not employed immediately before the relevant transfer and held that the Regulation relates only to contracts which subsist at the moment of transfer. Accordingly, the liability to make a redundancy payment rested with the Secretary of State. This decision is a troublesome one. By giving a very strict interpretation to the words of the Regulation the Court of Appeal has reduced the protection available to individual employees, which is, of course, the overriding purpose of the Regulations.

The House of Lords distinguished the *Spence* case in *Litster* v. *Forth Dry Dock and Engineering Co. Ltd* (1989). The employer went into liquidation and at 15.30 the employee was summarily dismissed. Later on the same day the assets of the business were purchased and some of the employees of the original employer were re-employed by the purchaser – but not the applicant. One issue before the House of Lords was whether the applicant was employed 'immediately before the transfer' for the purpose of an unfair dismissal claim. The House of Lords read into Regulation 5(3) additional words so as to insert after the words 'immediately before the transfer' the words 'or would have been so employed if he had not been unfairly dismissed'. The House of Lords felt that such a reading of the Regulation is entirely consistent with the overall scheme of the Regulations and is necessary to fulfil effectively the purpose for which they were made, i.e. giving effect to the Acquired Rights Directive. In interpreting Regulation 5(3) in this way the House of Lords did not criticise the decision in *Spence*, but distinguished it on the basis that in that case the employment of the employee was terminated before the actual transfer took place for a reason unconnected with the transfer.

8. Objection by the employee

Under Regulation 5(4A) it is provided that Regulation 5 shall not operate to transfer a contract of employment where the employee informs the transferor or transferee that he objects to becoming employed by the transferee. Where such an objection is made Regulation 5(4B) provides that the employee's contract will be regarded as terminated, but he shall *not* be regarded as having been dismissed by the transferor. These provisions were considered by the EAT in *Hay* v. *George Hanson (Building Contractors) Ltd* (1996). The EAT had some difficulty in interpreting the meaning of the word 'object', but nevertheless found that these particular provisions do not need to be approached in any artificial way. What is intended is to protect the right of the employee not to be transferred to another employer against his will; in this context the EAT construed the word 'object' as effectively meaning a refusal to accept the transfer, and that state of mind must be conveyed to the transferor or transferee. There is no particular procedure by which this needs to be done – it can be by either word or deed (or both) and each case must be looked at on its own facts to determine whether there was a sufficient state of mind to amount to a refusal to consent to the transfer. This does not mean that employees cannot *protest* about a proposed transfer without running the risk that this will be interpreted as an objection. The EAT found that to protest in advance of a transfer will not amount to an objection under the Regulations unless it is translated into an actual refusal to consent. This limitation is extremely important given the serious consequences of objection for an individual employee.

DISMISSAL

9. Dismissal on transfer

Under Regulation 8 it is provided that where, either before or after a relevant transfer, any employee of the transferee is dismissed for a reason connected with the transfer, the employee shall be treated as unfairly dismissed. However, under Regulation 8(2) where there is an economic, technical or organisational reason which entails changes in the workforce of either the transferor or the transferee, which is the reason for the dismissal, then that shall be regarded for the purposes of unfair dismissal law as being a substantial reason for the dismissal. This does not, of course, abrogate the responsibility of the employer to demonstrate that he has acted reasonably in dismissing for that reason.

As with many other aspects of these Regulations, the tribunals have struggled with the problem of interpreting unusual statutory language which has been imported from European law. The words 'economic, technical or organisational' sit uneasily in a UK statute. In *Gateway Hotels Ltd* v. *Stewart* (1988) it was made clear that the onus of proof is on the employer to establish an economic reason and it is not sufficient to deal with such matters in general terms. Illustrations of the ways in which the defence has been used are:

- An economic reason for dismissal was established when the transferee realised shortly after the transfer that the business could not be run economically with the original number of staff: *see Meikle* v. *McPhail* (1983).
- If the employer dismisses the employee believing that no transfer has occurred, the fact that there *may* have been an economic reason for the dismissal is irrelevant: *see BSG Property Services* v. *Tuck* (1996).
- Economic reasons must relate to the conduct of the business. However, if the economic reason is no more than a desire to obtain an enhanced price or to achieve a sale, it is not a reason which relates to the conduct of the business: *see Wheeler* v. *Patel and Golding* (1987).

10. Employer's duty to inform and consult with appropriate representatives

Under Regulation 10 it is the duty of an employer to consult with the appropriate representatives of employees who may be affected by the transfer. The employer is obliged to inform the representatives of the fact that the transfer is to take place, when and why it is taking place, the legal, social and economic implications for the affected employees, and any measures which will be taken in respect of those employees. For the meaning of 'appropriate representatives' *see* 14:17. If the employer fails to comply with Regulation 10 a complaint may be presented to an industrial tribunal by the appropriate representatives, or employees who are affected. The employer has a defence if he can show that there were special circumstances which rendered it not reasonably practicable to inform or consult and that he took all such steps which were reasonably practicable in the circumstances. The tribunal may make a declaration and 'order the employer to pay appropriate compensation' to affected employees.

16

SAFETY AND HEALTH AT WORK

INTRODUCTION

1. Introduction

The law relating to the safety and health of workers is derived from two sources:

(a) The common law principles developed by the courts with certain statutory interventions.

(b) The statutory provisions. Note should be made of the increasing number of provisions emanating from the EC (see Working Time Directive, 6:**13** above).

THE COMMON LAW

2. General principle

An employer owes a duty to his employees to provide a safe system of work: *Wilsons and Clyde Coal Co. Ltd* v. *English* (1938). If this duty is breached by the employer, and he has no defence available (*see* **8** below) he will be liable in damages to the injured employee. If an employee is injured by the negligence of a fellow employee, the employer may be liable on the basis of vicarious liability (*see* 2:**10**).

The employer's obligation may be divided into several aspects:

(a) duty to provide competent staff

(b) duty to provide a proper system of working

(c) duty to provide safe work premises

(d) duty to provide safe working equipment

(e) duty to provide adequate safety and protective equipment.

3. Duty to provide competent staff

If an incompetent employee injures a fellow workman an employer has failed to meet this duty and he will be liable to the injured employee, irrespective of any question of vicarious liability. It is no defence for an employer to say that he has delegated the selection of staff to another person.

4. Duty to provide a proper system of working

The employer must ensure that the method of work is safe. Thus he is normally regarded as being under an obligation to give adequate training in the work to be done, warning as to potential risks and dangers. However, if an operation is simple or if the particular employee has done a job on a number of occasions or the employer has given proper instructions, the employer may be relieved of liability: *Winter* v. *Cardiff RDC* (1950), *Wilson* v. *Tyneside Window Cleaning Co.* (1958).

A further aspect of this duty was discussed by the Court of Appeal in the case of *Johnstone* v. *Bloomsbury Health Authority* (1991). In this case a senior house officer employed in a hospital was required to work a standard week of 40 hours, but was also contractually required to be 'on call' for a further 48 hours a week. The court expressed the opinion that the employers could not require the doctor to work so much overtime as it was reasonably foreseeable that he might damage his health irrespective of the express terms of the contract of employment. Note that doctors are exempt from the provisions of the Working Time Directive (see 6:**13** above).

There has been a further recent development in this area. In *Walker* v. *Northumberland County Council* (1995) the High Court ruled that the implied term of the contract relating to a proper system of working related to the mental, as well as physical, system of working. Therefore the failure of the employer to relieve the workload of a social services manager who had already suffered one nervous breakdown, which then led to a second breakdown, was held to be in breach of this obligation. The decision is an important one in the context of the duty imposed on the employer in this regard.

5. Duty to provide safe work premises

An employer must take all reasonable steps to ensure that the working premises are as safe as possible: *Latimer* v. *AEC Ltd* (1953).

6. Duty to provide safe working equipment

At common law, distinctions were made between equipment obtained from a reputable supplier and otherwise and custom-built and standard equipment. These distinctions were removed by the Employers' Liability (Defective Equipment) Act 1969. The basic provision of the Act is that where an employee suffers personal injury in the course of his employment as a result of a defect in equipment provided by his employer for the purposes of the employer's business, and the defect is attributable wholly or partly to the fault of a third party (e.g. the manufacturer), the employer is liable to the employee. It should be noted that an employer who incurs liability by virtue of the Act may be able to claim from the manufacturer and/or the supplier. The provisions of the Act cannot be excluded by a contract of employment but the defence of contributory negligence is available to the employer (*see* **8** below).

7. Duty to provide adequate safety and protective equipment

In providing such equipment, the employer is expected to keep up with latest developments but it appears that the trend of the decisions has been to limit the meaning of the word 'provide' in this context.

In *Clifford* v. *Challen and Son Ltd* (1951) it was held that the employer had failed to provide safety equipment where it was only available if the employee walked to the works' store which was situated some distance from the actual work-place.

In *James* v. *Hepworth and Grandage Ltd* (1968) it was held that where an employer put up a notice about safety equipment (which the plaintiff was unable to read), this was sufficient for him to say he had performed his duty.

DEFENCES AVAILABLE TO THE EMPLOYER

8. Defences available to the employer

There are four circumstances in which the employer may be relieved of liability, either wholly or in part:

(a) *No negligence proved.* The employee must establish negligence by the employer without which the employer is not liable. Similarly, if the employer shows that the injury occurred because of some reason other than his negligence, he may escape legal responsibility: *see McWilliams* v. *Arrol & Co. Ltd* (1962).

(b) *Delegation of duty.* An employer may seek to defend an action by alleging that he has delegated the responsibility for performing the duty to a third party (e.g. an outside contractor) or to the employee himself. It appears that such a defence is no longer available although where the employer alleges that he has delegated the duty to the injured employee himself, this *may* indicate contributory negligence on the part of the employee (*see below*).

(c) *Volenti non fit injuria.* This defence occurs where the defendant alleges that the plaintiff consented to accept the risk of injury which in fact resulted, e.g. a boxer injured by a punch in a contest. In the context of employment, the courts today are extremely reluctant to permit reliance on this defence, although in extreme cases the defence may apply.

In *Imperial Chemical Industries Ltd* v. *Shatwell* (1965) three employees, experienced shot-firers, had specific instructions as to the manner of performing their work. In disregard of these instructions, two of the employees fired a shot causing injury to both of them. Held by the House of Lords: the action in respect of the injuries failed because, in view of the gross disobedience of the employees, the defence of *volenti non fit injuria* must be applied.

Note: When the defence succeeds, the entire action fails.

(d) *Contributory negligence*. The Law Reform (Contributory Negligence) Act 1945 provides that where an injured person has contributed to the injury by his own fault, his claim is not defeated (as was the position prior to the Act) but the damages awarded are reduced to 'such extent as the court thinks just and equitable having regard to the claimant's share in the responsibility for the damage'. It should be noted that in the sphere of industrial accidents the courts are often reluctant to make a finding of contributory negligence by an employee.

COMPULSORY INSURANCE

9. Compulsory insurance

Under the Employers' Liability (Compulsory Insurance) Act 1969, every employer carrying on business in Great Britain must maintain an approved insurance policy against bodily injury or disease sustained by an employee in circumstances where such injury or disease is deemed to 'arise out of and in the course of employment'. Copies of the insurance certificate must be displayed at the place of business. Failure to comply with the requirements of the Act is punishable by fine. Recently the Court of Appeal confirmed that breach of this duty does not give rise to a civil action: *Richardson* v. *Pitt-Stanley* (1995).

THE STATUTORY PROVISIONS

References in **10–24** below are, unless otherwise stated, to the Health and Safety at Work etc. Act 1974.

10. Scope of legislation

Prior to the passing of the Health and Safety at Work etc. Act 1974, which is largely based upon the recommendations of the Committee on Safety at Work chaired by Lord Robens (Cmnd. 5034), there was no legislation of general application relating to health and safety at work. Instead, legislation was based on the different kinds of places of work, e.g. Factories Act 1961; Offices, Shops and Railway Premises Act 1963; Mines and Quarries Act 1954 and, as such, a number of kinds of places of work fell outside the scope of any legislation. With the passing of the 1974 Act, although the previous legislation remains in force until such time as it is replaced by new regulations, virtually all persons who are at work or who are affected by work activities are now within the scope of legislation. In addition to imposing duties on employers, employees and the self-employed, the 1974 Act also places obligations upon manufacturers, suppliers, designers and importers of articles and substances used at work.

11. Nature of the legislation

The 1974 Act is essentially concerned with criminal sanctions (as opposed to the recovery of damages following an accident) which can apply even though no accident has occurred; the issue is whether the obligation has been broken. It is specifically provided that a breach of the 'general duties' (*see* **12** below) shall not give rise to civil liability but that breach of any regulation made under the Act (*see* **18** below) shall, unless otherwise stated, do so: s. 47.

The emphasis of the Act is towards prevention of accidents, and accordingly new powers have been given to the inspectors (*see* **20** below). The intention is also that industry should be self-regulating to a large extent (i.e. deal with its own problems) and, to this end, a system of safety representatives and safety committees has been introduced (*see* **13** below).

GENERAL STATUTORY DUTIES

12. Introductory

The 1974 Act imposes general duties on a number of different categories of persons. Most of these duties are qualified in that the obligation extends to that which is 'reasonably practicable'. The effect of this is to allow the person on whom the duty is placed to balance, on the one hand, the expense and effort involved in meeting that duty with, on the other, the risk involved: *Edwards* v. *NCB* (1949). Note, however, that it is for a person who alleges he has done that which is 'reasonably practicable' to establish it: s. 40.

13. Duties of employers

It is the duty of every employer to ensure so far as is reasonably practicable, the health, safety and welfare at work of his employees. In particular, he must have regard to:

(a) The provision and maintenance of plant and systems of work. In the case of *Tesco Stores* v. *Seabridge* (1988) the fact that two or three out of four screws were missing from a protective panel which covered live electric wires made a breach of s. 2 of the Act self-evident.

(b) The use, handling, storage and transport of articles and substances.

(c) The provision of information, instruction, training and supervision.

(d) The maintenance of the place of work and the provision and maintenance of means of access to and egress from such places.

(e) The provision and maintenance of a healthy and safe working environment and adequate welfare facilities and arrangements.

It can thus be seen that the common law obligations of employers are now, in broad terms, also contained in the criminal law. *See R.* v. *Swan Hunter Shipbuilders Ltd* (1981).

In addition, every employer, except those who employ less than five employees, has a duty to prepare (or revise) and bring to the notice of his employees, a written statement of his general policy with respect to the health and safety of his employees and the organisation and arrangements for carrying out that policy: *see Osborne* v. *Bill Taylor of Huyton Ltd* (1982).

The employer has additional obligations as regards safety representatives and safety committees, namely to consult with safety representatives. The Health and Safety (Consultation with Employees) Regulations 1996 now requires that this consultation must take place with elected worker representatives and not just with recognised trade unions (*see* 16:**5**). Such elected representatives are for health and safety purposes only. Finally the Regulations allow for consultation to take place with employees directly on health and safety issues. Therefore the whole workforce could be consulted as there is no small firm exclusion. The new Regulations run in parallel with the existing provisions. Such representatives have a number of powers including the right to inspect the work premises and to require the establishment of a safety committee: *see* the Safety Representatives and Safety Committee Regulations 1977 (SI 1977 No. 500) and the Code of Practice on Safety Representatives issued by the Health and Safety Commission. In addition the Regulations provide that safety representatives are to be allowed paid time off work 'for the purpose of undergoing such training … as may be reasonable in all the circumstances': reg. 4(2). (*See White* v. *Pressed Steel Fisher* (1980).)

No employer shall levy any charge on an employee in respect of anything done or provided in pursuance of the employer's statutory obligations: s. 9.

In addition to his obligations towards employees every employer has a duty to conduct his undertaking in such a way that persons not in his employment (i.e. outside contractors, other persons lawfully on his premises and the general public) are not exposed to risks to their health or safety. In *R.* v. *British Steel plc* (1995) the Court of Appeal held that the duty to persons, not in its employment, could not be delegated. British Steel were held liable for breach of the Act even though the incident had occurred as a result of the actions of two independent contractors who had not followed instructions properly. The decision illustrates the absolute nature of the obligation imposed by the Act. Furthermore, in prescribed cases, it is the duty of every employer to give such persons certain information about the way in which he conducts his undertaking.

14. Duties of the self-employed

It is the duty of every self-employed person to conduct his undertaking in such a way as to ensure, so far as is reasonably practicable, that he and other persons (not being his employees) are not exposed to risks to their health and safety. Furthermore, in prescribed cases, it is the duty of every self-employed person to provide certain information about the way in which he conducts his undertaking.

15. Duties of those who control premises

Every person who has control of premises (other than domestic premises) must ensure, as far as is reasonably practicable, that all means of access and egress and any plant or substance in the premises are safe and without risks to health as regards those persons who use the premises as a place of work.

A person in control of prescribed premises must use the best practicable means for preventing the emission into the atmosphere of noxious or offensive substances and for rendering harmless such substances as may be emitted.

16. Duties of manufacturers etc.

Manufacturers, designers, suppliers and importers of articles and substances for use at work have a duty to ensure, as far as is reasonably practicable, that such articles and substances are so designed, constructed etc. as to be safe and without risks to health when properly used. It should be noted, however, that there is a limited right for the manufacturer, importer or supplier to escape his obligation as regards articles by obtaining a written undertaking from the other party that certain steps will be taken to ensure the safe use of the article in question. In addition, manufacturers etc. have obligations to carry out certain research, testing and examination of articles and substances and to provide certain information about articles and substances for use at work.

17. Duties of employees

Every employee at work has a duty:

(a) to take reasonable care for his own and other persons' health and safety, e.g. to use safety equipment provided; and

(b) to co-operate with his employer and any other person to enable them to perform their statutory duties.

HEALTH AND SAFETY REGULATIONS

18. Nature of regulations

The Secretary of State is given power to make regulations on a wide range of matters. In so doing the provisions of previous legislation which remain in force (*see* **10** above) will gradually be repealed and replaced by regulations made under the 'umbrella' of the 1974 Act. In making such regulations, the Secretary of State acts on the advice of the Health and Safety Commission (*see* 1:**33**). Breach of a regulation is punishable as a criminal offence and, except in so far as may otherwise be provided, may also give rise to civil liability.

The regulations may deal with a wide range of matters, the most important of which are:

(a) The repeal or modification of existing statutory provisions.

(b) The exclusion or modification of the general duties in relation to a specific class of case.

(c) Making a specified authority responsible for the enforcement of any statutory provision.

(d) The provision of exemptions from any requirement or prohibition.

(e) Specifying a class of person who may be guilty of an offence.

(f) The imposition of requirements and prohibitions in relation to the design, construction, manufacture, use etc. of articles and substances for use at work.

Therefore these regulations involve the whole range of matters dealt with in health and safety legislation.

CODES OF PRACTICE

(Sections 16 and 17.)

19. Purpose of Codes

In order to provide practical guidance to those persons who have obligations under the 1974 Act or other relevant statutory provisions, the Health and Safety Commission may approve and issue Codes of Practice with the consent of the Secretary of State. These Codes therefore clearly form an important part of the law relating to health and safety at work.

Breach of a provision of a Code does not of itself render a person liable to criminal or civil proceedings but, in criminal proceedings, the provisions of a Code of Practice are admissible in evidence to show that an offence has been committed. The same may also be true of civil proceedings.

ENFORCEMENT

(Sections 18–26.)

20. Enforcing authorities

In general terms, enforcement of the 1974 Act and the other statutory provisions lies with the Health and Safety Executive (see 1:35). However, the Secretary of State may require local authorities to enforce certain provisions.

All enforcing authorities have the power to appoint inspectors. Inspectors have a considerable number of powers including the right:

(a) to enter premises and make examinations and investigations

(b) to take samples of and detain articles and substances

(c) to require information to be given.

21. Improvement notice

If an inspector is of the opinion that a person is contravening a statutory provision or has done so and the contravention is likely to be continued or repeated, he may serve an improvement notice upon him. The notice must specify which provision and how it is being broken and requiring it to be remedied within a specified period of not less than twenty-one days. An appeal against such a notice may be made within twenty-one days to an industrial tribunal. The tribunal may cancel, affirm or amend the notice. The lodging of an appeal has the effect of suspending the operation of the notice until the appeal has been dealt with.

22. Prohibition notice

If an inspector considers that an activity involves a risk of serious personal injury, he may serve a prohibition notice directing that the activity in question cease until the matter is remedied. Such a notice may either take immediate effect or be deferred until the end of a specified period. An appeal against a prohibition notice may be made within twenty-one days to an industrial tribunal which has the power to cancel, affirm or amend it. The lodging of an appeal has the effect of suspending the operation of the notice only if the tribunal so directs.

OFFENCES AND PENALTIES

(Sections 33–42.)

23. Offences

A wide range of offences may be committed under the 1974 Act, the most important of which are contravening one of the general duties (*see* **12** above) or a health and safety regulation (*see* **18** above), preventing an inspector from carrying out his duties and contravening an improvement or prohibition notice. The list also includes a number of others, such as falsely pretending to be an inspector!

24. Penalties

Upon conviction in summary proceedings in the magistrates' court, the maximum punishment is a fine of £400 or, in certain cases, £1,000. If proceedings are brought upon indictment, the Crown Court may impose an unlimited fine and, in certain cases, a maximum of two years' imprisonment.

In addition, the court may order that the offence be remedied, e.g. by requiring an article or substance to be forfeited.

25. Victimisation on off-shore installations

A further piece of legislation has recently come into effect: the Off-shore Safety (Protection Against Victimisation) Act 1992. The Act was introduced as a result of the report into the Piper Alpha Disaster by Lord Cullen. The disaster concerned an explosion on an oil rig in which 165 workers died. The effect of the legislation is to protect employees working on off-shore installations against victimisation when acting as safety representatives or members of safety committees.

NO SMOKING POLICIES

One of the areas of development in employment law has been that of policies to deal with problems arising out of the employment relationship. Safety is no exception and in this respect no smoking policies need to be examined.

26. Why have such a policy?

In 1983 the Royal College of Physicians estimated that at least 90% of deaths from lung cancer and chronic bronchitis were due to smoking. Further the question of 'passive' smoking has received much recent publicity and the Independent Scientific Committee on Smoking and Health estimated that as a result of living with smokers, non-smokers have a 10–30% increased risk of contracting lung cancer.

27. Implementation

For a smoking policy to be introduced, the views of employees must be sought. Any policy must have available in it a series of smoking cessation programmes in order to help employees give up.

28. Resistance

What happens if a person fails to comply with a no smoking policy? Can that person be fairly dismissed? Two contrasting cases will illustrate the difficulties. In *Watson* v. *Cooke, Webb and Holton Ltd* (1984) it was held that the dismissal of W for failing to comply with a no smoking policy was unfair for two reasons. Firstly, the introduction of a no smoking rule represented the imposition of a completely new term of the contract which amounted to a fundamental breach of the original contract. Secondly, the method of implementation was unreasonable as W had not been consulted and alternatives were not examined.

The above must be compared with the decision in *Rogers* v. *Wicks and Wilson* (1988). It was held that R was not unfairly dismissed for failing to comply with a no smoking policy. Three reasons were given; firstly, there was no implied term allowing smoking as it was not essential to allow R to carry out his work. Secondly, even if smoking was a contractual term the employer, by giving four months notice, had acted lawfully by offering to re-engage on new terms. Finally, the employer had acted reasonably in imposing such a ban when there was increasing evidence showing the harmful effect of smoking.

Both the above are industrial tribunal cases and they need to be now looked at in the light of the Scottish EAT decision in *Dryden* v. *Greater Glasgow Health Board* (1992). D was a nursing auxiliary who smoked. Up to 1991 the employer had set aside areas for smoking. In 1991, after consultation, the employer decided to prohibit smoking. The employee resigned and claimed unfair dismissal on the ground that the introduction of the no-smoking policy amounted to a constructive dismissal. The EAT held that there was no implied term allowing her to smoke. Further it decided that the new policy amounted to a works rule which did not have contractual effect and so did not amount to constructive dismissal.

The case clearly shows the introduction of a no-smoking policy, provided a reasonable procedure is used, is not going to found an action of unfair dismissal.

RIGHTS AND OBLIGATIONS

29. Employee rights

Section 44 of Employment Rights Act (ERA) 1996 states that an employee has the right not to be subjected to any detriment by the employer if he or she carried out activities in connection with preventing/reducing risks to health and safety at work, having been designated by the employer to do so or performed function of a health and safety representative or member of a safety committee. Similar provision applies to dismissal or selection for redundancy: ss. 100 and 105 ERA 1996.

This principle is further supported by the House of Lords' decision in *R.* v. *Associated Octel Ltd* (1997) where it was held that an employer was responsible for the acts of an independent contractor as the duty under the Act could not be delegated. A number of cases have been decided on the application of these provisions. In *Barton* v. *Wandsworth Council* (1994) an employee was held to have been unfairly disciplined when he complained about the introduction of new working practices which he felt, as an ambulance driver, could affect the safety of the public. The EAT in *Tedeschi* v. *Hosiden Besson Ltd* (1995) stated that the burden of proof was on the employee to show he had been dismissed for health and safety reasons.

There are further grounds on which an employer cannot take action against an employee including leaving a place of work in circumstances which the employee believes to be dangerous. Such a situation would have to be judged with reference to all the circumstances.

30. Health and safety at work regulations

An important step was taken by the implementation of the Management of Health and Safety at Work Regulations 1992 [SI 2051 1992]. These are designed to implement the Framework (89/391/ EEC) and Temporary Workers (91/383/ EEC) Directives of the European Community. The regulations contain a number of important obligations for both employers and employees, which in summary are as follows:

(a) Employers shall make suitable assessment of the risks to the health and safety of employees and others affected by work activities.

(b) Employers shall make arrangements to ensure health and safety.

(c) Employers shall establish procedures to be followed in the event of serious and imminent dangers.

(d) Employers shall provide comprehensible and relevant information to employees on risks, preventive measures and emergency procedures.

(e) Employers shall ensure that employees are provided with adequate health and safety training on recruitment or when exposed to new or increased risks.

(f) Employees have duties to use equipment safely and to comply with the employer's instructions and restrictions.

The Regulations came into force in January 1993.

17

THE LAW RELATING TO TRADE UNIONS

References in this chapter are to the Trade Union and Labour Relations (Consolidation) Act 1992 – the 1992 Act.

INTRODUCTION

1. Scope of the chapter

In this chapter, consideration is given to the legal status of trade unions and to those legal rules which affect the relationship between a trade union and its members.

2. Definition

A 'trade union' is an organisation (whether permanent or temporary) which: 'consists wholly or mainly of workers of one or more descriptions and is an organisation whose principal purposes include the regulation of relations between workers of that description or those descriptions and employers or employers' associations': s. 1 of the 1992 Act.

It should be noted that organisations whose purposes include such functions are excluded from this definition if their principal purposes do not include them: *Midland Cold Storage* v. *Turner* (1972); *Carter* v. *Law Society* (1973).

3. Legal status

Under s. 10 of the 1992 Act a trade union 'shall not be, or be treated as if it were, a body corporate', i.e. it has no separate legal personality. Thus in *EETPU* v. *Times Newspapers* (1980) it was held that a trade union did not have sufficient personality to be capable of being defamed; nevertheless under s. 10 it is provided that a trade union may make contracts, sue and be sued in its own name and be prosecuted.

4. Administrative matters

A trade union is required to keep proper accounting records and to make an annual audited return to the Certification Officer: ss. 28–31 of the 1992 Act.

LISTING AND CERTIFICATION

5. Listing

As noted in 1:**18**, the Certification Officer maintains a list of trade unions which satisfy the definition given in **2** above. If the Certification Officer refuses to enter the name of an organisation on the list or proposes to remove it, an appeal may be made to the Employment Appeal Tribunal (*see* 1:**9**).

6. Certification as independent

Any trade union may apply to the Certification Officer for a certificate that it is an 'independent trade union': s. 6 of the 1992 Act. The Certification Officer grants such a certificate if he is satisfied that the union falls within the following definition:

> 'a trade union which—(a) is not under the domination or control of an employer or a group of employers or of one or more employers' associations; and (b) is not liable to interference by an employer or any such group or association (arising out of the provision of financial or material support or by any other means whatsoever) tending towards such control': s. 5 of the 1992 Act.

In deciding whether to grant such a certificate, the Certification Officer is concerned to ensure that the union has achieved genuine and effective freedom: *Blue Circle Staff Association* v. *Certification Officer* (1977); *Squibb United Kingdom Staff Association* v. *Certification Officer* (1979).

In *A. Monk & Co. Staff Association* v. *Certification Officer* (1980) an application from the staff association for a certificate of independence was rejected by the Certification Officer for a number of reasons. All the association's officers and members were employed by the same company; the association depended on facilities provided by the company (office premises, free check-off facilities and time-off for attendance at meetings) removal of which would make it difficult for the association to continue to function; the association had a weak negotiating record. The EAT allowed the appeal and ordered a certificate to be issued. It found that on balance the association was not vulnerable to interference, tending towards control, by the employer and that the association would be able to survive if the facilities provided by the employer were withdrawn. Although the collective bargaining record of the association had been based on methods more old-fashioned and less militant than those of other trade unions, there was evidence that the association had doggedly pursued its own methods and aims. If the Certification Officer refuses to grant a certificate, the union may appeal on a point of fact or law to the Employment Appeal Tribunal but no appeal will lie by a third party against the Certification Officer's decision to grant a certificate: *GMWU* v. *Certification Officer and Another* (1977).

7. Significance of independence

A certificate of independence is conclusive evidence in any proceedings of the fact that a trade union is independent: s. 8(1) of the 1992 Act. There are a number of important advantages in being an independent trade union (as opposed to being a non-independent union), the most important of which are as follows:

(a) The members and officials of independent trade unions have certain rights (*see* Chapter 8).

(b) Representatives of independent trade unions are entitled to have certain information disclosed to them (*see* 18:5).

(c) An employer must consult with the representatives of an independent trade union prior to dismissing employees as redundant (*see* 14:17).

(d) An independent trade union may apply for financial assistance in connection with certain secret ballots and may request that such a ballot be held on the employer's premises (*see* **16** below).

(e) An independent trade union has the right to be informed about and consulted about transfers of business under the Transfer of Undertakings (Protection of Employment) Regulations 1981 (*see* 18:8).

> *Note*: As a result of the Collective Redundancies and Transfer of Undertaking (Protection of Employment) (Amendment) Regulations 1995, and the Health and Safety (Consultation with Employees) Regulations 1996, the rights in **(b)**, **(c)** and **(e)** above are now extended to elected representatives as well as to trades unions.

THE POLITICAL FUND

8. Meaning of the term

The original rules relating to the application of the funds of a trade union for political purposes were established by the Trade Union Act 1913. Amendments to these rules have been introduced by the 1984, 1988 and 1990 Acts, all of which are now consolidated in the 1992 Act.

9. Consent of members required

A trade union must obtain the consent of its members before its funds may be used for specified political purposes and there must be a majority in favour of such a use. Section 3 of the TURER Act, 1993, introduces into the 1992 Act the same requirements as to security of political final ballots as those of union elections—see **16** below. A resolution to establish the fund must be passed in accordance with the rules approved by the Certification Officer (CO). Section 74 of the 1992 Act states that a ballot on a political resolution must be held in accordance with the rules of the trade union as approved by the CO.

Further, the 1992 Act requires that a trade union must ballot its members at least every 10 years on whether they wish to retain the political fund of the union. All members must be given the opportunity to vote. Section 75 of the 1992 Act requires that all ballots must be subject to independent scrutiny and that each voting paper must state the name and address of the independent scrutineer.

10. Disputes relating to the political fund

The 1992 Act gives the High Court jurisdiction to hear complaints about the conduct of a political fund ballot. Sections 80 and 81 of the 1992 Act extend the potential liability of a trade union in that a member can complain that either a ballot held or a proposed ballot breaks the rules laid down by the Certification Officer. The effect of a declaration that the union has failed to comply with the rules is that an enforcement order may be made requiring the union either to remedy the defect or hold an appropriate ballot.

11. The specified political objects

The specified political objects of the fund are contained in section 72 of the 1992 Act. The objects are:

(a) Contribution to the funds of, or payment of expenses incurred by, a political party.

(b) Provision of any service or property for use by a political party.

(c) The registration of electors or the selection of candidates for political office.

(d) The maintenance of any holder of a political office.

(e) The holding of any conference or meeting by or on behalf of a political party or of any other meeting at which business of a political party is transacted.

(f) The production, publication or distribution of political literature, film or advertisements which seek to persuade a person to vote for, or not vote for, a political party or candidate.

MEMBERSHIP AND RULES

12. Membership

Broadly speaking, it is for a trade union to determine who is eligible for membership of it and whether a person shall continue to be a member: *see Boulting* v. *ACTAT* (1963) *and Faramus* v. *Film Artistes' Association* (1964). However, a trade union must not, in exercising such rights, act contrary to the Sex

Discrimination Act 1975, s. 12 or the Race Relations Act 1976, s. 11. In addition, it would seem that a trade union must adhere to the rules of natural justice and thus cannot expel a member without giving him a right to be heard, proper notification of the charges against him and adequate opportunity to refute those charges. But *see Cheall* v. *APEX* (1983), discussed at **14** below. In addition, the person presenting the case against the member should not also be involved in the decision to expel him.

Section 69 of the 1992 Act provides that in every contract of membership of a trade union, there shall be an implied term by which the member, on giving reasonable notice and complying with any reasonable conditions, is entitled to terminate his membership of the union.

13. Rules

The rules of a trade union constitute a contract between the union and its members and thus, if they are broken, an individual member may seek redress in the courts. The miners' strike of 1984–85 brought sharply into focus the legal position of such rules, e.g. *Taylor* v. *NUM (Yorkshire Area)* (1985); *Taylor* v. *NUM (Derbyshire Area)* (1985); *Clarke* v. *Chadburn* (1985). The cases show that, as a general principle, the courts are prepared to intervene where there has been a breach of the rules. The majority of these cases concerned the position of working miners.

Section 64 of the 1992 Act strengthens the position of members in relation to the rules of a trade union. Section 64 states that members now have a right not to be unjustifiably disciplined by their union, and provides that discipline is unjustifiable for specified conduct. The specified conduct includes failure to participate in or support industrial action; making or intending to make a true allegation that the union has acted contrary to its rules; and seeking or proposing to seek advice or assistance from the Commissioner of Rights of Trade Union Members (*see* 1:**19**), the Certification Officer, or any other person. The 1993 Act amends the 1992 Act to add further items to this list including failing to agree, or withdrawing agreement, to the payment of union subscriptions via a check-off arrangement; becoming or proposing to become a member of another union and working, or proposing, to work with people who are not trade union members.

In *Knowles* v. *Fire Brigades Union* (1996) two full-time fire-fighters were disciplined by their union because they accepted, in breach of union policy, additional employment as retained (part-time) fire-fighters. The Court of Appeal held that the policy of the union did not amount to industrial action and therefore the union had not breached s. 64.

The section also talks of a member suffering 'any other detriment'. It has been decided that naming a person as a strike-breaker in a union publication may be a detriment: *National and Local Government Officers' Association* v. *Killorn and Simm* (1990). A further case concerning NALGO illustrates the strictness of the provisions. In *NALGO* v. *Courtney-Dunn* (1992) union members employed as social workers sought to be exempt from industrial action. They were expelled but then reinstated. However, they claimed compensation on the basis that the union had not done everything necessary to reinstate them as NALGO had not restored the check-off mandate. It was held that NALGO had failed in its duty and compensation was awarded accordingly.

A complaint may be made to an industrial tribunal, concerning the above, by virtue of s. 66 of the 1992 Act.

Section 63 of the 1992 Act further provides that where High Court proceedings relate to certain grievances which a member began to pursue against his union under its rules more than six months before applying to the court, the court is not to dismiss or adjourn the proceedings on the ground that further procedures for resolving the grievance are available under the union's rules.

14. The Bridlington Agreement

The Trade Union Congress agreed (at Bridlington) in 1939 a number of principles broadly designed to prevent 'poaching' of members of one union by another union. Where a breach of these principles is alleged the matter is referred to the Disputes Committee of the TUC which, if it finds the complaint proved, will usually order that the union in breach terminates the membership of the individual member.

Most trade unions incorporate a model rule into their constitution enabling them to terminate the membership of a member if that is necessary to give effect to a decision of the Disputes Committee. In *Cheall* v. *APEX* (1983) the House of Lords ruled that the requirements of public policy do not prevent trade unions from entering into arrangements which they consider to be in the interests of their members and such arrangements may include agreeing to be bound by a determination of the Disputes Committee. In addition it was held that there was no denial of natural justice in failing to allow the individual member to make representations on the matter of expulsion from membership, as the duty of the union was to act in the best interests of its members as a whole, which in this type of case means acting in accordance with the Bridlington Agreement principles and the decision of the Disputes Committee.

However, it was acknowledged that different considerations may apply if the effect of the expulsion is to put the individual's job in jeopardy because of the existence of a closed shop.

15. Exclusion from membership

Section 14 of the TURER Act 1993, amends ss. 174–177 of the 1992 Act, which covers the right not to be unreasonably excluded or expelled from a trade union. Previously the provisions only applied when a union membership agreement (closed shop) was in force. The new provisions now give a general right to all individuals not to be excluded or expelled from a trade union. There are a number of exceptions to this principle with the most important being that the provision does not apply if the exclusion or expulsion is entirely attributable to the individual's conduct. However, the term 'conduct' is a very limited concept in that it does not include conduct for which a member has the right not to be disciplined by a trade union under s. 65 of the 1992 Act.

For the position on unfair recruitment see **12** above.

In *NATSOPA* v. *Kirkham* (1983) K voluntarily retired from the newspaper industry in 1968 and withdrew from the union. Several years later he wished to restart employment in the industry (in which a closed shop operates) and he was readmitted to membership of the union, but only in a casual worker category. Accordingly he could not get regular employment in the industry. On K's complaint of being unreasonably excluded from membership of a union, the EAT held that in order for K to have a valid complaint under the Act he had to show that the branch or section from which he was excluded was specified in the union membership agreement which created the closed shop. In this case the only organisation specified in the union membership agreement was the union as a whole, and it could not be said that K had been refused membership of the union. Accordingly, the complaint failed.

In *McGhee* v. *Midland British Road Services Ltd* (1985) it was held that a trade union member who resigns from his union cannot complain that he was constructively expelled by reason of the union's behaviour to him.

The new legislation was interpreted in *NACODS* v. *Glunchowski* (1996). G was suspended from membership of the union because of complaints about his business activities. The EAT held that suspension from membership did not amount to exclusion. There was a distinction between suspension from the benefits of membership of a union and the actual exclusion from membership. G had no complaint under s. 174. It should be noted that the right under s. 174 of the 1992 Act is in addition to other statutory and common-law rights (*see* **12** above).

If a person wishes to complain that this statutory right has been infringed, a complaint must be presented to an industrial tribunal normally within six months of the act of which he complains. If the tribunal finds the complaint well-founded, it will make a declaration to that effect. An appeal lies to the Employment Appeal Tribunal on a question of law or fact. In addition, an industrial tribunal may award compensation to the complainant. If the trade union refuses to comply with the terms of the declaration, a further claim for compensation may be made to the Employment Appeal Tribunal. The 1993 Act does not change the previous remedies under the 1992 legislation, as outlined above. Consequently if the applicant makes a further claim for compensation to the EAT then the minimum award is £5,000.

TRADE UNION BALLOTS

16. Secret ballots for trade union elections

Section 46 of the 1992 Act imposes a duty on every trade union to ensure that every person who holds a position, as listed below, must have been elected by a secret ballot of all members. Further, such a person must be re-elected at least once every five years. The positions to which the provisions apply are: member of the executive, any position by virtue of which a person is a member of the executive, president and general secretary. The term 'member of the executive' includes those who, under the rules and practice of the union, are entitled to attend and speak at meetings of the executive other than in an advisory capacity. Section 49 of the 1992 Act further requires a trade union to appoint a qualified independent person to act as a scrutineer for the above elections. The existing duties of the scrutineer include the duty to make a report about the conduct of the election. There is now the further duty of inspecting the register of names and addresses of the members of the trade union. The scrutineer is obliged to inspect the register whenever it appears to be appropriate to do so and in particular where either a candidate or union member suspects that the union has failed to keep the register up-to-date. Section 51 of the 1992 Act provides that ballots for the above positions should be held by postal voting only. Section 2 of the 1993 Act inserts a new s. 51A into the 1992 Act. The new provision requires unions to appoint one or more independent persons to undertake the storage, distribution and counting of the voting papers used in the election. Further s. 6 of the 1993 Act inserts a new s. 24A into TULR(C)A 1992, which imposes a duty of confidentiality not to disclose the name or address of any member on the membership register.

Section 55 of the 1992 Act allows an individual member to apply to either the Certification Officer or the High Court for a declaration that the union has failed to comply with the provisions of the Act. Section 56 of the 1992 Act does not preclude a member from making a subsequent application to the High Court in respect of the same matter even though it was originally referred to the Certification Officer.

17. Secret ballots before industrial action

See Chapter 19 on the Law of Industrial Conflict.

18. Control of the funds and property of a trade union

Three sections of the 1992 Act are relevant to this topic. Section 28 imposes a duty on a trade union to keep its accounting records available for inspection for a period of six years. Any member may inspect them for any period of membership within 28 days of making a request, subject to payment of charges notified before inspection is arranged.

Further regulation of the funds and financial affairs of trade unions have been introduced by the TURER Act 1993. The purpose of these new requirements is to ensure that union members can ascertain the position of their union's finances.

Section 32 of the 1992 Act requires a trade union to send an annual return to the Certification Officer giving details of the union's accounts; s. 8 of the 1993 Act inserts the further requirement that this information must include details of the salary and other benefits paid to each member of the executive, the president and general secretary. In addition to the annual return, a new s. 32A of the 1992 Act requires a union to prepare a financial statement for its members. The financial statement must include such matters as the total income and expenditure of the union as a whole and also the same information relating to any political fund of the union.

Section 15 of the 1992 Act makes it unlawful for a trade union to indemnify an individual in respect of penalties for 'relevant offences' or contempt of court. No union funds or property can be used for these purposes. An offence is a relevant one unless the Secretary of State says it is not. A member may bring proceedings against the union.

Finally, s. 16 gives the Court wide powers over the trustees of a union, including their removal and the appointment of a receiver, if any member satisfies the Court that the trustees have permitted the unlawful use of a union's property or are proposing to do so. Clearly this gives a trade union member wide powers over the use of union funds and property.

18

THE LAW OF COLLECTIVE BARGAINING

References in this chapter to 'the 1974 Act' are to the Trade Union and Labour Relations Act 1974 and to 'the 1975 Act' are to the Employment Protection Act 1975. The legislation is now consolidated in the Trade Union and Labour Relations (Consolidation) Act 1992.

INTRODUCTION

1. Historical

Prior to 1971, there was no legal obligation upon an employer to allow his employees to join trade unions (*see* 8) and no obligation to 'recognise' a trade union or to negotiate with it. The Industrial Relations Act 1971 introduced provisions giving rise to such rights on the part of employees and trade unions but these were repealed in 1974. The 1974 Act and the 1975 Act contained provisions concerning the legal effect of collective agreements, the recognition of trade unions and the disclosure of information to recognised trade unions. The provisions on recognition of trade unions were repealed by the Employment Act 1980 so that there is now no legal machinery of general application whereby an employer may be compelled to recognise a trade union for collective bargaining purposes. The legislation is now contained in the 1992 Act. However, where the Transfer of Undertakings (Protection of Employment) Regulations 1981 apply, an employer who acquires a commercial undertaking will be deemed to recognise any independent trade union previously recognised by the transferor (reg. 9(2)(a). It is open to the transferee to rescind or vary that recognition (reg. 9(2)(b)).

2. Collective bargaining

The term 'collective bargaining' refers to the process by which representatives of a trade union(s) negotiate with an employer(s) or employers' association about a wide range of matters including the terms and conditions of employment of employees and the procedures by which disputes should be settled. The result of such negotiations, the legal effect of which as between the parties is considered at **4** below, may be a collective agreement which may be incorporated into the contract of employment of an individual employee (*see* 4:**9**).

LEGAL EFFECT OF COLLECTIVE AGREEMENTS

3. Definition

The term 'collective agreement' is defined as an 'agreement or arrangement made by or on behalf of one or more trade unions and one or more employers or employers' associations' relating to a number of specified matters, e.g. terms and conditions of employment, termination of employment, matters of discipline, facilities for trade union officials: s. 178(1) of the 1992 Act.

4. Legal effect

The matter is governed by s. 179(1) of the 1992 Act which provides that a collective agreement: 'shall be conclusively presumed not to have been intended by the parties to be a legally enforceable contract unless the agreement:

(a) is in writing, and

(b) contains a provision which (however expressed) states that the parties intend that the agreement shall be a legally enforceable contract'.

Thus, unless there is a provision to the contrary in it, a collective agreement is not legally enforceable by the parties to it: *see Monterosso Shipping Co. Ltd* v. *International Transport Workers Federation* (1982). It should be remembered, however, that collective agreements may achieve an indirect legal effect via the individual contract of employment and may be enforced as such by the individual employee: *see* 4:**9–11**. Further, a number of single union agreements which include legally binding collective agreements, particularly in relation to no strike clauses, have recently been negotiated.

DISCLOSURE OF INFORMATION

5. Basic principle

For the purpose of all stages of collective bargaining, it is the duty of an employer to disclose to the representatives of any independent trade union (*see* 17:**6**) recognised by him, all such information relating to his undertaking without which the representatives would be, to a material extent, impeded in carrying on such collective bargaining, and which it would be in accordance with good industrial relations practice to disclose; *see* ss. 181 and 182 of the 1992 Act. In determining this latter point, regard must be had to the ACAS Code of Practice 'Disclosure of Information to Trade

Unions for Collective Bargaining Purposes'. If requested by the representatives, the information must be in writing. Many of these rights are now extended to elected representatives as a result of recent regulations (*see* 17:7).

6. Information which need not be disclosed

The employer is not required to disclose:

(a) any information the disclosure of which would be against the interests of national security

(b) any information which he could not disclose without contravening a prohibition imposed by law

(c) information which he has received in confidence

(d) information relating specifically to an individual

(e) information the disclosure of which would cause substantial injury to the employer's business for reasons other than its effect on collective bargaining

(f) information obtained by the employer for the purpose of bringing or defending any legal proceedings.

The employer is not required to produce, or allow the inspection of, any document other than a document prepared for the purpose of confirming or conveying information where this would involve an amount of work or expenditure out of all reasonable proportion to its value in the conduct of collective bargaining.

In *Scottish Courage Brewing Ltd* v. *Amalgamated Engineering and Electrical Union (AEEU)* (1996) the Central Arbitration Committee (*see* 7 below) ordered the employers to disclose to the Union details of overtime payments and schedules worked by a particular group of employees. The CAC felt that this information was not confidential and the fact that the union would find out the wages of individuals was not a valid ground for refusing disclosure. The union wanted the information in order to secure a fairer distribution of overtime.

7. Enforcement

If an independent trade union considers that an employer has failed to disclose information which he is required to disclose, it may present a complaint to the CAC (*see* 1:15). If the CAC considers that the matter could be settled by conciliation, it must refer the matter to ACAS. Otherwise, the CAC examines the complaint and if it finds it well-founded, it must issue a declaration stating:

(a) the information in respect of which the complaint is well-founded

(b) the date on which the employer refused or failed to disclose the information; and

(c) a period (not less than one week) within which the employer ought to disclose the information.

If, after that period, the employer still fails to disclose the information, a further complaint may be presented to the CAC. If it finds the complaint well-founded, the CAC may make an award in respect of the employees covered by the application. Such an award requires that the employer observe terms and conditions of employment as specified by the CAC in respect of those employees. The award takes effect as part of individual contracts of employment and may be enforced as such until superseded or varied by a further award or an improved agreement between the employer and trade union/employees concerned.

8. Disclosure and consultation of the transfer of a business

The Transfer of Undertakings (Protection of Employment) Regulations 1981 (as amended) state that there is a duty to consult with 'appropriate representatives' on certain matters relating to the transfer of a business. The nature of this duty was changed by the collective Redundancies and Transfer of Undertakings (Protection of Employment) (Amendment) Regulations 1995. Previously the duty to consult only concerned representatives of 'recognised trade unions' but the Government was forced to introduce the new requirement when the ECJ in *Commission of the European Communities* v. *United Kingdom* (1994) held the existing provisions to be in breach of European Law.

The Regulations require the employer to consult on certain matters, relating to the transfer, including: details of when and why the transfer is to take place; the legal, social and economic implications of the transfer for employees and any measures which may be taken by the transferor or transferee in relation to employees when an employer envisages that measures will be taken in respect of employees; it also has a duty to consult with 'appropriate representatives'

The Regulations do not state how the selection of these representatives should take place. This provision was challenged in *R.* v. *Secretary of State for Trade and Industry ex p. UNISON* (1996) on the basis that the Regulations do not comply with the appropriate EC Directives. It was held that the Directives imposed a primary duty to consult and inform. Therefore there was no obligation to produce a detailed mechanism on how such representatives should be elected.

If an employer fails to meet these obligations a complaint may be made by the trade union to an industrial tribunal which may make a declaration and award appropriate compensation, up to a maximum of four weeks pay, to the affected employees.

19

THE LAW OF INDUSTRIAL CONFLICT

References in this chapter, unless otherwise stated, are to the Trade Union and Labour Relations (Consolidation) Act 1992.

INTRODUCTION

Historically, it was very difficult for industrial action to be organised or carried out without criminal and/or civil liability arising as regards the organisers and/or those participating. A series of Acts, culminating in the 1992 Act, has limited the extent to which such liability arises so that mere industrial action, i.e. strikes etc., without accompanying violence, threats or other acts unlawful in themselves, is now largely free from legal consequences, subject to the provisions outlined below relating to balloting.

The effect of the legislation is that 'mere industrial action' has a very limited focus and trade unions must adhere to very complex legislation in order to be immune. Therefore, there is no 'right' to take industrial action in English law.

TRADE DISPUTE

1. Significance

In terms of potential legal liabilities, it is of the utmost significance whether an act is done 'in contemplation or furtherance of a trade dispute', since the statutory immunities discussed below only apply in such circumstance. If an act falls outside the scope of a trade dispute, the immunities cease to operate and the full rigour of the law applies.

2. Definition

Section 244 of the 1992 Act defines a trade dispute as 'a dispute between workers and their employer which relates wholly or mainly to one or more of the following:

(a) Terms and conditions of employment, or the physical conditions in which any workers are required to work.

(b) Engagement or non-engagement, or termination or suspension of employment or the duties of employment, of one or more workers.

(c) Allocation of work or the duties of employment as between workers or groups of workers.

(d) Matters of discipline.

(e) The membership or non-membership of a trade union on the part of a worker.

(f) Facilities for officials of trade unions.

(g) Machinery for negotiation or consultation, and other procedures, relating to any of the foregoing matters, including the recognition by employers or employers' associations of the right of a trade union to represent workers in any such negotiation or consultation or in the carrying out of such procedures'.

The present position is that the dispute must relate 'wholly or mainly to' one of the specified matters. It is now clear that where the connection with one of the s. 244 matters is only slight, any dispute will not be a trade dispute within the statutory definition. *See also Hadmor Productions Ltd* v. *Hamilton* (1982) and *Universe Tankships Inc. of Monrovia* v. *International Transport Workers' Federation* (1982). An example of the way in which the narrower definition substituted by the 1982 Act operates is found in *Mercury Communications Ltd* v. *The Post Office Engineering Union* (1983). Under the Telecommunications Act 1981 the Secretary of State is empowered to license telecommunications systems. Early in 1982 such a licence was issued to Mercury, allowing them to establish a rival telecommunications system to British Telecom. The effective operation of the Mercury system requires some degree of interconnection with the BT system so that subscribers on both systems can communicate with each other. The trade union was opposed to such a process of liberalisation and took industrial action. This took the form of instructing members not to connect Project Mercury to the BT system. The management of BT subsequently effected some interconnection themselves and the union thereupon instructed its members to black BT services at Mercury's own premises. Mercury sought interlocutory relief to restrain the union from calling industrial action preventing the interconnection of the systems. The Court of Appeal at the interlocutory stage was clear that on a trial on the main issue it was likely that the conclusion would be reached that the dispute here was not a 'trade dispute' under the amended s. 244 of the 1992 Act. This was because, although the union feared some job losses as a result of this process of liberalisation, the actions of the members were mainly due to political objection to the breaking of the monopoly of a nationalised industry. Accordingly, interlocutory relief was granted.

In the case of *London Borough of Wandsworth* v. *National Association of Schoolmasters and Union of Women Teachers* (1993) the Court of Appeal held that the proposed action by the trade union concerning the boycotting of tests relating to the National Curriculum was a trade dispute. The Court of Appeal upheld the decision of the High Court that the dispute was concerned with teachers' workloads and consequently came within the definition contained in s. 244 of the 1992 Act. The Court of Appeal felt there was sufficient evidence to justify this decision despite the acknowledged hostility of the union towards testing.

3. 'In contemplation or furtherance'

To be within the statutory definition the act must be 'in contemplation or furtherance of' a trade dispute: s. 219 of the 1992 Act.

(a) *Contemplation.* The act must not be one of mere 'coercive interference' but instead be directed towards something which is 'impending or likely to occur': *Conway* v. *Wade* (1909); *BBC* v. *Hearn* (1977). Thus the mere fact that a trade union official has in mind a certain desired objective is not sufficient – he must be acting with a particular dispute in view.

(b) *Furtherance.* The test of whether an act is done in furtherance of a trade dispute appears, as a general rule, to be subjective. As long as the person committing the act in question honestly believes that it assists in achieving the objectives of the dispute then he acts in furtherance of the dispute, even if the belief is an unreasonable one: *see Express Newspapers Ltd* v. *McShane* (1980).

The position of secondary industrial acts will be dealt with in **8** below.

LIABILITY IN TORT

4. Introduction

A number of different civil liabilities (i.e. tortious) may arise out of industrial action although it can be seen that many of these will be protected if the act falls within the statutory definition of 'in contemplation or furtherance of a trade dispute' (*see* **1** above).

5. Breach of contract

A number of the provisions referred to in this section are concerned with breaches of contracts of employment and other contracts, e.g. a contract for the supply of goods. This includes any breach of contract, e.g. if an employee goes on strike without giving proper notice to terminate the contract, refuses to work contractually-agreed overtime or takes part in a 'go-slow' or refuses to do work that he is contractually obliged to do. However, a 'work-to-rule' or 'work-to-contract' is not a breach of contract since this is a literal performance of the terms of the contract although there is a breach if the limits of the contract are exceeded: *Secretary of State for Employment* v. *ASLEF (No. 2)* (1972).

6. Inducing breach of contract

Any person who knowingly induces another person to break a contract with a third party *prima facie* commits the tort of inducing breach of contract. In the area of industrial conflict, inducing breach of contract normally has one of three forms:

(a) Direct inducement by a trade union official who induces an employee to break his contract of employment with his employer.

(b) Direct inducement by a trade union official who induces a supplier of the employer with whom the dispute lies to break that contract of supply.

(c) Indirect inducement (sometimes called 'procurement') by a trade union official who induces an employee of the supplier to break his contract of employment with his employer, with the result that the contract of supply between the supplier and the employer (with whom the dispute lies) is broken.

In *Lumley* v. *Gye* (1853) a singer was contracted to sing at the plaintiff's theatre. The defendant persuaded the singer not to sing at the plaintiff's theatre but to appear for him instead. Held: the defendant was liable for inducing a breach of contract between the plaintiff and the singer. The scope of this tort has been extended to include any intentional uses of unlawful means aimed at interfering with the trade or business of the plaintiff. Another example of this tort is provided by the decision in *Falconer* v. *NUR and ASLEF* (1986), where F was prevented from travelling from Sheffield to London because of a rail strike caused by the action of the two train unions. A secret ballot had not been held. F obtained damages for two nights' hotel accommodation and other incidental expenses incurred as he had to travel a day earlier in order to fulfil business appointments.

7. Immunity

This will be given in cases such as *Lumley* v. *Gye* by s. 219 of the 1992 Act. It needs to be borne in mind that this immunity can be lost if there is no ballot (*see* below). However, even if there is a ballot, immunity can be lost in two important situations. Firstly, immunity will be lost where the industrial action in question consists of unlawful picketing, i.e. picketing outside the scope of the immunity contained in s. 220 of the 1992 Act. Secondly, where the action is deemed to be unlawful secondary industrial action, immunity will be lost.

8. Secondary industrial action

Secondary industrial action occurs where the person induces / interferes with the contract of employment of another, where the employer under the contract of employment is not a party to the trade dispute. For example: the employees of Company X are taking industrial action for better wages (the primary dispute). Company Y supplies Company X; the employees at Y are asked to take sympathetic action – this will be deemed to be 'secondary action'.

Any immunity for secondary action is now governed by s. 224 of the 1992 Act. Section 224 consolidates the changes introduced by s. 4 of Employment Act 1990 which repealed the existing position as contained in s. 17 of the Employment Act 1980. The current position is that there is no immunity for secondary industrial action, save for two exceptions contained in s. 224 of the 1992 Act. Firstly, s. 224(3) retains the immunity for the actions of certain picketing activities. Therefore, where the secondary action is a consequence of lawful picketing, that is by pickets at their own place of work (see **18** below) and any secondary effects were not the main purpose of the picketing, then immunity will remain. Secondly, s. 234(5) states that any primary action in a dispute which has secondary effects elsewhere retains immunity. The latter is wider than merely picketing but it is clear that to retain immunity the action must relate to the primary dispute alone.

9. Other situations where immunity is lost

Three further situations need to be mentioned where immunity can be lost:

(a) A person induces or attempts to induce an employer to incorporate a clause in a commercial contract requiring the contractor to use union (or non-union) labour only: s. 222(3) of the 1992 Act.

(b) A person induces or threatens to induce an employee to break his contract of employment so as to interfere with the supply of goods or services and the reason for inducing or threatening the breach is that the work to be done in connection with the supply of goods or services is done by union (or non-union) labour, or the supplier does not recognise or negotiate with a union: s. 225 of the 1992 Act.

(c) Section 222(1) of the 1992 Act removes immunity where one of the reasons for the industrial action is that an employer employs, or proposes to employ, a person who is not a member of a trade union. Immunity is also removed where the trade union pressurises an employer into treating a person less favourably because of his non-membership.

10. Intimidation

The tort of intimidation consists of a threat to do an illegal act which causes damage to another person. It was generally considered that this was limited to threats to do crimes or torts but in *Rookes* v. *Barnard* (1964) the House of Lords held that a threat to break a contract of employment constituted an 'unlawful act' for the purposes of the tort of intimidation.

However, it is now provided that:

'An act done by a person in contemplation or furtherance of a trade dispute shall not be actionable in tort on the ground only . . . (b) that it consists in his threatening that a contract (whether one to which he is party or not) will be broken or its performance interfered with, or that he will induce another person to break a contract or interfere with its performance': s. 219(1) of the 1992 Act.

Of course, threats of assault etc. in any context constitute the tort of intimidation. It should be noted that where two or more persons join together to threaten an unlawful act, the question of conspiracy may also arise (*see* **11** below).

11. Conspiracy

The tort of conspiracy consists of an agreement by two or more persons to commit an unlawful act (e.g. assault) or a lawful act by unlawful means (e.g. threatening to assault an employer in order to obtain a reduction in working hours).

In *Quinn* v. *Leathem* (1901) L, a butcher, employed non-union labour. The union threatened X, a supplier of meat to L; X complied. Held: this was an actionable conspiracy since the object of their actions, namely the financial harming of L, was unlawful.

In *Rookes* v. *Barnard* (*see* **10** above), it was held that a threat to break a contract was unlawful means and therefore there was an actionable conspiracy.

The scope of the tort of conspiracy has been narrowed somewhat, at least where unlawful means are concerned, by the decision of the House of Lords in *Lonrho Ltd* v. *Shell Petroleum Co.* (1982) where it was held that in addition to showing that unlawful means have been used, the plaintiff must also show that the defendants acted for the purpose of injuring the plaintiff's interests.

Section 219(2) provides: 'An agreement or combination by two or more persons to do or procure the doing of any act in contemplation or furtherance of a trade dispute shall not be actionable in tort if the act is one which, if done without any such agreement or combination, would not be actionable in tort.' Thus, liability for conspiracy can only arise if unlawful means are used or if the object of the conspiracy is an act unlawful in itself. A breach of contract or an interference with a contract is not normally regarded as an unlawful act or unlawful means for this purpose.

REMEDIES

12. Damages

As with any other tort, the plaintiff may seek damages against the defendant. If damages are awarded, the object of the award will be to put the plaintiff back into the position as if the tort had not been committed.

Where a trade union is sued successfully in its own name a scale indicating the maximum amount of damages payable has been laid down by s. 22 of the 1992 Act:

Union Membership	Limit on Damages
Less than 5,000	£10,000
5,000–25,000	£50,000
25,000–100,000	£125,000
over 100,000	£250,000

It should be noted that these limits do not apply in respect of actions for personal injury arising out of negligence or the ownership or occupation of property.

13. Injunction

An *ex parte* injunction is one where one party makes an application to a court in the absence of the other. If granted, the effect is to render unlawful the commencement or continuation of the industrial action in question. It is expressly provided that a court shall not grant such an injunction if the party against whom it is sought claims, or the court considers it likely he would claim, that he acted in contemplation or furtherance of a trade dispute, unless all reasonable steps have been taken to give that person notice of the hearing and the opportunity to be heard: s. 221(1) of the 1992 Act.

If an application is made for an interlocutory injunction and the party against whom it is sought claims that he acted in contemplation or furtherance of a trade dispute, the court, in exercising its discretion whether or not to grant the injunction, must have regard to the likelihood of that party establishing that his acts were protected by the various statutory immunities discussed above: s. 221(2) of the 1992 Act, and *see Star Sea Transport Corporation of Monrovia* v. *Slater* (1978).

If a trade union fails to comply with an injunction it will be held to be in contempt of court. There is no limit to the amount a trade union can be fined for being in contempt. In the miners' dispute (1984–85) the funds of the NUM were eventually sequestrated by the court as the union had persistently refused to comply with the terms of the injunction imposed by the court. See generally s. 23 of the 1992 Act.

14. Balloting before industrial action

Section 226 of the 1992 Act requires a secret ballot to be held before official industrial action was first authorised in order for a trade union to be immune. The immunity for unofficial industrial action will be dealt with in **18** below. The requirements of the balloting provisions are contained in ss. 227–230 of the 1992 Act. In addition the 1992 Act has given rights to individual members of a trade union in relation to non-compliance with the balloting provisions.

15. The balloting provisions

The 1992 Act, s. 226, states that an act done by a trade union to induce a person to take part in industrial action is not protected unless the industrial action has the support of a ballot. The requirement to ballot extends, by virtue of s. 235, not only to workers under a contract of employment but also to workers who are working on a casual or self-employed basis. The position of new members, i.e. members who had subsequently joined the relevant union after the ballot was held, was clarified in *London Underground Ltd* v. *National Union of Rail, Maritime and Transport Workers* (1996). The Court of Appeal held that a union is entitled to call new members out on strike, even though they had not been balloted.

The first authorisation of the action must take place within four weeks of the ballot being held. The relevant date for these purposes, in terms of the four-week period, is the last day upon which votes can be cast. In *RJB Mining (UK) Ltd* v. *National Union of Mineworkers* (1995) the voting in a strike ballot had closed at 10 am on 16 May. The ballot therefore ceased to be effective at midnight on 12 June (four weeks later). The Union called its members to start the action on 13 June. The Court of Appeal granted an injunction restraining the action as it started outside the four-week period.

By s. 234 of the 1992 Act a trade union may apply to the court for an order to set aside the four-week period if the ballot is in some way being challenged. However, there is a maximum of only a further eight weeks under this provision. A simple 50 + 1 per cent majority of those who voted is sufficient for immunity. The 1992 Act (as amended) states that a union is no longer free to induce its members to take industrial action immediately. Section 234(A) of the 1992 Act now requires that the trade union give the employer at least seven days notice of any intended action. This notice must be in writing and specify the employees of a particular employer whom the union intends to call upon to take action.

Section 17 of the TURER Act 1993 amends s. 230 of the 1992 Act to require industrial action ballots to be fully postal. Consequently all voting papers must be sent by post to each member and returned in the same manner.

Three further points should be noted about the 1992 legislation:

(a) The 1992 Act defines industrial action as 'any strike or other industrial action by persons employed under contracts of employment'. Therefore, a ballot must be held even though the industrial action does not breach or interfere with a contract of employment.

(b) A new s. 231A of the 1992 Act is introduced as a result of the provisions of the TURER Act 1993. Trade unions are now required to give notice to employers during the various stages involved in calling industrial action. Consequently the union must tell the employer that it intends to hold the ballot; specify the date on which the ballot will commence and who will be entitled to vote in the ballot. In *NATFHE* v. *Blackpool and The Fylde College* (1994) the Court of Appeal held that this notice must allow the employer to be able to identify individually the employees covered by the notice. Often employers will be able to do this via the check-off system, i.e. union subscriptions deducted through PAYE. However if this is not possible then the union must list the individual members concerned. Further within three days of the start of the ballot the trade union must send a copy of the ballot paper to the employers involved.

The 1992 Act (as amended) also now requires the trade union to inform the employers involved as to the details of the ballot result, for example number of individuals answering Yes or No to the question being asked. Further, for ballots involving more than 50 members at a particular workplace then an independent scrutineer must be appointed in order to oversee the conduct of the ballot.

(c) The ballot paper must now ask whether the voter is prepared to take part in a strike or is prepared to take part in action short of a strike. Both questions must be asked separately in the 1992 Act. Also every voting paper must contain the following statement: 'if you take part in a strike or other industrial action, you may be in breach of your contract of employment'.

(d) The general principle is that a separate ballot must be held for each workplace and immunity will only be given where the workplace voted by a majority to take industrial action. There are exceptions to this general principle where employees are employed by one employer, on common terms, and everyone is given the entitlement to vote; however, the scope of the exceptions is by no means clear.

16. Code of Practice on Balloting

(Industrial Action Ballots and Notice to Employers, which came into force in November 1995, and replaced the previous code of practice.)

The Code of Practice introduces some important changes and seeks to provide 'practical guidance' on pertinent issues relating to industrial action ballots. Amongst the most important changes are: all industrial action ballots to be fully postal; independent scrutiny of such ballots when they involve more than 50 union members; a requirement to give seven days notice of the intention to hold a ballot and the passing of information to the employer of who is to be balloted; the need to give the employer seven days notice of any industrial action which is to be taken following a ballot.

Whilst the code does not impose any legal obligations, it is admissible in evidence before any court, tribunal or the CAC: s. 207 of the 1992 Act.

17. Rights of individual members in respect of industrial action ballots

Section 62 of the 1992 Act allows a member who has been induced to take part in industrial action which has not been authorised with the support of a ballot to apply to the court for an order. The action must be endorsed by 'a responsible person' within the trade union and this is defined by s. 20 of the 1992 Act. The court has discretion to give an order it 'considers appropriate': s. 62(3) of the 1992 Act. Again the 1992 Act has widened the potential liability of a trade union which fails to follow the balloting provisions.

The above provisions as to balloting were aimed at controlling so-called official industrial actions which were approved of by the trade union. The law, until 1990, did not seemingly control unofficial industrial action and this was outside the scope of the legislation. However, the Employment Act 1990 changed the position and this is now governed by the 1992 Act.

Section 20 of the 1992 Act extends liability in tort to virtually all types of industrial action. A trade union will be responsible if the industrial action is authorised or endorsed by a committee or officer of the union. This provision applies even though the rules of the trade union do not allow this to happen. Consequently if the industrial action is, say, approved of by an *ad hoc* strike committee the union will be prima facie liable in tort.

A trade union can avoid liability for unofficial action if the provisions of s. 21 of the 1992 Act are satisfied. Liability can be avoided if the action is repudiated by the principal executive committee or general secretary of the union. The repudiation must go to all members and be in writing. The evidence of repudiation must not merely be words but supported by the actions of the appropriate officials. A subsequent ballot may give the industrial action immunity provided the initial unofficial action has been repudiated.

18. Rights of other individuals in respect of industrial action

A novel principle is now contained in s. 235(A) (as amended) of the 1992 Act which gives individuals a right, in certain circumstances, to bring court actions restraining unlawful industrial action even though they are not directly involved in the dispute itself.

An individual may make a claim if the trade union is likely to do an unlawful act in inducing any person to take part in industrial action and the action will prevent or disrupt the supply of goods and services. The above is novel in that the individual concerned does not have to personally suffer any damage. Clearly an injunction is the only appropriate remedy.

19. Picketing

The term 'picketing' describes the conduct of persons who seek to persuade other persons to take a certain course of action or not to do something, usually entering work premises or delivering supplies during industrial action. As with industrial action, above, the law only provides immunity for pickets (from the consequences of both the civil and criminal law) if the picketing is within the provisions of s. 220 of the 1992 Act.

Section 220 provides that:

'(1) It shall be lawful for a person in contemplation or furtherance of a trade dispute to attend –

(a) at or near his own place of work; or
(b) if he is an official of a trade union, at or near the place of work of a member of that union whom he is accompanying and whom he represents, for the purpose only of peacefully obtaining or communicating information, or peacefully persuading any person to work or abstain from working.'

The following points should be noted:

(a) The picketing must be within s. 220, otherwise immunity is lost.

(b) The words 'at or near his own place of work' are intended to stop secondary picketing (i.e. picketing a person other than at his own place of work). Two cases illustrate the difficulties of this wording. Firstly in *Moss* v. *McLachlan* (1985) it was held that police were under a duty to stop 'flying' pickets from Kent going to pits in Nottinghamshire during the 1984–85 miners' dispute. The reason for this decision was that, as the police suspected that a breach of the peace might occur, this imposed a duty on them to prevent one occurring. Secondly, in *News Group Newspapers Ltd* v. *Society of Graphical and Allied Trades* (1986) it was held that employees dismissed by the plaintiff could not picket at Wapping, to where their work had been moved, as it was not their former place of work.

(c) The Secretary of State for Employment has issued a Code of Practice on Picketing. This Code, which has legal status (*see* 1:**20**), states that 'pickets and their organisers should ensure that in general the number of pickets does not exceed six at any entrance to a workplace; frequently a small number will be appropriate'. In *Thomas* v. *National Union of Mineworkers (South Wales Area)* (1986) an injunction was granted to working miners limiting the number of pickets to six where mass picketing had taken place during the miners' dispute of 1984–85. The case would seem to suggest that the Code now states the legal position as to the number of pickets.

(d) It appears that the police have considerable discretion in respect of picketing.

In *Piddington* v. *Bates* (1961) a police constable informed pickets that two were sufficient at a particular place. The defendant did not agree and attempted to push past the constable. He was arrested and charged with obstruction of a police officer in the execution of his duty, in that the constable had reasonably anticipated a breach of the peace. Held: the defendant was guilty in that the court would not say that the constable had no reasonable grounds for anticipating the breach of the peace.

In *Tynan* v. *Balmer* (1967) forty pickets, including the defendant, were walking on the highway with a view to preventing supplies being delivered to a factory. A police officer requested the defendant to disperse them but he refused. He was arrested and charged with obstruction of a police officer in the execution of his duty. Held: the defendant was guilty because the conduct of the pickets amounted to an obstruction of the highway which the police officer could seek to end. The argument that the pickets had to obstruct the highway to force drivers to stop in order that they could attempt peaceful persuasion was rejected.

20. The Public Order Act 1986

The 1986 Act replaces the existing legislation on public order, mostly contained in the 1936 Act. The 1986 Act creates five new statutory offences, namely riot (s. 1); violent disorder (s. 2); affray (s. 3); causing fear or provocation of violence (s. 4) and causing harassment, alarm or distress (s. 5). Perhaps the most important for the control of pickets is s. 5 which has been described as a 'catch all' provision and states that the offence is committed where a person, within the hearing or sight of a person likely to be caused harassment, alarm or distress thereby:

(a) uses threatening, abusive or insulting words or behaviour, or disorderly behaviour, or

(b) displays any writing, sign or other visible representation which is threatening, abusive or insulting.

In terms of picketing, s. 5 may well have an important role to play. The Act also gives powers (ss. 11–14) for marches, processions and static assemblies to be controlled, and there is a power for marches to be banned.

INDEX